NATURAL KINDS

For Penny, Catherine and David

Natural Kinds

T. E. WILKERSON
Reader in Philosophy
University of Nottingham

Avebury

Aldershot • Brookfield USA • Hong Kong • Singapore • Sydney

Published by
Avebury
Ashgate Publishing Limited
Gower House
Croft Road
Aldershot
Hants GU11 3HR
England

Ashgate Publishing Company
Old Post Road
Brookfield
Vermont 05036
USA

British Library Cataloguing in Publication Data

Wilkerson, T. E.
      Natural Kinds
      I. Title
      111

ISBN 1 85972 131 1

Library of Congress Catalog Card Number: 95-79580

Printed in Great Britain by Antony Rowe Ltd,
Chippenham, Wiltshire

Contents

Acknowledgements

Some of the material in this book has appeared before, or is directly descended from material that has appeared before, in the following places:

(1) 'Natural Kinds and Identity, A Horticultural Enquiry', *Philosophical Studies*, vol. 49, pp. 63-69; © 1986 by D. Reidel Publishing Company; reprinted by permission of Kluwer Academic Publishers;

(2) 'Natural Kinds', *Philosophy*, vol. 63, 1988, pp. 29-42;

(3) 'Species, Essences and the Names of Natural Kinds', *Philosophical Quarterly*, vol. 43, 1993, pp. 1-19.

I am very grateful to the editors and publishers of those journals for allowing me to use and develop the material.

I wish to give special thanks to Jonathan Harrison, who first encouraged me to start work on this book; and to Brian Carr, who gave me invaluable help when I was producing camera-ready copy.

T.E.W.   Nottingham, 1995.

1 What exists?

Two pictures of reality

What exists? And what counts as a true description of what exists? Those who have a special fondness for physics will suppose that the answers to those questions are simple and straightforward. They will say that the entities that exist are the entities mentioned in physical theory, and that true descriptions are true descriptions couched in the language of physics. Inevitably there are footnotes and complications, but they arise only because we can never be quite sure that the concepts and laws of contemporary physics are the correct concepts and laws, that they accurately reflect the structure of physical reality. But we do not need to worry too much about the footnotes and complications. For the purposes of this discussion we can imagine a perfect physics, and with suitable minor amendment repeat the original answers to our questions. The entities that exist are the entities mentioned in the perfect physics, and true descriptions of what exists are true descriptions couched in the language of the perfect physics.

For all sorts of reasons, I cannot sensibly predict the content of a perfect physics. So for the rest of this book I shall simply assume for the purposes of argument that the basic entities of physics are packets of energy, united by various forces which may or may not be reducible to a single force. In any case, I think it is unlikely that any future revolution in physics is likely to undermine my general philosophical project. Given that background assumption, the physicist will offer us the following outline picture of reality, and of the proper description and explanation of reality. The whole universe consists of a vast complex arrangement of packets of energy, and at any given time one vast complex arrangement (an initial state) will give rise to another vast complex arrangement (an outcome), according to the laws of physics. There is absolutely no reason for anyone working with this picture to focus closely on certain local concentrations of energy, or to treat them as special entities of some kind. Nor indeed is there any reason for anyone working with this picture of reality to exploit or develop any descriptive or explanatory concepts that are not included in, or reducible to, the concepts of physics.

Now it is curious and puzzling that many otherwise intelligent and rational people neither talk nor behave as though that conception of reality, and that account of the proper description and explanation of reality, were true. They neither talk nor behave as though the entities that exist are exclusively the entities mentioned in physics, and they neither talk nor behave as though true descriptions of those entities are true descriptions couched in the language of physics. To begin with, they manifest a powerful interest in certain local concentrations of energy, and as the concentrations become larger and more complex, their interest, if anything, tends to increase. For example they become interested in concentrations called 'atoms' and in arrangements of atoms called 'molecules', and before we know where we are, they have created Departments of Chemistry to ponder such concentrations. Certain complex strings of molecules give rise to the science of biology and in turn to a profound interest in highly complex concentrations of energy, such as ants, chimpanzees, elm trees and, of course, human beings. In their everyday lives they make, and talk of making, highly ornamental concentrations of energy, such as tables, chairs, paintings, sculptures and other artefacts. Moreover, when all these comparatively large and complex concentrations arrange themselves in certain ways, they start to talk of yet other entities: of families, households, tribes, states, nations; of firms, cartels and economies; of herds, colonies and swarms.

So we seem to have the makings of answers to our original questions that are quite different from the physicist's answers. First, we otherwise intelligent and rational people seem to work with a much richer and more heterogeneous range of entities than are offered by the physicist. Included in our list are, for example, atoms, molecules, genes; various material objects, especially plants and animals; families, households, tribes, states and nations; firms, cartels and economies; herds, colonies and swarms. Moreover, perhaps there is already a suspicion that we have a quite special interest in one group of entities, namely middle-sized material objects, and particularly in plants and animals. Second, when we otherwise intelligent and rational people try to describe and explain the properties and behaviour of our various entities, at various levels of concentration and complexity, we employ a wide and heterogeneous range of descriptions and explanations, many of which have no apparent connection with the descriptions and explanations of the physicist. At the level of atoms and molecules we turn to chemistry, and when the molecules are of a certain kind, complexity and arrangement, to biology. Confronted by that baffling entity, the human being, we use psychological descriptions and explanations, and, since humans organize themselves into families, clubs, societies and nations, we are soon engaged in political, sociological and economic description and explanation. Sometimes we use the explanatory resources of the social sciences to talk about organized groups of non-human animals, such as swarms of bees, colonies of ants, herds of deer, schools of whales and communities of apes and monkeys. Just as prima facie we treat clubs, societies and nations as individual entities, and attribute beliefs and other propositional attitudes to them, so prima facie we sometimes treat swarms, colonies and herds as individual entities. It might seem an exaggeration to say that we attribute propositional attitudes to swarms, colonies and herds, but we certainly use the language of agency. We say that they are stationary or on the move, are attacking or defending themselves. And if, as I suspect, agency logically requires beliefs and desires, then swarms, colonies and herds have propositional attitudes.

Very roughly, the distinction between various kinds of entity and various levels of description and explanation corresponds to a difference of size and complexity between comparatively bigger and more complex things, and comparatively smaller and less complex things. Bigger and more complex things are composed of smaller and less complex things. It would be wonderful if we could treat the descriptive and explanatory language used at a higher level merely as a summary or generalization of the descriptive and explanatory language used at some lower level. That is, it would be wonderful if we could argue that, since big things are composed of small things, the laws governing the behaviour of the big things must summarize or generalize or simplify the laws governing the behaviour of the small things. If we confine our attention to physics, there seems to be no objection to our doing just that. Quantum physicists who explain the behaviour of very tiny things, who at that level connect initial state with outcome according to statistical laws, suppose that the same laws, in a suitably generalized form, govern the behaviour of the very large billiard ball that I am trying vainly to propel into a woefully large and humiliatingly adjacent pocket. It may well be true that quantum indeterminacies are unlikely to show up at the level of whole billiard balls, but it is nonetheless true that the behaviour of the billiard ball is governed by quantum-statistical laws, rather than by the deterministic laws of a Newtonian physics.

But as soon as we broaden our attention, and think about academic disciplines other than physics, that supposition looks very implausible. Description and explanation of big things cannot be treated as a summary or generalization or simplification of description and explanation of small things. In all sorts of ways, there seems to be no fit, even loose and approximate, between our remarks about entities at one level and our remarks about entities at another. Let me give four illustrations of this absence of fit. The first illustration concerns the notion of identity. If big things were made of little things, and if the description and explanation of the features of the big things were merely a summary or generalization or simplification of the description and explanation of the features of constituent little things, then the identity of the big things would depend directly on the identity of the constituent little things. More formally, the criteria of identity of an entity at a given level would depend directly on the identity of its constituents (entities of the next lower level).

Admittedly there are one or two arcane examples which appear to support that principle: in set theory the identity of a set is determined by the identity of its members. But such examples are extremely problematic. For example it is not at all clear that the members of a set can sensibly be regarded as its constituents, and it is in any case absurd to raise questions about the identity of a set through change. So I think that we can leave such examples on one side, and continue to argue that the identity of an entity typically does not depend on the identity of its constituents. For example my identity clearly does not depend on the identity of my constituents, whether we construe my constituents as quite large, such as arms, legs, kidneys and lungs, or whether we construe them as quite small, such as individual cells or groups of cells. My identity is not affected by my having a heart or kidney transplant; nor is it affected by the continual alteration and degeneration of the matter of which I am composed, by digestion, excretion, loss of hair and tooth enamel, and so on. Mutatis mutandis, the same point can be made about the identities of many other entities, for example clubs, societies and nations. All of these can retain their identities despite a constant change of members; and conversely the members of a club, society or nation can retain their respective identities even when, as a result of some social or political catastrophe, the club, society or nation disappears.

A second illustration concerns our habit of attributing psychological features to entities such as families, clubs, societies, nations, and indeed to swarms of bees and ant colonies. 'The British view is that discussions should take place'; 'The club is trying to expand'; 'The bank is very embarrassed by its debt'; 'The swarm is preparing for attack'; 'The colony is on the march.' Many will argue that such remarks should not be taken literally, because such supposed entities are not entities at all, and are therefore logically incapable of having psychological features. Others will argue that any remarks about the propositional attitudes of the whole group are parasitic on remarks about the propositional attitudes, if any, of the members. But I am not sure that we should dismiss such idioms so swiftly, particularly before we have discussed important general issues about the notion of an entity. I shall return to those issues later on, and for the moment will merely point out that the psychological features we attribute to clubs, societies, firms, nations, etc., cannot be analysed in terms of, or reduced to, the psychological features of their constituent parts (e.g. their members, employees or citizens). No doubt under highly autocratic régimes the wishes, intentions and attitudes of the club or nation coincide with those of the chairman or Führer. But typically that is not so, particularly in democratic organizations, where there are complicated constitutional arrangements for arriving at decisions, and where bargaining and compromise are unavoidable. One can easily imagine circumstances in which the bank is extremely embarrassed even though none of its employees are, or in which a nation is anxious to open negotiations, even though most of its members are unrepentantly belligerent.

The third illustration (of a lack of fit between remarks about entities at one level and entities at another) concerns the problem of intensionality. One fashionable example of this problem is to be found in the philosophy of mind. Many philosophers have argued that psychological sentences have a quite different logic from, for example, the sentences one finds in the natural sciences. Psychological sentences, they claim, are typically intensional, while physical, chemical and biological sentences are typically extensional. What are the tests of extensionality? One test is that an extensional sentence permits extensional generalization: ascription of a property to an individual implies the existence of an individual with that property. Another test is the substitution test: in an extensional sentence, for any expression one can substitute an extensionally equivalent expression salva veritate. But psychological sentences apparently fail both tests. For example consider the sentence 'Fred believes that Charles Dickens met Mr Pickwick'. It fails the first test, the existential generalization test, since it does not imply that there is something (Mr Pickwick) such that it is believed by Fred to have been met by Charles Dickens. And it also fails the second test, the substitution test, since it does not imply 'Fred believes that the author of *American Notes* met Mr Pickwick'. Fred may not know that Dickens wrote *American Notes*.

As it stands, that point about intensionality is very muddled. It is just not true that natural scientists do not use intensional sentences and intensional explanations. It is not even true that physicists do not use intensional sentences and intensional explanations. Indeed, if Aristotle and Dennett are to be believed, intensional descriptions and explanations turn up all over the place. One of Aristotle's 'four causes', or four kinds of explanatory feature, is the 'telos', or purpose, or end, or proper point, of something: what it is for. He seems to have found it useful to apply that kind of explanation to almost anything that had any kind of structure, however rudimentary. Although we are much less prodigal, there are at least two good reasons for expecting to find intensional explanations in the natural sciences — and I include folk natural science for these purposes. The first reason is that we commonly use functional explanations, particularly in biology, and functional explanations are very reminiscent of Aristotelian teleology. We often use functional explanations in biology, in characterizing organs or other parts of a plant or an animal. What is a heart? It is a pump. What is a hand? It is a gripping device. What is a leaf? A power station. Such descriptions fail the first test for extensionality, because there are circumstances in which hearts don't pump (e.g. where that function has been taken over by an artificial pump during an operation) or in which hands don't grip (e.g. where I am coddled by an army of servants and am never required to grip anything at all), or in which the leaf does not produce any energy (because there is insufficient light). In a rather similar way, many descriptions of artefacts are typically intensional, since they characterize the artefact's function, what it is for, its proper use, rather than what it actually does. A thermostat is a temperature regulator, even when it isn't connected to the system, or is overridden by the householder. A chair is a single seat for one, even when it is carefully protected from possible use in the museum. Even if we look at academic physics, there is no shortage of examples of functional concepts that resist purely extensional analysis. For example when we talk about resistors and capacitors we are talking about the function or purpose of a component, rather than what it actually does. (Indeed, even the expression 'component' is itself used intensionally here. A component is something whose function, or proper purpose, is to be a part of a complex structure.)

The second reason for expecting to find intensional sentences in the natural sciences is that scientists often produce causal explanations, and causal explanations are typically intensional and fail the substitution test. Take a simple example from folk physics, which could easily be cleaned up and reformulated in the language of serious physics. Suppose I sit on a chair and it collapses under my weight. The appropriate causal explanation will look something like this:

C1:   The downward pressure from a 14 stone massive body
        caused the chair to collapse.

If we now substitute one extensionally equivalent expression for another, we get:

C2:   The chair's being sat upon by Mrs Wilkerson's only son
        caused the chair to collapse.

But C1 is true and C2 is false. C1 picks out the crucial causal mechanism, namely the relation between pressure and load-bearing capacities, whereas C2 threatens to bestow magical powers upon me, or upon my mother. The collapse is caused by my weight, not by my parentage. We cannot substitute extensionally equivalent expressions salva veritate.

If intensional explanations turn up all over the place in the natural sciences, is there anything more to be gained from thinking about intensional contexts? I think that there is a great deal to be gained. For the reasons I have just given, we cannot argue that explanations in the natural sciences are extensional, and that explanations in the social sciences are intensional, but we can reasonably argue that explanations in the social sciences characteristically involve a particular kind of intensional explanation. For they typically involve the use of *normative* concepts of one sort or another — concepts of what is rational, right, desirable, sensible, obligatory, justified or (conversely) of what is irrational, wrong, undesirable, stupid, to be avoided, unjustified, and so on. Those concepts in turn are connected with the concepts of intention, of purpose and of reasons for acting. All these concepts seem particularly remote from the concepts of the natural sciences. There are superficial parallels but they are only superficial. For example functional explanations in biology may be expressed in the language of purposes, but that has nothing to do with the notion of purpose that informs explanations of human action. Indeed, the biological story about the purpose of particular features could be translated into a very complicated story about the evolution of groups of individuals by natural selection and the causal role of various features of a phenotype in the process of evolution and survival. But the notion of purpose that informs explanation of human behaviour is intimately connected with the notions of a motive, an intention and a reason for action.

So I say once again that there is one group of intensional concepts, namely normative concepts, that are used, and only used, at comparatively high levels of explanation. They have no place in the natural sciences in general, or in physics in particular. The physicist is concerned to explain the occurrence of certain events (outcomes), given certain other events (initial states). The initial state in no way justifies the outcome, makes it rational or irrational, desirable or undesirable, sensible or stupid. But it is difficult to see how the social sciences could function at all without a rich repertoire of normative concepts. We are constantly judging our own behaviour and the behaviour of others against the background of legal and moral rules, or rules of economic and political strategy, and trying to make behaviour intelligible in the context of social rules and conventions. To abandon that repertoire would be to abandon the social sciences.

The fourth illustration (of a lack of fit between remarks about entities at one level and remarks about entities at another) highlights important differences between explanations at different levels, though the explanations may appear on the surface to be very similar. As I pointed out above, we use causal explanations at all the levels I have mentioned. Physicists, chemists and biologists are concerned to discover which physical, chemical and biological effects issue from which physical, chemical and biological causes; the professional or amateur psychologist looks for the causes of my behaviour, and tries to explain and predict it from knowledge of my beliefs, desires and attitudes; the sociologist, economist and political scientist all try to discover what causes what in the great social scheme of things.

If we delve beneath the surface, however, we find that there are a number of significant differences between lower- and higher-level explanations. To begin with, it is strictly false that physical explanations are causal explanations. On one standard interpretation of quantum physics, physical laws are best regarded as statistical generalizations which express the probability of an outcome given an initial state. And even if we refused to be fussy about the interpretation of quantum physics, and continued to talk loosely of causal explanations in physics, the 'cause' in each case would be the total initial state of the universe and the 'effect' the total subsequent state of the universe.

In contrast, higher levels of explanation have a quite different structure, in at least three respects.[1] First, we often pick out one element of the initial state as the 'cause', leaving all the other elements on one side as background conditions. The cause of the accident was my driving fast, though clearly the accident could not have happened without many other background conditions (the presence of other cars, the mechanical condition of the cars, the absence of protective barriers, etc.). The cause of the match's igniting was my striking it on the box, though nothing would have happened without further conditions (a rough strip on the box, the presence of oxygen, a dry atmosphere, the absence of chemical or physical inhibitors, etc.). It is not at all clear how or why we are so selective. Sometimes the cause is an event that is abnormal or unexpected or generally out of the way. Sometimes it is an event that is extremely normal, perhaps the event or condition that it is easiest for us to produce. Sometimes we seem to appeal to the Principle of the Final Straw: the cause is the final event in a long and accumulating sequence of events and conditions that eventually produced the effect.

Second, in some causal explanations the so-called cause is not even part of the fabric of the universe at all, but an absence, or a failure, or a refraining. The cause of the breakdown was the lack of petrol. The cause of the accident was my failure to see the warning notices, or my neglecting to ponder the consequences of the new road plan, etc. 'For want of a nail the shoe was lost, For want of a shoe the horse was lost ... .' Third, our interest in causes at higher levels of explanation is often irretrievably connected with an interest in moral or legal responsibility, or at least with an interest in outcomes that are potentially within someone's control, or are someone's legal or moral responsibility. We say that the dangerous driver caused the collision, even though it would not have happened at all had the innocent driver stayed at home. We fasten on to the bad driving or the failure to read a warning notice precisely because those are factors that we believe to be within someone's control, or to be someone's responsibility.

I shall now sum up the results of this section. I have been using a notion of levels of explanation, where levels are more or less determined by degrees of size and complexity, and I have argued that description and explanation of things at higher levels cannot in general be treated as a summary or generalization or simplification of description and explanation of things at the very lowest level, the level of physics. There seems to be no sort of fit, even loose and approximate, between our remarks about entities at one level and our remarks about entities at another. And the looseness of fit is evident if we consider a) the notion of identity; b) our habit of attributing psychological features, including propositional attitudes, to complex entities such as families, clubs, societies, nations, swarms and colonies; c) our use of one important group of intensional expressions, namely those with normative content; and d) our approach to causal explanation.

Explanatory liberalism

Let us now recall our original questions: What exists? And what counts as a true description of what exists? We discovered that there are at least two different answers to those questions. On the one hand, we are offered the desert landscape of physics, and invited to see the universe as a vast and complex arrangement of energy. On the other hand, we are offered a complicated and messy landscape in which all kinds of description and explanation jostle for our attention. They include physical, chemical, biological, psychological, economic, political and sociological descriptions and explanations. According to the first picture, we have no particular reason to focus on certain local concentrations of energy rather than others, for absolutely any packet of energy, large or small, concentrated or liberally scattered, will still obey the laws of physics and make a contribution to each transformation of the universe from initial state to subsequent state. According to the second picture, we will often find our attention drawn to certain special entities, particularly middle-sized material objects in general and to human beings in particular. They in turn are constituents of yet other entities, such as families, clubs and nations — or, in the cases of certain insects, of swarms and colonies. Finally we noted that the two pictures of reality are so different that there seems to be no way of treating the second picture as simply a summary or generalization or simplification of the first.

Is the fact that we have two answers to our questions, two pictures of reality, a cause for puzzlement or dismay? One familiar group of philosophers,[2] whom I shall call explanatory liberals, would argue that it is not. They would claim that the point of explanation is to make sense of what has happened, and to predict with moderate accuracy what is going to happen next. In order to do that, they would say, we must be ready to accept different kinds of explanation, at different levels, and in turn to accept different kinds of entity. Moreover, try as we might, we cannot sensibly concentrate our interest in the world around us into one channel. We inevitably develop an interest in the physical properties of things, in their chemical and biological properties, in the psychological properties of our fellows, and the economic, political and social organizations of which they are the most important constituents. We have so many different explanatory purposes, and the entities whose features we want to explain come in so many different shapes and sizes, that it is neither surprising nor embarrassing that the range of descriptions and explanations available to us is so wide and heterogeneous. So the two answers to our original questions, and the two associated pictures of reality, should not be thought of as incompatible. On the contrary, the physical picture is admirably suited to one explanatory purpose, and the other, much more prodigal, picture is admirably suited to a much wider and heterogeneous range of entirely different explanatory purposes.

What are the arguments for explanatory liberalism? It might seem that I have already given one argument in the previous section, in arguing that the second, much richer, picture of reality cannot be reduced to, or treated as a summary or generalization or simplification of, the physicist's picture. But that argument is not, as it stands, an argument for explanatory liberalism. It shows that there are two pictures of reality, but it does not show that we have good reasons for employing both of them. Astrological theories, and psychological theories that refer to witches or Aristotelian humours, cannot be reduced to the language of physics, but we would be very unwise to use them. We need to ask why we should not eliminate modern social sciences, in the way in which we have eliminated various scientific superstitions. Part of the answer will be a story about the general criteria of scientific acceptability. For example theories about astrological forces, witches and humours are flatly inconsistent with observation and never yield reliable predictions. They are quite literally useless. In contrast, social scientists do seem to be grappling with real entities, in some sense of 'real', and their explanations cannot be eliminated on the ground that they deal in compelling myths. And some social scientists, notably economists and psephologists, do seem to produce quite useful predictions, with a reasonable amount of success. But why should we not eliminate the social sciences for a quite different reason, namely that they deal in merely superficial properties, which at best supervene on the fundamental physical features of the world? Why should we not insist with the physicist that the real causal powers of the world are purely physical, and that in any fully developed account of the world the features of interest to social scientists will collapse into the fundamental physical features?

I shall have much more to say about causal powers and superficial properties later on, but nothing I say will imply that we could or should dispense altogether with non-physical explanations. There are at least three connected reasons for being an explanatory liberal. One reason is this. So far I have used a notion of levels of explanation, which are determined roughly, though not exactly, by the size and complexity of the entities in question. Sociological and economic explanations, for example, belong to quite a high level and are applicable only to entities that, from the physicist's point of view, are fairly large and complex. Now, if we are to explain anything, we need to regard certain events or states of affairs as instances of general laws, and we need therefore to detect patterns and regularities. But pattern and regularity are in part a function of level. That is, we may detect a certain pattern or regularity at one level, to which nothing even approximately corresponds at some lower level:

> Martians might be able to predict the future of the human race by Laplacean methods, but if they did not also see us as intentional systems, they would be missing something perfectly objective: the *patterns* in human behaviour that are describable from the intentional stance, and only from that stance, and that support generalizations and predictions.[3]

For example, we might attribute fear to a human being, a dog, an octopus or a crab, because their behavioural dispositions are remarkably similar. The attribution of fear would in no way be undermined by the discovery that the physical processes (e.g. brain processes) characteristic of a fearful human are quite different from those characteristic of fearful dogs, and different again from those characteristic of fearful octopuses or crabs. The pattern shows up at the level of the whole animal, the level of behavioural dispositions, but may be quite invisible at some suitably lower level. Nor therefore can the relevant explanatory feature at the higher level be reduced to some explanatory feature at some lower level.

This first reason leads us directly to a second, for the account of the first reason touched on a thought about the possibility of multiple realizations of a single feature. For example modern functionalists rightly value a distinction between function and realization. They regard psychological states as functional states, and they stress that one and the same function can be performed by an indefinitely large number of pieces of physical machinery,

by many different physical realizations. For example, many humans believe
that water is tasteless. Given that some are male, some female, that all are
genetically slightly different, that different groups of them speak different
languages, it is highly improbable that they are all in the same physical state
when they believe that water is tasteless. Moreover, functionalists will say,
we must leave room for much more extreme possibilities, for example that
beings who have nothing even remotely like a human brain and nervous
system might be functionally similar to us, and therefore capable of sharing
our beliefs and other psychological states. So there may be many different
realizations of the same function. But (and here is the important point for
our present purposes) the distinction beween function and realization is
inevitably a distinction between different levels of explanation. The function
emerges at the level of the whole person, and will often be invisible at the
level of the realization. Any attempt to characterize the multiple realizations
of the function forces us to retreat to some lower level of explanation, such
as the level of physical structures in the brain and nervous system. In short,
if psychological explanations and predictions are concerned with functional
role, rather than with realization, then psychology must be primarily
concerned with explanation at a fairly high level.

A third reason for using explanations at higher levels is that purely
physical explanations in terms of packets of energy are often in practice quite
useless, even when we are dealing with comparatively simple pieces of
machinery. It is in practice impossible for me to predict the behaviour of my
car by calculating the likely outcome of the present state of the entire
universe. I would be dead long before I had collected even a tiny fragment
of the information about the initial state of the universe. I would be wiser to
stick to the folk physics of large machines, and to ponder the general
connection between my turning an ignition key and the car's starting. Or
consider one of Dennett's favourite examples.[4] If I am trying to decide what
my chess opponent will do next (and it doesn't matter in the least whether
my opponent is a human machine or an artificial machine), it would be
impossible to apply the 'physical stance', to calculate the likely result of the
present physical state of the whole universe, including his/her/its present
physical state. Normally, successful prediction is guaranteed if and only if
I apply the 'intentional stance', and play on the assumption that my opponent
is a rational agent who is trying to win the game.

We can illustrate these three points by taking other examples from the
social sciences. For example economists are interested in patterns of
economic change, in changes in the rate of inflation, or the rate of
unemployment, or the rate of bankruptcy, but typically none of these patterns
show up neatly at some lower level, for example at the level of individual
firms or individual workers and businessmen. At the level of a whole

economy the rate of unemployment will vary in a way intelligible to macroeconomists, and it both affects and is affected by other economic variables also discernible at that level, such as the rate of investment, consumer demand, the prime lending rate, and so on. But nothing neatly corresponds to those variations at even the next lower level. If I may paraphrase a remark by that great economist and philosopher, Harold Wilson, now Lord Wilson of Rievaulx, to each individual worker the rate of unemployment is always either 100% or zero. As with our psychological examples, we must distinguish function (macroeconomic performance of the whole economy) from realization (the interrelated entities at some appropriate lower or microeconomic level, such as individual firms or banks or individuals, which together 'realize' that function). Furthermore, we can imagine different realizations of one and the same function. That is, we can imagine all kinds of different arrangements of workers, firms, businessmen, statisticians, etc., which realize the same macroeconomic organization, an economy with a certain GNP, a certain rate of growth, a certain rate of unemployment, and so on. The similarity between the different arrangements, the recurrent pattern, will be visible at the macroeconomic level of the whole economy, but at microeconomic levels we may be struck only by differences, between numbers and sizes of firms, between distributions of workers, between working methods, and so on. Finally, it would in practice be quite pointless to attempt to base economic predictions on information about the total physical state of the universe at a given time. Predictive success can be guaranteed if and only if we adopt the 'economic stance', and assume that individuals, firms and other bodies are attempting to achieve various economic goals in the face of scarcity, competition and other obstacles.

Before leaving this section, I should briefly add a fourth reason for thinking that we could not consistently refuse to use explanatory concepts that were not part of the language of physics. Earlier I noted that physics makes no provision for normative concepts, for notions such as a reason for acting, for what is desirable, rational, sensible, justifiable, for what accords with a rule or convention, and so on. Physicists simply tell us what follows what, not what justifies what. It follows that physics makes no provision for agency, for the notion of an agent is logically irretrievably connected with the normative notions I have just mentioned. Now any decision to restrict our explanatory repertoire, to abandon all concepts other than the concepts of physics, would either be self-defeating or inexpressible. If I were to justify my decision (to use only the language of physics) by appealing to philosophical reasons, the decision would be self-defeating, because the notion of a reason for a decision is not part of the language of physics. If, on the other hand, I simply stop using normative concepts altogether, then

I have no way of expressing what I have done and why I have done it. The very existence of an argument about the status of physics entails that there is more in this life than physicists can dream of. Paradoxically, even the physicist is constantly making decisions about what he ought to do, whether certain evidence supports some hypothesis, whether he is acting in a rational or sensible manner, but no such decisions can be expressed in the language of physics.

An objection to explanatory liberalism

That, then, is explanatory liberalism: we should and must embrace useful explanatory generalizations wherever they appear, and should cheerfully accept a wide range of explanatory laws and concepts, since different laws and concepts will be required in different contexts, for different purposes, and at different levels. We should not be worried or puzzled by the fact that explanations that prove to be highly successful at a comparatively high level (e.g. the explanations offered in the social sciences) cannot be neatly connected or reduced to explanations at some lower level, and particularly to explanations in the language of physics. Furthermore, if we are worried about what exists, and about which entities we should pick out in our description and explanation of the world, the explanatory liberal will offer us a wide range of entities. An entity will be any item that is the value of an individual variable at any level of explanation in any discipline.

In the rest of this book I shall be defending a view that falls short of unmitigated explanatory liberalism. I shall argue that, although we cannot work exclusively with the physicist's very restricted view of the world, not all explanations are on the same footing. Some have a special status. Part of the explanatory liberal's explanatory repertoire is far more significant than the rest, because it picks out members of natural kinds. In the rest of this chapter I shall prepare us for the fray by examining three general objections to explanatory liberalism. The first objection is that, despite their liberalism, despite their attempts to accommodate a wide range of logically different kinds of explanation, there is something that explanatory liberals fail to explain, namely the relation between explanations at one level and explanations at another. It surely cannot be an accident that something described at one level as a local concentration of energy is also, at another level, a quantity of chemical elements and compounds, and at another, a producer or consumer or citizen or whatever. There may well be good reasons for supposing that patterns and features at higher levels cannot be closely tied or reduced to patterns or features at lower levels, but surely there must in principle be an account of the relation between the various levels, and an explanation of how arrangements of entities at a lower level yield arrangements of entities at a higher level. After all, as I pointed out earlier, the distinction between levels corresponds roughly to a difference of size and complexity. Big things are composed of little things, and the bigger the entity, the higher the appropriate level of explanation. The relation between the bigger and the smaller, the higher level and the lower, cannot be a matter of magic!

In order to reply to this objection I shall help myself to something originally invented by my distinguished friend and colleague, Robert Kirk, namely the Strict Implication Thesis.[5] There are many compelling reasons for supposing that the world in which we live contains, and only contains, physical objects with physical properties. This is what Kirk calls 'minimal physicalism'. There are equally compelling reasons for supposing that many of our ontological, descriptive and explanatory concepts are logically quite different from the ontological, descriptive and explanatory concepts of physics. I have talked about levels of explanation and levels of existence. I have alluded to the possibility of multiple realizations of a single function, and the connection with levels of explanation and levels of existence. We can now combine all these disparate thoughts into a single thought, the Strict Implication Thesis: the totality of physical facts strictly implies the totality of facts, including psychological, economic, political and sociological facts — facts about families, nations, colonies and swarms, and so on. Necessarily, any two possible worlds exactly similar in every physical respect are exactly similar in every respect.

As Kirk discovered, the Strict Implication Thesis is very puzzling to some philosophers. Some will perhaps wonder how a set of physical sentences can strictly imply a set of conceptually different and conceptually much richer set of sentences, whose members include psychological, economic, political and sociological sentences, many of which are imbued with the normative concepts to which I referred earlier. Other philosophers will perhaps be puzzled because the Thesis seems in effect to be a claim that mind and body are necessarily connected, and many prominent physicalists have explicitly argued that the relation between minds and bodies (e.g. between minds and brains) is contingent.[6] So I shall briefly explain the point of the Strict Implication Thesis, and make clear what it excludes, what it allows, and why we should accept it. First, it allows that expressions used to characterize physical facts as such, and expressions used to characterize psychological and sociological facts as such, may well be logically very different, and that the second may well be irreducible to the first. As I argued earlier, in discussing normative concepts, psychological and sociological sentences may well have a conceptual richness that distinguishes them from physical sentences. But that in itself does not undermine the suggestion that the set of true physical sentences strictly implies the set of all true sentences. It will be puzzling only to those who have a very primitive view of strict implication, and expect the consequent of every example of such implication to be somehow 'contained' in the antecedent. Second, we should note that the Thesis allows two physically different worlds to share the same psychological, economic, political and sociological features. That is, the strict implication only runs one way. The totality of physical facts strictly implies the totality of facts, but not conversely. If the totality of 'other' facts (e.g. the psychological and sociological) facts were different, then the totality of physical facts would be different. But there could be an indefinitely large number of different sets of physical facts, each of which strictly implied one and the same totality of facts (including psychological or sociological facts). Different realizations, same functions.

The main suggestion that the Thesis is designed to exclude is the suggestion that there could be two worlds, physically exactly similar, but with different psychological, economic, political or sociological features. Indeed the main argument for the Thesis is 'minimal physicalism', the claim that the world in which we find ourselves contains, and only contains, physical objects and their physical properties. The minimal physicalist cannot allow any variation, for example, in the psychological facts without some variation in the physical facts. If there are only physical substances, the suggestion that two worlds could be physically similar but psychologically different is wholly mysterious. The mystery would only be dissipated by introducing something even more mysterious, namely non-physical substances or non-physical properties, which are only contingently connected with the physical substances and physical properties. In other words, it would be dissipated only by abandoning minimal physicalism in favour of Cartesian dualism or epiphenomenalism. But if a change in, for example, psychological and sociological facts strictly implies a change in physical facts, then, by contraposition, the totality of physical facts strictly implies the totality of facts.

So there is no special mystery about the connections between facts at one level and facts at other levels. Indeed, if we were able to display a hierarchy of levels in each explanatory context, we could illustrate a corollary of the Strict Implication Thesis, namely that the totality of facts at any given level strictly implies the totality of facts at all higher levels. I am not particularly anxious to tighten the talk of levels, and I suspect that it might prove impossible to display a neat hierarchy in each explanatory context, so I will not press the corollary. But the Strict Implication Thesis itself helps us to see how we might connect the physicist's picture of reality with the explanatory liberal's, without forcing the explanatory liberal to abandon descriptions and explanations that cannot be reduced to those of the physicist.

A Kantian argument from Strawson

Let us now turn to a second objection to explanatory liberalism. It consists in an attempt to show that some entities have a special status, and reflects a long philosophical tradition stretching back through Kant to Aristotle. The entities that supposedly have that special status are medium-sized material objects. The argument I wish to consider can be found in chapter 1 of P.F. Strawson's *Individuals*. In the barest outline it goes like this. In talking to ourselves and others, we make identifying reference to objective particulars, to such things as people, pieces of furniture, to historical events and processes such as the battle of Waterloo, or the decline and fall of the Roman Empire. If we are to guarantee successful reference, our identifying reference must in principle uniquely identify one particular rather than one exactly similar. We need for example to distinguish two exactly similar twins, or to distinguish two exactly similar renderings of Beethoven's 'Choral' Symphony. As techniques of mass production make abundantly clear, two particulars can share exactly the same sensible properties, such as colour, shape, size, and so on. So the only way to offer the guarantee of successful reference is to identify the particular as having a certain spatial and temporal position. Compare Kant:

> difference of spatial position at one and the same time is ... an adequate ground for the *numerical difference* of the object.[7]

The two twins are numerically different, or the two performances of the symphony are numerically different, because they are either at different places at a given time, or at different times at a given place. So uniquely identifying reference is possible only within a system of spatio-temporal coordinates.

But how is such a system established? Rather in the way that Leibniz described: places and times are defined in terms of spatio-temporal relations between material objects. So our description of the object that concerns us should include an account of its spatial and temporal relations to other objects. But it is always logically possible that the universe is exactly symmetrical, that the material objects in one half of the universe, together with their spatial and temporal relations, are mirrored exactly by other material objects, together with their spatial and temporal relations, in the other half. (Imagine a chess board which has an 'Equator' running down one of the longest diagonals.) So any description of one object, including a reference to its relations to other material objects, will pick out two objects, both the object that concerns us and the object in an exactly similar position on the other side of the universe. In order to distinguish one particular from its mirror particular, we must make demonstrative reference to certain material objects, which will act as conventional fixed points of reference, and will underpin our system of spatio-temporal co-ordinates. That is, we must eventually abandon the attempt to identify all objects solely by the use of complex descriptions, and locate some of them, or the objects related to them, simply by *pointing*. In short, identifying reference to objective particulars requires awareness of material objects in space and time. Thus material objects have a special status, for, unlike entities of every other kind and level, they underpin the system of spatio-temporal co-ordinates which in turn underpins our ability to talk about objective particulars at all.

One response to this argument is tempting but muddled. It is tempting to argue that this argument is a transcendental argument, that is, an argument that purports to set out the necessary conditions of a possible experience, and that, like all transcendental arguments, it is in spirit anti-realist. It is therefore inconsistent with the general realist spirit which has been implicit in my discussion so far, and which will be increasingly explicit in what follows. The argument is anti-realist, it will be said, because it makes the existence and features of reality dependent on the existence and features of sentient beings. More specifically it makes the special ontological status of material objects dependent upon the referential requirements of our language. So the argument may reveal a great deal about our *thought* about reality, but reveals nothing about reality.

That response, as I said, is muddled. It may well be true that many transcendental arguments are in spirit anti-realist, and can be made valid only if we suppose that the reality to which they refer is in some sense dependent upon us and our theories about it. Indeed that was the central thought in Kant's 'Copernican Revolution'. He claimed that a priori knowledge of reality is certainly available, but only if we attach a transcendental idealist or, as we would say, anti-realist sense to 'reality':

> If intuition must conform to the constitution of the objects, I do not know how we could know anything of the latter a priori; but if the object (as object of the senses) must conform to the constitution of our faculty of intuition, I have no difficulty in conceiving such a possibility.[8]

But I do not think that Strawson's argument suffers that fate. He is not committed, for example, to rejecting the realist's conception of material objects, as existing wholly independently of our thoughts about them. Quite the contrary. Rightly or wrongly, he clearly thinks of material objects realistically, and is merely concerned to argue that our reference to objective particulars logically depends on our awareness of certain material objects.

A much better response (which is easily confused with the first response) is as follows. This chapter has been concerned with ontological questions, with questions about what entities there are. I argued that we have to admit a rather complex and heterogeneous set of entities if all our reasonable explanatory ambitions are to be properly satisfied. In considering objections to explanatory liberalism, we have in effect begun to ask whether some entities have a special ontological status, whether any are in some sense ontologically primary. And I suggest that the main difficulty in Strawson's argument is that it is not, after all, an argument for ontological primacy, but an argument for epistemological primacy. He has not shown that the existence of material objects is particularly important in the scheme of things, but rather that our *knowledge* of their existence is necessary for our *knowledge* of the scheme of things. If we were not able to use certain material objects to fix a system of spatio-temporal co-ordinates, we could not have knowledge of objective particulars at all. That leaves open the possibility that there are other entities, which are no more or less important than material objects in the scheme of things, but which have a minor role to play in our knowledge of the world. Perhaps Martians, who are notoriously very different from ourselves, regard swarms, ant colonies, families, nations and clubs as epistemologically central, and show little or no interest in medium-sized material objects. So Strawson's argument gives us no conclusive reason to move from unmitigated explanatory liberalism.

An Aristotelian objection

In order to approach the third general objection to explanatory liberalism, we need to think more carefully about the notion of an entity. I observed earlier that, from the physicist's point of view, one concentration of energy is no more or less an entity than any other. From that point of view there is nothing to prevent our treating as an entity any old bucketful of energy, even a bucketful widely scattered in space and time, for example, an entity consisting of my left foot, the most remote hydrogen atom in the galaxy, the first nylon shirt, the nearest manuscript of Leviticus, and the potassium atoms in Queen Victoria's body at the time of her death. I think we would be wise to introduce some general constraints on the notion of an entity.

One plausible constraint is that a genuine entity should have some structural unity, where the structural unity is visible at some level of description or explanation. Random bucketfuls of energy have no such structural unity. If we allowed random bucketfuls to count as entities, we would deprive the notion of an entity of all content. That consideration immediately leads to another. If a genuine entity has a certain structural unity, it has criteria of identity, criteria that determine how such entities should properly be counted, and how they can retain their identity through change. And that consideration yields yet another. Anything with a certain structural unity and with criteria of identity is something of a certain kind. That is, it has certain properties that make it one kind of thing rather than another. It follows that its general determining properties, those that make it a member of a kind, can be described and explained in terms of appropriate generalizations. If the entity is capable of persisting through change, then its changes must be subject to scientific laws. (But for the moment I want to leave open questions about the essential features of a scientific law.)

To sum up, then, I suggest that a genuine entity must at least fulfil the following conditions:

(1) It must have a certain structural unity;
(2) It must have criteria of identity which determine how entities of that kind should be counted. If it is the kind of entity that can persist, its criteria of identity must determine when it comes into and goes out of existence and, if it is capable of change, the criteria must also determine and constrain its identity through change; and
(3) Its characteristic features and its characteristic changes must be governed by scientific laws.

Let us recall some of my main examples of entities of various kinds, and consider how many of them fulfil those conditions. Atoms and molecules seem to fulfil them, and can therefore reasonably be regarded as entities. So do medium-sized material objects, and particularly plants and animals. Sadly and obviously, sub-atomic entities do not fulfil them. There is no sense in talking of the structural unity, or the persistence through change, of an electron, a quark or a quantum of energy. So at best we have a constraint on atomic and supra-atomic entities, and we may wonder why we should accept the constraint in some cases but not in others. An Aristotelian might respond that, at the very least, it is a very striking fact that all entities other than the sub-atomic have those three general features, and the fact should be commemorated in some way. No-one can sensibly insist a priori that every entity must have the same general features. By all means let us abandon the strong language of constraints and conditions, but we should still argue that atomic and supra-atomic entities typically have the three general features in question. Furthermore, that move will in due course allow us to reveal an important difference between some of the entities and others. So, in this courteous and accommodating spirit, I ask once again how many such entities actually fulfil the conditions, and immediately report that atoms, molecules and medium-sized material objects fulfil them. But what about alleged entities such as families, clubs, societies, nations, swarms and ant colonies? They all have a certain structural unity, they all have criteria of identity, and their behaviour can be described and explained by appealing to generalizations familiar to scientists of various kinds, notably sociologists, bee-keepers and entomologists. The explanatory liberal will urge us to include them — and many other entities — in our general ontological inventory.

But (and here we come to the third general objection to explanatory liberalism) those nourished on a diet of Aristotle and Kant will regard such entities with considerable suspicion, and will argue that their existence is at best secondary, dependent or derivative. Their existence depends on the existence of medium-sized material objects, and in particular on the existence of plants and animals. It is precisely those medium-sized material objects that are the genuine entities, that have an ontologically central and primary role in the scheme of things. If we move down a level, and contemplate the parts or elements or constituents of the genuine entities, we find that the parts or elements or constituents (fingers, kidneys, arms, leaves, flowers, etc.) exist as such only insofar as they contribute to the structural unity of the complete animal or plant or other medium-sized material object. If, on the other hand, we move up a level or two, and contemplate families, clubs, societies or nations, we find that we are only dealing with well-organized collections of people. Since the families, clubs, societies and nations could not exist if there were no people, and since the people could exist in the absence of families, clubs, societies or nations, people — and, mutatis mutandis, other medium-sized material objects — clearly have a special ontological status.

If that view could be sustained, we would have a third answer to our original questions: What exists? And what counts as a true description of what exists? Against the physicist we could argue that we can legitimately introduce entities, concepts and laws that are not the entities, concepts and laws of physics. But against the explanatory liberal, we could insist that certain entities have a special status. But what are the arguments for that view? What are the arguments for the view that, among all the many entities accommodated by explanatory liberalism, some entities have a special status? I shall consider three.

The first argument should remind us of Aristotle's opaque remark in the *Categories* that substance signifies a 'this':

> Every substance signifies a certain 'this'. As regards the primary substances, it is indisputably true that each of them signifies a certain 'this'; for the thing revealed is individual and numerically one.[9]

It is the argument that medium-sized material objects, and particularly plants and animals, have clear criteria of identity and individuality. There are very definite grounds for deciding whether we have one and the same chimpanzee we started with, or one and the same elm, or one and the same human being. In contrast, if we move down to a lower level, to the level of arms or toe-nails or kidneys, or to a higher level, to the level of families, clubs, societies and nations, the notions of identity and individuality are much less secure. If we move down to the level of arms or toe-nails or kidneys, the problem is that such 'entities' no longer exist as such, once they have been detached from the whole organism, or once the organism has died. A detached arm is no longer an arm, a detached kidney is no longer a kidney, and so on. Their identity as arms or kidneys depends entirely on their making a relevant contribution to the life of the whole complex structured and living organism:

> no part of a dead body, such I mean as its eye or its hand, is really an eye or
> a hand ... when the soul departs, what is left is no longer an animal, and ...
> none of the parts remain what they were before, except in mere configuration
> ... Similarly, the true object of architecture is not bricks, mortar or timber,
> but the house; and so the principal object of natural philosophy is not the
> material elements, but their composition, and the totality of the substance,
> independently of which they have no existence.[10]

Furthermore, of course, if we go a very long way down, to the level of particles or packets of energy, the notions of identity and individuality no longer apply, for the notion of a persisting substance no longer applies. If, on the other hand, we move up to a higher level, to the level of families, clubs, societies and nations, we find it equally difficult to apply the notions of identity and individuality. History suggests, for example, that there are no very tight or generally acceptable criteria of identity for nations. The criteria that do exist have much less to do with the features of the nation in question than with the attitudes of other nations: roughly, a nation is almost any group of people that can persuade other similar groups to treat it as such.

This first argument is unconvincing for three reasons. The first reason is that it is no good to set up medium-sized material objects as paradigm examples of objects with clear criteria of identity and individuality, for philosophers since Hobbes have shown relentless ingenuity in producing puzzle cases that cast serious doubt on any suggested criteria of identity. Transplant surgery, Parfitian puzzle cases[11] and (as I shall reveal in chapter 6) even the mundane demands of amateur gardeners, all raise serious doubts about the prospects of stating completely determinate criteria of identity for medium-sized material objects in general, and for plants and animals in particular. A second reason for rejecting the argument is that it is preposterous to suggest that parts of medium-sized material objects, such as arms, toe-nails and kidneys, or structured and organized collections of those objects, such as families, clubs, societies and nations, lack criteria of identity and individuality. No-one in practice has serious difficulty in counting components temporarily separated from complete machines, such as carburettors, tyres, taps and tap washers. There may be something to be said for the view that a carburettor is strictly not a carburettor until bolted to an engine, and no doubt Aristotelian mechanics will talk of 'potential carburettors', but there is nothing at all to be said for the view that it cannot be counted under some appropriate description or other. Equally, in normal social and historical circumstances, no-one has any difficulty in distinguishing one family from another, or one club from another, or one nation from another. A certain family or club or nation may persist for many centuries, despite the deaths and births of its members, despite geographical relocation of the family (after emigration) or the club (after the purchase of new premises) or the nation (e.g. after refoundation in Israel in 1948).

The third reason for rejecting the argument is that, even if it were true, it would not give us an overwhelming reason for treating medium-sized material objects as special or primary entities in the scheme of things. We would at most have discovered that at one level the notions of identity and individuality have a particularly appropriate and comfortable application. But we already know from our talk of levels that concepts may apply at one level without necessarily applying at others. Indeed we already know that, quite often, new concepts emerge at higher levels. So, even if we managed to show that the notions of identity and individuality applied particularly neatly at the level of medium-sized material objects, we would not thereby show that that level was ontologically special or primary. Someone will no doubt point out that, in saying that, I have implicitly abandoned one of the general constraints on the notion of an entity, for I suggested that an entity must have criteria of identity. I will simply plead guilty. I have already argued that the notions of identity and individuality, and the associated notion of substance, will have little or no application to the basic entities of physics, to particles or packets of energy, and so I am already committed to conceding that those notions may apply at certain levels of entities but not at others.

A second argument for allowing a special ontological status to plants and animals would go as follows. We need to think carefully about the relation between structured, unified entities and their constituent parts. It is striking that plants and animals, though clearly composed of constituents, change and develop as organic entities. That is, they change and develop if and only if they retain their organic structure. The components may change, as the result of normal metabolic change or as the result of abnormal transplant surgery, but they persist as total, structured, unified organisms. But once they are divided into their constituent parts, neither they nor their constituents survive. A detached heart or kidney or leg or root or petal or leaf soon decomposes beyond recall. In contrast, so-called entities such as ant colonies, swarms of bees, families, clubs, societies and nations may go out of existence without their constituents' going out of existence. Even when the club has broken up, the members still press on. When the nation is destroyed, because of some historical catastrophe, the individual citizens survive. When the ant colony or the swarm of bees is disturbed by an enthusiastic but myopic gardener, the individual ants and bees rush about, confused but undoubtedly existent. We should draw the conclusion that the entities capable of survival in these various kinds of dissolution, namely whole plants and animals, have a special ontological status.

If I may be permitted a short digression, I would like to note in passing that those who enjoy firing textual missiles at their opponents will be sadly embarrassed at this point. This whole section is concerned with an Aristotelian objection to explanatory liberalism. It is Aristotelian because, in the *Categories* and the *Metaphysics,* Aristotle seems clearly to defend the view that medium-sized material objects, and especially plants and animals, have a special ontological status. Many of the points I have made I have borrowed, in letter or spirit, from Aristotle. It is therefore dispiriting to note that he appears to take an entirely different view in the *Politics,* and cheerfully treats all organic wholes in the same way, whatever their size, complexity or level:

> The state is by nature clearly prior to the family and to the individual, since the whole is of necessity prior to the part; for example if the whole body be destroyed, there will be no foot or hand, except homonymously, as we might speak of a stone hand ... the individual, when isolated, is not self-sufficing, and therefore he is like a part in relation to the whole.[12]

In a political context, it would seem, the entity with a special ontological status is the whole state, and positively not the individual. The only hint of the doctrine of the *Metaphysics* occurs a little later, and that hint is by no means unambiguous:

> The family may be said to be more one than the state, and the individual than the family.[13]

Let us now return to the main track. We were considering the second argument for the view that plants and animals have a special ontological status. The central thought was that special status should be granted to those entities whose constituent parts cannot survive the dissolution of the whole of which they are the constituents. And I can think of two difficulties. One difficulty is that, if we look carefully at examples of the so-called constituent parts of biological organisms, both whole organisms and well-structured colonies or swarms, the survival of constituents after the dissolution of the entity of which they were the constituents seems to be entirely contingent and unsystematic. Ants and bees do not in general survive after the destruction of the colony or the swarm, and kidneys do not in general survive the dissolution of the kidney's owner. On the other hand, humans do generally survive the destruction of their families, clubs and nations, and advances in medical technology will soon make it possible to preserve the parts of otherwise moribund individuals for use in future transplant operations.

A second difficulty is that there is an interesting group of animals whose behaviour suggests that we should not put too much weight on the distinctions between whole and constituents, or between individual organism and organs, or between colony and individual. Sponges consist of masses of specialized cells organized in a complex way to form a primitive organism. They are for example organized in such a way that they can draw in water containing fine food particles in one place, and expel water at another. Yet the individual cells are perfectly capable of an independent existence. If for example the sponge is filtered through a fine sieve, the individual cells will be separated and will survive — though curiously they will in time pay an unconscious tribute to Aristotle by reorganizing themselves into something resembling the original sponge. Here we seem to have a clear case of a single whole, with determinate criteria of identity, but whose constituents are quite capable of an independent existence.

So the second Aristotelian argument must be abandoned and we must turn to a third, which will provide our agenda for chapter 2. We might try to found the special ontological status of at least some medium-sized material objects, namely plants and animals, on their having what Aristotle called 'natures'. Aristotle's own notion of φύσις was a fairly narrow one, and was central to an account of the ability of substances to move themselves and to undergo change, but I shall follow a common philosophical practice and use 'nature' to refer to the intrinsic properties which make something a member of a certain natural kind, and which determine its behaviour and development. A chimpanzee is a chimpanzee, a daffodil a daffodil, an elm tree an elm tree, in virtue of their respective 'natures' or intrinsic properties, properties which determine the behaviour and development of chimpanzees, or daffodils, or elm trees. Furthermore, the doctrine of natures is connected by Aristotle, and will be connected by me in chapter 2, with a doctrine about independence. Aristotle argued, and I shall attempt to argue, that what makes a chimpanzee a chimpanzee, or a daffodil a daffodil, or an elm tree an elm tree, is its intrinsic nature, that is, a feature that does not depend on the existence of something else. It does not in any way depend on a relation between the chimpanzee, daffodil or elm tree, and something else. In contrast, what makes something a table or a bed or a house depends crucially on its relation to something else. For example something is a bed if and only if it can act as a comfortable nocturnal resting place for human beings; something is a house if and only if it provides permanent shelter for human beings, and so on. So, if all that is correct, we have discovered a curious feature of at least some medium-sized material objects, namely plants and animals, a feature which promises to give them a special ontological status.

Their being what they are depends on their intrinsic features, on their 'natures', and on nothing else. Crudely, the rest of the world could change as dramatically as it wished, but things of *that* kind would still be things of *that* kind.

I intend to pursue this argument at much greater length in chapter 2, but I am happy to admit straightaway that it faces very serious objections. I cannot deny that the connected notions of a 'nature', an intrinsic property, and of ontological independence, are extremely slippery. To begin with, there is an obvious sense in which the existence of plants and animals depends on the existence of something else, for it depends on the existence of constituent parts. Indeed historically that consideration was taken by many philosophers as an excellent reason for refusing to regard medium-sized material objects as substances, and for connecting the notions of substance and simplicity. The argument went like this. A substance is necessarily something whose existence does not depend on the existence of something else; but a material object is a complex of constituents, and so the existence of a material object depends on the existence of its constituents; therefore a material object (and more generally any complex object) is not a substance. In other words, a substance is necessarily simple.[14]

One possible reply to that move (and here I anticipate some of the argument of chapter 2) is to distinguish two kinds of dependence, a dependence of constitution and a dependence of relation. A's being *constituted* by B, C, D, etc. is quite different from A's being *related* to B, C, D, etc. At any given moment A can exist only if its constituents exist, though of course over a period of time the constituents may change, because of metabolic change, transplant or repair. In contrast, if we now think about the dependence of relation, it is clear that at any given time, A could exist even though the objects to which it is related did not exist. For example, I could exist even if my friends and acquaintances, my books and furniture, did not exist. So we can now repeat the original claim, making it clear at every stage that, in talking about dependence, we are talking about the dependence of relation, not the dependence of constitution. A chimpanzee or a daffodil or an elm tree is what it is in virtue of its intrinsic properties, not in virtue of a relational dependence upon something else. In contrast, a table or a chair or a house depends for its existence, qua table or chair or house, on a relation to something else, namely a functional relation to a possible user.

It is interesting, however, that, even if that reply went some way towards showing that some plants and animals have a special ontological status, it would also appear to show that swarms of bees and ant colonies have a similar status. For a swarm or a colony is what it is in virtue of certain intrinsic properties, and its existence as a swarm or a colony, though clearly depending on the existence of constituent bees or ants, does not depend on its being related to anything else. The two cases seem to run along exactly parallel lines. At any given time the existence of a plant or animal depends on the existence of its constituent parts, but equally at any given time the existence of the swarm or colony depends on the existence of constituent bees or ants. Change the rest of the world as much as you wish, thereby changing the relational properties of the plant or animal as much as you wish, the chimp is still a chimp, the daffodil is still a daffodil, the elm is still an elm. Change the rest of the world as much as you wish, thereby changing the relational properties of the swarm or colony as much as you wish, the swarm is still a swarm and the colony is still a colony.

A rather similar worry seems to arise from pondering the notion of a nature, an intrinsic property or set of properties which makes plants and animals the plants and animals they are, and which determines their behaviour and development. The problem is not that plants and animals don't have such natures (though I shall have some trouble defending that thought in chapter 5), but rather that other entities also seem to have natures of their own. For example, the explanatory liberal will say, many of the entities studied by social scientists have characteristic natures: families, tribes, nations, industrial proletariats; perfect markets, stock exchanges, hunter-gatherer economies; aristocracies, democracies, oligarchies; and so on. Just as it is the task of natural scientists to discover the physical, chemical and biological natures of things, so it is the task of social scientists to discover the psychological, sociological, political and economic natures of things. After all, social scientists use general descriptive and explanatory language, make predictions and test their theories against the facts of social history, rather in the way in which natural scientists use general explanatory and descriptive language, make predictions and test theories by experiment.

So we are for the moment at a stand. According to the explanatory liberal, there are many kinds of entities, of many different levels, and we must be prepared to countenance a correspondingly wide range of explanatory concepts. The objection to such liberalism is that, although there are undoubtedly many kinds of entities, and many kinds of explanatory concept, some entities have a special status, because they are members of natural kinds. The obvious reply is to say that many entities can be said to belong to natural kinds, for any serious academic discipline devoted to explanation and prediction will in effect be devoted to discovering the 'natures' of the entities central to the discipline. I say that we are for the moment at a stand, because we quite clearly need to know much more about the notion of a natural kind. I shall turn to that problem in a new chapter.

Notes

1   Cf. H.L.A. Hart and A.M. Honoré (1959), passim.
2   Daniel Dennett seems to me to be a good example. Cf. his (1978) and (1987), passim.
3   D. Dennett (1987), p. 25.
4   See D. Dennett (1978), pp. 237-8.
5   See R. Kirk (1994), p. 74 ff.
6   See J.J.C. Smart (1963), passim.
7   Kant (1781/87), A263/B319.
8   Kant, op. cit., Bxvii.
9   Aristotle, *Categories*, 3b10-12.
10 Aristotle, *De Partibus Animalium*, 641a3-4; 641a19-20; 645a33 - 645b1.
11 See D. Parfit (1984), chs. 10-12.
12 Aristotle, *Politics*, 1253a19-22 and 26-7.
13 Aristotle, *Politics*, 1261a20.
14 Cf. the discussion of the thesis of the second Antinomy, in Kant, op. cit., A434-42/B462-70.

2 Natural kinds

What is a natural kind?

In chapter 1, I asked what exists. I compared and contrasted two answers to the question. On the one hand, there were those with a special interest in physics, whose ontology included only those entities mentioned in physical theory. On the other hand, there were those I dubbed explanatory liberals, who were prepared to countenance any entity that fulfilled certain very general conditions, and any entity that appeared in a serious descriptive and explanatory discipline. The very general conditions were that the entity should have clear criteria of identity, that it should have a certain structural unity, and that it should lend itself to description and explanation in terms of relevant scientific generalisations. In order not to prejudge too many of the crucial philosophical issues, I placed no constraints on what should count as a serious descriptive and explanatory discipline, and (at least provisionally) left room for all sorts of entities available to explanatory liberals, in particular the entities of the social sciences.

In this second chapter, I want to discuss something that is likely to turn up in both ontologies. Whether we incline to the view that the only genuine entities are physical, or whether we believe that entities may be physical, chemical, biological, psychological, economic, political, etc., we may well wish to cater for so-called natural kinds. Indeed, any version of metaphysical realism requires a commitment to natural kinds in some fairly weak sense of 'natural kind'. I take metaphysical realism to be the view that there is a distinction between reality or 'nature', on the one hand, and our beliefs and theories about it, on the other. If all goes well in our scientific work, our beliefs and theories will converge upon the truth; if not, not. But in either case, according to the metaphysical realist, we must use a broad distinction between the features that reality actually has, and the features we ascribe to it. In writing a book about natural kinds, I am assuming the truth of metaphysical realism. I make the assumption, not because I suppose it to be uncontroversial, but simply because one cannot take on the whole of philosophy at one go, and because I wish to concentrate on one small group of interconnected problems. Now, if we are realists, we are bound to consider how things are 'in nature', and to wonder whether the kinds distinguished in our theories are natural kinds. To use Plato's familiar analogy, we must wonder whether we are carving at the joints of nature. Moreover, it will follow that some of the entities and features mentioned in our theories have a special status. For, if our theories are true, those entities and features are 'natural'. That is, they are not merely theoretical entities and theoretical features, but are parts of reality independent of our theories.

That, as I said, offers a very weak account of a natural kind: in this weak sense, natural kinds are determined by all and any features that are logically independent of our beliefs and theories. A stronger account is likely to be much more interesting than that. But what sort of stronger account is available? In what 'interesting' sense are there natural kinds? As we shall see, the concept of a natural kind has a long history. Many of the important doctrines can be detected in Aristotle, were revived by Locke and Leibniz, and have again become fashionable in recent years. There has been considerable general agreement about paradigm examples: the kinds *electron, proton, neutron, narcissus, chimpanzee, stickleback, carbon, gold* and *water* are natural kinds, and the kinds *table, nation, banknote* and *rubbish* are not. Equally it has been generally agreed that, if there are natural kinds, they fall into at least two groups. There are kinds of stuff, such as *carbon, gold, water, cellulose*, and there are kinds of individual, such as *tiger, chimpanzee, stickleback, narcissus*. As we shall see in the next chapter, we may have to provide at least one further category to accommodate some of the entities of physics, medicine and other disciplines. Sadly, agreement does not extend much further. It is impossible to discover a single account of natural kinds in the literature, and different discussions focus on different doctrines without writers or readers being aware of the fact. In this chapter I shall attempt to find a defensible distinction between natural and non-natural kinds.

Where should we begin? One obvious answer is that the notion of a natural kind must first be tied to that of a real essence, understood as a property or set of properties both necessary and sufficient for membership of the kind. Whether we are talking about kinds of stuff (*gold, water, cellulose*) or kinds of individual (*tiger, chimpanzee, stickleback*), members of natural kinds have real essences, properties which make them members of the relevant kind, and without which they could not be members of that kind. Thus gold must have a certain real essence (which we may for the moment suppose to be its having the atomic number 79) if and only if it is to be gold; and a chimpanzee must have a certain real essence (which, again, we may for the moment suppose to be its having a certain genetic constitution) if and only if it is to be a chimpanzee. The word 'real' is there, of course, to remind us that the account of natural kinds is offered within the general framework of metaphysical realism. The essences of natural kinds are quite independent of our thought about them, and any essential features that are merely essential de dicto, and merely reflect the structure of our thought, rather than the structure of reality, are irrelevant to the matter in hand.

But that answer doesn't take us very far. It appears perhaps to take us far, but only because of my careful and very restricted choice of illustrative examples. If a natural kind is merely a kind with a real essence, and if a real essence is merely a property or set of properties necessary and sufficient for members of the kind, then there will be an enormous number of natural kinds. The only significant cause for scepticism would come from those who have accepted Wittgenstein's account of family resemblances, and who are therefore sceptical about the whole project of defining general words in terms of necessary and sufficient conditions. Those who do not share that kind of scepticism will simply be left with an enormous number of natural kinds. If we can in principle state the conditions necessary and sufficient for something's being a table, a greeting, a theory, a string quartet, a number, a nation or a banknote, then they will all count as members of natural kinds. Clearly that is absurd, and we must stiffen the account.

I suggest that, if we are to produce an interesting account of natural kinds, we should insist that members of natural kinds, and the corresponding real essences, must lend themselves to scientific investigation. It is possible to have a science of gold, water and cellulose, or of tigers, chimpanzees and sticklebacks, because it is possible to produce suitable theoretical generalisations about their behaviour. It is precisely because gold has a certain atomic number that it has certain characteristic properties (its being malleable, fusible, etc.); it is precisely because a chimpanzee has a certain genetic constitution that it has certain characteristic properties (e.g. a characteristic way of growing and reproducing itself); and so on. Gold cannot change into water or cellulose and chimpanzees cannot change into tigers or sticklebacks. In contrast, it is impossible to have a science of tables or greetings or nations or banknotes. Tables are made of so many different materials, come in so many shapes and sizes, that there are no very definite constraints on their properties and behaviour. Greetings, nations and banknotes are governed by so many different legal, political and moral conventions that they do not lend themselves to any sort of precise scientific investigation. By the same token, we should insist that natural kind predicates are inductively projectible, whereas other predicates are not. If I know that a lump of stuff is gold, or that the object in front of me is a narcissus, I am in a position to say what it is likely to do next, and what other things of the same kind are likely to do. I know for example that the gold cannot turn into water, and that the narcissus will not in due course produce tomatoes. Moreover, since membership of the kind is determined by a real essence, I know that no other piece of gold could be persuaded to turn into water, and that no other narcissus could be persuaded to produce tomatoes. Certain outcomes, including counterfactual outcomes, are ruled in, and others are ruled out, by the real essences of gold or of narcissi. In contrast, if I know that the stuff in front of me is rubbish, or that the object over there is a table, I am in no position to say what it is likely to do next, nor what things of the same kind are likely to do. This heap of rubbish might be inflammable, because it contains unwanted animal fat, but another heap of rubbish will not be inflammable, because it contains nothing but brick rubble. This table will shortly collapse, because it has woodworm, but that one is virtually indestructible, because it is made of stainless steel. Conversely, perhaps in Greenwich Village or on Twin Earth this heap of assorted waste might be regarded as an interesting objet d'art, and that object with a flat upper surface and four regularly-spaced lower projections might be used as a writing implement. Because there are no very specific real essences that make rubbish rubbish, or tables tables, I cannot even in principle make sound inductive projections about rubbish as such or tables as such.

So (to repeat) if an account of natural kinds is to be at all interesting, it is no good merely to tie the notion of a natural kind to that of a real essence; we must insist that members of natural kinds, and the corresponding real essences, must lend themselves to scientific generalisation. But there is still more to be said. Historically, the real essences of natural kinds have been thought of as intrinsic, rather than relational, properties. Nothing I have said so far actually commits me to that view. In saying that a natural kind has a real essence, a property that is necessary and sufficient for membership of the kind, and in insisting that the real essence must be a property that lends itself to scientific investigation and inductive projection, I have left open the possibility that it is some relational property. And indeed, scientists clearly take a keen interest in the relational properties of things, and characterize them in terms of their relational properties: an electron is a particle with a negative charge, which orbits the nucleus of an atom; an acid is a proton-donor; a gene is a complex molecule which governs the properties of the phenotype; and so on.

However, I wish to argue that we must close off that possibility, and insist that the real essences of natural kinds are intrinsic properties, not relational properties. The reason is that scientific generalisation rests on an account of the causal powers of things, and causal powers must be constituted or realized by their intrinsic properties. No doubt we often express causal powers as just that: powers or dispositions to behave in certain ways in certain circumstances. Moreover, in doing so, we inevitably allude, directly or indirectly, to the relation between one individual or quantity of stuff and another. So for example in talking about acids as proton-donors we are alluding to the results of potential chemical reactions between the acid and other substances. But all of this story, about the dispositions or powers of things, and their relations to others, must rest on a story about their intrinsic properties. If we fail to produce a story about intrinsic properties, we are left with a mystery, with the unexplained brute fact that various objects are related in various ways. And since the number of possible relational properties will be very large indeed, our scientific generalisations will be at best very messy and at worst unmanageable. The only way of cutting through the mess is to suppose that all dispositional properties must be constituted or realized by categorical properties, and that all causal powers lie ultimately in the intrinsic properties of things.

Three comments

So we now have three general and interconnected conditions which any interesting account of natural kinds must satisfy. The first condition is that membership of a natural kind is determined by a real essence, a property or set of properties necessary and sufficient for membership of the kind. If that condition is to be interesting, it must be stiffened by a second condition, namely that natural kinds, and their real essences, lend themselves to scientific generalisation. And the third condition is that, since scientific generalisation involves exploring the causal powers of things, and since causal powers must be constituted or realized by intrinsic properties, the real essences of natural kinds must be intrinsic rather than relational properties. Before moving on, I must add three quite important comments — all, I hope, in the interests of clarity.

The first comment returns us to my remarks about tables and rubbish. I said that we cannot even in principle make sound inductive projections about rubbish as such or tables as such. The phrase 'as such' is very important. Obviously I can make safe predictions about the behaviour of my table or rubbish heap under certain circumstances. I know the likely outcome of putting my kitchen table on the bonfire, or of leaving a heap of vegetable waste undisturbed in a hot climate. But the point is that, in making my predictions, I am exploiting the fact that every object, or quantity of stuff, will belong to at least one natural kind, even if it also belongs to one or more non-natural kinds. My predictions rest, not on any facts about membership of non-natural kinds, but on facts about membership of natural kinds. I am not predicting the behaviour of the table *as a table*, but rather its behaviour *as a quantity of cellulose*, and I am not predicting the behaviour of the rubbish-heap *as a rubbish-heap*, but rather its behaviour *as a quantity of decomposing vegetation*. As Aristotle remarked,

> a bed and a coat and anything else of that sort, qua receiving these designations ... have no impulse to change. But in so far as they happen to be composed of stone or of earth or of a mixture of the two, they *do* have such an impulse, and just to that extent.[1]

We need constantly to acknowledge those important expressions 'qua', 'insofar as', and 'just to that extent'.

The second comment consists in an admission that an account of natural kinds which involves a notion of real essences, and which ties that in turn to those of scientific generalisation and inductive projectibility, will inevitably include a highly controversial account of scientific laws. Defenders of such an account (and I am one) will argue that scientific laws are necessary truths, which articulate certain de re necessities in nature. It may not be at all obvious why a concern with inductive projectibility should be connected with an interest in de re necessities in nature, but curiously the connection was most eloquently explained by Hume, who was profoundly sceptical about both of them. In his long and penetrating account of causation, induction and probability in Book I, Part III of the *Treatise*, he in effect argued that rational inductive practices rest on the assumption that, in general, preceding events are necessarily connected with succeeding events. If we are to have a rational expectation that one event, and no other, will happen next, we have to assume that it *has* to happen, given the immediately antecedent state of the universe. As philosophers interested in the problem of induction, we must then make a difficult choice. Furthermore, there are only two positions available. On the one hand, we can follow Hume, and despair of making any sense of the notion of a necessary connection between distinct existences. But then, like Hume, we must argue that induction is not a rational procedure, and that, although we may have very strong expectations about the future, they are not rational expectations. On the other hand, we can follow, for example, Leibniz and Kant, and insist that our inductive practices are rational, on the ground that objects have real essences, which determine how they must behave. That is, we can insist that there are necessary connections between distinct existences. But we must then make sense of natural or de re necessity. That is the course I propose to take, and I shall attempt to plot the course in chapter 3.

For the moment I shall merely repeat that there are only two positions available. The many empiricists who have applauded Hume's attack on the notion of de re necessity, and yet have claimed to justify induction, are deceiving themselves. John Mackie, for example, in his otherwise admirable analysis of causation, attempts to distinguish two senses of 'necessity'. Necessity$_1$, which he accepts, is the feature (whatever it may be) that distinguishes causal from non-causal sequences. Necessity$_2$, which he rejects, and which Hume rejected, is the supposed warrant for an a priori inference, for example, the power in a cause which allows us immediately to infer that the effect will follow.[2] The expression 'a priori' is perhaps unfortunate, for Hume's and Mackie's opponents will almost certainly claim that metaphysical necessities in nature are discovered a posteriori. That is, although the necessities in question are indeed necessities, they do not occupy a fundamental and unassailable position in our conceptual scheme, and they certainly do not occupy a fundamental and unassailable position in any conceptual scheme. Nor are they discovered, or even discoverable, without any aid from observation. It would be better to say that, since the necessities are indeed necessities, as soon as I discover them a posteriori, I have an excellent reason, on pain of absurdity, to predict one outcome and no other. But let all that fussiness about 'a priori' pass. The central objection to Mackie's suggestion is that necessity$_1$ and necessity$_2$ collapse into one another. The supposed warrant for an a priori inference from one event to another is precisely the natural necessity that distinguishes causal from non-causal sequences, and which is grounded in the real essences of things, which in turn govern their behaviour.

   The third comment is a request that we should not put too much weight for the moment on the word 'scientific'. That is, in claiming that natural kinds lend themselves to scientific generalisation, I do not want to interpret 'scientific' so narrowly that I confine science to the natural sciences. As we saw in chapter 1, according to the explanatory liberal, there are many sciences other than physics, chemistry and biology, and many entities that can be investigated, described and explained in the language of the social sciences. In view of what I said in my second comment above, that would of course entail that the laws of the social sciences are necessary truths and articulate de re social scientific necessities. But I shall have more to say about this issue in the next chapter, and for the moment will leave open the possibility that some of the kinds dear to social scientists are natural kinds.

Nature, convention, artifice and culture

How then should we distinguish between natural and non-natural kinds? One apparently promising thought arises from pondering metaphysical realism, and the associated distinction between the features of reality that are independent of ourselves and our theories, and the features of reality that prove to be merely features of our theories or beliefs about it. Perhaps we need a distinction between the classifications that are given to us by nature, and the classifications that are somehow up to us, that reflect our peculiar wants, interests and preoccupations. Many philosophers have therefore thought it useful to discuss distinctions between natural and conventional kinds,[3] or between natural and artificial kinds,[4] or between natural and culturally generated kinds.[5] Thus, for example, banknotes are banknotes, and nations are nations, in virtue of human conventions. If there were no such conventions, there would be no banknotes and no nations, and if there were rather different conventions, more or fewer things might count as banknotes, or nations might be individuated differently: we might sensibly treat cheques as banknotes, or individuate nations more by sociological, religious or linguistic criteria, than by political or geographical criteria.

Similarly, if we turn to the notion of an artificial kind, we might argue that tables are tables, and pencils are pencils, because they have been manufactured specifically to fulfil certain functions for human beings. If there were no human beings, with peculiar interests and concerns, and with the ability to fashion useful artefacts, there would be no tables and no pencils. There might, because of some cosmic accident, be objects of medium size with flat upper surfaces and four regularly-shaped lower projections, or wooden cylinders with a core of soft black material, but in the absence of humans they would not be tables or pencils. Perhaps in other galactic societies similar objects are weapons of war or foodstuffs. More generally, all these examples are examples of culturally generated kinds, since their existence depends both causally and logically on the existence of certain cultures. They clearly depend causally on the existence of certain cultures, since they are the direct result of the development of human societies with various technological skills. Moreover, as we shall see later on, they also depend logically on the existence of certain cultures. That is, in any analysis of coins or banknotes or artefacts there will be an essential reference to the peculiar and historically parochial needs of human beings.

Unfortunately, none of these distinctions, between nature and convention, or between nature and artifice, or between nature and culture, will quite give us what we want. Remember our three general conditions: natural kinds are determined by real essences; members of natural kinds, and the associated real essences, characteristically lend themselves to scientific investigation; and real essences consist in intrinsic rather than relational properties. But there are many kinds that fulfil those conditions, and yet whose members are produced artificially, or, more generally, are culturally generated. The point has become particularly striking over the last century, with the construction of oil refineries and the invention of plastics. Polystyrene, pvc, kerosene, petrol, diesel fuel, etc., are certainly artefacts, but they have real essences, properties that make them the kinds of thing they are; they lend themselves to scientific investigation by organic chemists; and the real essences that determine the kinds consist in intrinsic chemical properties. They are all causally dependent on the existence of a certain historically parochial industrial culture, and some of them are described in a vocabulary that makes explicit their logical dependence on the existence of a certain culture: for example we talk of lighter fuel and of diesel oil.

Conversely, there are many kinds that fail to fulfil the three conditions, and yet are neither conventional nor artificial nor culturally generated. Gardeners talk cheerfully of seedlings, saplings, trees, shrubs, bushes, climbers, perennials, annuals, pot plants, and so on, but none of those terms pick out a real essence; none are likely to appear in reports of serious scientific investigation; and none refer to a kind determined by an intrinsic property. One and the same plant will grow as a tree under one set of conditions and as a shrub under others (e.g. many *Eucalyptus* and *Acer* species). One and the same plant will be an annual or pot plant in a temperate European climate and a shrub in a hot African climate (e.g. *Pelargonium* species). One and the same plant is a shrub in western Ireland and a hardy perennial in Nottingham (e.g. *Fuchsia magellanica*). None of those terms pick out an intrinsic property and none of them correspond, even approximately, to any botanical classification, whether at the level of varieties, or of species, or of genera, or of families, or of orders. For example, there is no intrinsic property of botanical interest that is shared by a seedling fern and a seedling cabbage. Yet none of the terms has any connection with convention, artifice or culture. No doubt it is a convention that we use the sound 'tree', rather than some other sound, to pick out trees, and all such sounds causally depend on cultural organisation, but that point is of no interest. It is equally a culturally generated convention that we use the sound 'gold', rather than some other sound, to pick out gold. But it is not a culturally generated convention that a particular substance is gold, and it is clear that it is not a culturally generated convention that something is a tree or a shrub or a bush or a climber, or whatever. Nor are trees, shrubs, etc., artefacts, however much loving care and attention we fanatical gardeners may lavish on our plants.

It is interesting that, mutatis mutandis, exactly the same point can be made about many geographical and meteorological kinds. They fail to fulfil our three conditions, but are neither conventional nor artificial nor culturally generated. Geographers talk of beaches, cliffs, mountains, valleys, seas and volcanoes. Meteorologists talk of depressions, anti-cyclones, winds, thunderstorms, clouds and hurricanes. But the terms do not pick out things with real essences, they do not figure in scientific generalisations, and they do not pick out any relevant intrinsic properties. One and the same lump of material will count as a mountain in one environment, as a valley floor in another, and as part of the sea bed in yet another. One and the same reaction counts as a thunderstorm if it happens on a large scale in the open air, but if it happens under the bonnet of my car it is called a short circuit and my car fails to start. On Earth thunderstorms involve water vapour, but perhaps on Venus they involve ammonia and on Twin Earth quite other gases. On Earth mountains and cliffs are made from a fairly narrow range of stony materials, but on Twin Earth perhaps they could be made from plasticine or Stilton cheese. But none of those things are typically artefacts, and I cannot think of any relevant convention or other culturally generated fact that makes a mountain a mountain, or a sea a sea, or a thunderstorm a thunderstorm, or a depression a depression. Mountains, seas, thunderstorms and depressions are just not like nations and banknotes.

Perhaps at this point we should pause for a moment, for some readers will already have found my remarks at best perplexing and at worst ridiculous. I have argued that there are many kinds that fail to fulfil our three conditions, and yet are neither conventional nor artificial nor culturally generated. Members of those kinds do not have real essences, they do not lend themselves to scientific investigation, and they do not share relevant intrinsic properties. There can be no science of trees and shrubs, of mountains and cliffs, of anti-cyclones and thunderstorms. But, it will be objected, that claim is patently absurd. All the examples are taken from well-established and highly respected scientific disciplines, from agriculture and horticulture, from geography, geology and meteorology. Surely I cannot seriously defend the view that they are not, after all, proper scientific disciplines. The scientific work, the theoretical generalisations, the successful explanations and predictions, are there for all to see! Furthermore, it will be said, we can make provision for such scientific disciplines with the aid of explanatory liberalism. According to the explanatory liberal, entities can only be individuated, and their behaviour explained and described, at a particular level of size or structure. Description and explanation are possible only if the phenomena to be described and explained exhibit a certain regularity and pattern, but patterns, like entities, are themselves relative to level. What emerges as a clear pattern at one level may well be invisible at some lower level. As far as our present disciplines are concerned (agriculture, horticulture, geography, geology, meteorology, etc.), they are very much concerned with general patterns that only emerge at a fairly high level. But since, at that level, description and explanation are so successful, I must surely accept that they are serious scientific disciplines.

In reply, I am happy to concede that farmers and gardeners, geographers, geologists, meteorologists and many others — such as civil engineers, computer scientists and builders of steam engines — do excellent scientific work and produce highly respectable explanations and predictions. But, paradoxical though it may seem, that concession does not undermine my claim that strictly there can be no science of trees and shrubs, of mountains and cliffs, of anti-cyclones and thunderstorms. We need to ask why gardeners, geologists and the rest manage to do such excellent work. It is no good appealing to the thought that entities, descriptions and explanations are relative to level, that the explanatory apparatus of a science may only make sense, and only yield useful predictions, at a certain level of size or structure. That argument looks plausible only in those cases where the entities visible at a higher level obviously depend very directly on patterns visible at some lower level, but where the explanatory apparatus of the science in question cannot in practice be reduced to some suitable explanatory apparatus at a lower level. For example, an excellent reason for taking biology seriously is that the biological properties of things obviously depend directly on their physical and chemical properties. But the explanatory apparatus of biology cannot in practice be reduced to the explanatory apparatus of physics or chemistry or both.

Similarly, we might decide to take seriously the explanatory apparatus of one or more of the social sciences on rather similar grounds. The thought would be that sociological patterns are emergent in a very strong sense: they are detectable at a certain level of size or structure, but cannot be reduced to, or even closely connected with, patterns at some lower level. And one symptom of such emergence would be that social scientists were noticeably reluctant to ground their disciplines on sciences that deal with entities of some lower level (e.g. on physics, chemistry and biology).

I shall have more to say about the social sciences in the next chapter, and I shall also have more to say about the notion of a level, but I hope that I have said enough to justify my surprising suggestion that many of the kinds that feature in agriculture, horticulture, geology, meteorology, etc., are not natural kinds, because they do not have real essences and do not lend themselves to scientific generalization. The general point to bear in mind is that the explanatory apparatus of such disciplines, though no doubt relative to a fairly high level of size or complexity, is not emergent. It is, as it were, perpetually provisional, and is constantly being reduced to, or connected with, or supplanted by, the explanatory apparatus of some discipline characteristically concerned with entities of some lower level, notably physics, chemistry and biology.

Given that general point, I can now answer the objection in three stages. First, the sciences of agriculture, horticulture, geography, geology and meteorology rest squarely on sciences that are directly concerned with real essences. Geology and geography would be impossible if there were no physics and chemistry of the various elements and compounds that constitute our planet. Meteorology would be impossible if there were no science of gases, of electricity, of the behaviour of massive bodies in gravitational fields. Agriculture and horticulture would be impossible without physics, chemistry and biology. Cliffs, as such, do not have real essences, but sandstone, limestone and granite do. Clouds, as such, do not have real essences, but gases such as oxygen, hydrogen and water vapour do. Trees, as such, do not have real essences, but elms, oaks and beeches do.

Second, agriculture, horticulture, geology, etc., involve the application of physics, chemistry and biology to specific cases, and especially to cases where local conditions are comparatively stable and constant. For example, those who are interested in the erosion of cliffs by the sea are confronted with one fairly homogeneous liquid, salt water, one fairly stable gaseous mixture, air, and a restricted range of stony materials, such as sandstone, chalk, limestone or granite. Their work would be incomparably more difficult if the sea in certain places consisted of crude oil or pure alcohol, or if the coast were littered with deposits of polystyrene foam or Stilton cheese. Similarly, meteorologists would find their professional lives unbearably difficult if the Earth's atmosphere contained some clouds of water vapour, some of ammonia, some of methane, or if there were large and unsystematic variations in the force of gravity from time to time or place to place. It is interesting to recall that, when the first spacecraft first landed on Mars and sent back pictures of the surface, geologists were baffled. The Martian environment was so very different from the terrestrial environment that they were quite unable to explain even superficial geographical and geological features. Similar bafflement seems to have greeted the recent collision between Jupiter and a very large comet: the structure and composition of Jupiter is so different from that of Earth that it is very difficult to make sense of what is going on.

Third, it is significant that the sciences we are discussing rely heavily on statistical methods. Meteorology is a particularly striking example. It is in practice impossible to predict weather patterns from a complete state description of the world, or part of the world, at a given time, with the aid of the laws of physics and chemistry. There are so many possible variables that it is impossible to complete the calculations. (Indeed, that very simple thought has recently inspired the new science of chaos theory.) It is, however, possible to use statistical methods with considerable success. Forecasters collect detailed information about key indicators at various places — wind speed, temperature, air pressure, humidity, etc. — and consult detailed records of weather patterns over many years. Roughly speaking, they comb their records until they find a day that was just like today, and they are then confident that the weather over the next few days will develop just as it did all those months or years ago. The improvement in weather forecasting over the last few years has had very little to do with a greater understanding of physical and chemical changes in the atmosphere, with an understanding of real essences. It has been due largely to the collection of more, and more accurate, information and to the introduction of computers. Both developments have allowed more sophisticated statistical comparisons between one day's weather and another's.

The third point is tightly connected to the first two, and thereby to our general discussion of natural kinds, for this reason. Statistical methods work only on two assumptions: that the various items of interest (clouds of water vapour, electrical disturbances, etc.) have real essences under some description, and that the general background conditions are comparatively constant and stable. We could not transfer our weather forecasts (or, mutatis mutandis, our geological, geographical, agricultural and horticultural predictions) to places where either of those assumptions proved to be false, where there were no underlying real essences to be discovered, or where background conditions were inconstant and mutable. So we could not use our expertise to make weather forecasts on Venus or Twin Earth, or to plan our voyage on the good ship 'Lollipop', since, notoriously, bonbons play on the sunny shore of Peppermint Bay.

Therefore I claim, again, that a satisfactory account of natural kinds must fulfil three main conditions: members of natural kinds must have real essences, natural kinds must lend themselves to scientific investigation, and real essences must consist in intrinsic properties. I conclude that the distinctions between the natural and the conventional, between the natural and the artificial, and between the natural and the culturally generated, do not quite give us what we want. I also conclude that disciplines such as geography, geology, agriculture, horticulture and meteorology are strictly not scientific disciplines, and are not concerned with natural kinds, in my 'strong' sense of 'natural kind'. Perhaps another point has emerged once again in the course of the discussion, namely that the word 'natural' is potentially misleading. Trees, shrubs, annuals and perennials are all natural in a perfectly ordinary, weak and uninteresting sense of 'natural', as are pebbles, volcanoes, rivers, glaciers, cliffs, thunderstorms, anti-cyclones and fronts. Anyone interested in 'nature', that is, anyone wedded to any version of metaphysical realism, would take an interest in such things. But none of them have real essences, and none are likely to yield any relevant theoretical generalisations. A perfectly ordinary sense of 'natural' is not enough. It is time to take a deep breath and start again.

Natural and nominal kinds

Sometimes a distinction is drawn between natural and nominal kinds, in a deliberate attempt to tie the account of natural kinds to Locke's distinction between real and nominal essences. According to that account, a real essence is a property that is essential to a thing, and makes it the kind of thing it is. A nominal essence is a property or set of properties that is typical of things of the same kind, is apt to feature in dictionary definitions of the relevant general name, and is the property or set of properties that we find it convenient to rely on in our ordinary everyday classifications. For example (to borrow one of Locke's own examples), the real essence of gold is its having the atomic number 79, and its nominal essence is its being rather heavy, yellow, fusible, malleable, and soluble in aqua regia. The real essence of a tiger is its having a certain genetic constitution (close to, but crucially different from, those of many other large cats), and its nominal essence is its being a fierce, black and yellow striped quadruped, with whiskers, strong teeth and a tail, and found in India.

Those are of course examples of members of natural kinds. According to this account, a natural kind is one determined by a real essence, and a purely nominal kind (such as the kinds *table*, *nation* and *banknote*) is determined solely by a nominal essence. In the case of natural kinds, it is argued, there is both a connection and a certain looseness of fit between real and nominal essences. There is a connection, because the real essence directly explains at least a substantial part of the nominal essence. It is no accident that an element with the atomic number 79 is fairly heavy, fusible and malleable, and it is no accident that an animal with the genetic constitution of a tiger looks and behaves as it does, and lives in India rather than, say, Antarctica. Plant and animal breeders constantly tinker with the genes of populations in an effort to produce plants and animals with the right sort of nominal essence, for example, plants with more attractive flowers or foliage or greater resistance to disease, dogs that will win dog shows, cattle that will produce leaner meat, and so on. On the other hand, there is inevitably a certain looseness of fit between real and nominal essences, for two reasons. One reason is that some members of a natural kind will lack at least part of the relevant nominal essence. Gold becomes brittle at low temperatures, and congenitally abnormal tigers may have three legs or no tail, or may be white and whiskerless. In some extreme cases, part of the nominal essence may be possessed by none of the members of the kind. Chemically pure gold is white, and the supposed golden colour of gold is due to minute traces of copper. The second reason is that there are individuals that substantially possess the nominal essence of a certain natural kind, but are not members of it. There were marsupial wolves and tigers in Australasia, but they were only remotely related to wolves and tigers. *Hebe cupressoides*, as the name suggests, looks and behaves just like a cypress, but is in fact a hebe.

One way of distinguishing between natural and nominal kinds (traces of which are found in Locke) goes as follows. In the case of natural kinds it is possible, and indeed necessary, to distinguish real from nominal essences. The nominal essence merely reflects our interest and convenience, and encapsulates useful criteria of recognition, but we suppose that, in nature, there are certain kinds of thing, with appropriate real essences. So, for example, in attempting to classify oaks, gold and sticklebacks, we are attempting to reflect the joints of nature. The extension of the natural kind name is determined by the real essence of the kind, not by its nominal essence. The real essence is the intrinsic property that unites all oaks, or the intrinsic property that unites all sticklebacks, or the intrinsic property that unites all samples of gold. In contrast, in the case of purely nominal kinds the distinction between real and nominal essences collapses, for we do not pretend to produce a classification that conforms to nature. A nominal kind is merely a kind determined by a group of features that, for one reason or another, we find it useful or convenient to associate. As far as we know, there are no relevant kinds in nature to which our classification could conform. There are no corresponding real essences underpinning our classification of tables, coins and banknotes, and we are free to associate various groups of properties together, and to classify things by such nominal essences, in whichever way seems useful and convenient. Ultimately the extension of the general name is determined by decision:

> these *essences of the species of mixed modes are* not only *made* by the mind, but made *very arbitrarily*, made without patterns, or reference to any real existence. Wherein they differ from those of substances, which carry with them the supposition of some real being, from which they are taken, and to which they are conformable.[6]

Questions about the proper classification of gold, tigers, oaks and sticklebacks should be answered by discovering real essences, certain de re necessities in nature. But questions about the proper classification of tables, coins, coffee cups and sinking funds can only be answered by reflecting on the de dicto peculiarities of our language, and on the distinctions we find it useful, or convenient, to adopt.

The distinction between natural and nominal kinds is undoubtedly better than the distinction between natural and conventional kinds, or between natural and artificial kinds, or between natural and culturally generated kinds. For it promises, among other things, to yield an account of the awkward examples I introduced in the last section. They were examples of kinds that are certainly not 'natural' in the strong sense that I am trying to identify, but are independent of convention, artifice and culture — kinds such as *tree, shrub, pot plant, annual, river, glacier, cloud.* If the distinction between natural and nominal kinds proved fruitful, we could say that, since none of those awkward examples are examples of kinds determined by real essences, they are purely nominal kinds. Having given their nominal essences, and perhaps having explained why we find it useful and convenient to collect precisely such-and-such properties in each nominal essence, there is nothing more we need to say.

Unfortunately the promise cannot be kept, for two reasons. First, the notion of a nominal essence is obscure. It is not clear, for example, how we are to decide which properties are to count as part of the real essence of a thing, and which are to count as part of its nominal essence. Nor is it clear whether a given property could turn up both in the real and in the nominal essence. The criteria offered are a very mixed bag: the nominal essence consists of those properties thought of as typical of the objects in question; or it consists of properties which often appear in dictionary definitions of the kind; or they are the properties that we rely on in our ordinary everyday classifications, and that are often straightforwardly observable. Locke, who frequently identifies nominal essences with abstract ideas, explains that the sorting of objects

> under names *is the workmanship of the understanding, taking occasion, from the similitude* it observes amongst them, to make abstract general *ideas*, and set them up in the mind, with names annexed to them, as patterns or forms.[7]

But in a scientifically educated community, any account of a nominal essence (e.g. in a good dictionary) is apt to include some reference to the real essence of the object, to the intrinsic properties in which a scientist is interested. For example, in our culture many of those invited to talk about water or sulphuric acid would say that water is H_2O and that sulphuric acid is H_2SO_4. There will be a clear distinction between real and nominal essences only in a community where there is a great gulf fixed between the scientific élite and everyone else, and in which the gulf is reflected in a systematic gap between ordinary and scientific vocabularies.

Second, as I have already hinted in my gloss on Locke, many philosophers who have used a distinction between natural and nominal kinds have given the definite impression that a nominal essence, and therefore the classification of purely nominal kinds, depends directly on human interests, conventions or convenience. Locke is an excellent though extreme example, for he frequently identifies nominal essences with abstract ideas, and is therefore committed to the view that purely nominal kinds are determined by the psychological tendencies and biasses of human beings:

> the *essence* of each *genus* or sort comes to be nothing but that abstract *idea* which the general or *sortal* ... name stands for. And this we shall find to be that which the word *essence* imports in its most familiar use. [It] may not

unfitly be termed ... the *nominal essence*.

    The measure and boundary of each sort or *species*, whereby it is constituted that particular sort and distinguished from others, is what we call its *essence*, which *is* nothing but that *abstract* idea *to which the name is annexed*; so that everything contained in that *idea* is essential to that sort. This, though it be all the *essence* of natural substances that we know or by which we distinguish them into sorts, yet I call it by a peculiar name, the *nominal essence*.[8]

Other philosophers, though not sharing Locke's account of abstract ideas, still give the definite impression that nominal essences, and therefore purely nominal kinds, depend on human interests and conventions. For example Schwartz talks of a nominal essence as a 'linguistic essence',[9] and Mackie describes it as 'a set of criteria of recognition'.[10] That impression is unfortunate, as we can see if we return to some of my previous examples, to trees and shrubs, to rivers and glaciers, to clouds and thunderstorms. I have argued that they are not, as such, members of natural kinds, because their membership of the kind is not determined by a real essence. But equally their classification does not merely reflect the de dicto peculiarities of our language, and thereby the peculiar interests, psychological habits, conventions and preoccupations of human beings. So they do not count as members of purely nominal kinds. In some (admittedly weak) sense of 'natural', it is just a brute natural fact that certain plants have a single woody stem, which branches some feet from the ground, and that others produce a mass of branches very close to the ground; that water rises from the ground on land masses, and flows within more or less confined limits to the sea; that quantities of water vapour collect in the lower part of the Earth's atmosphere; and so on. These facts are no doubt often reflected in our classifications, and therefore in facts about our interests, conventions and preoccupations, but they are logically independent of them. There is a 'natural' distinction between trees and shrubs, or between rivers and glaciers, even if none of us have the wit or the wish to draw it. Once again we must look elsewhere for a satisfactory account of natural and non-natural kinds.

Natural and dependent kinds

I have already implied that one of the most interesting discussions of natural kinds is to be found in Locke's *Essay* (and, indeed, in corresponding sections of Leibniz's *New Essays*[11]). Not merely does Locke attempt a careful analysis of the distinction between real and nominal essences, but he is clearly aware of the important consequences for the philosophy of science. If the distinction can be sustained, science becomes a search for real essences, and scientific laws are to be understood as de re necessary truths about the properties that determine membership of natural kinds, and their important role in governing the behaviour of individual members. It is therefore sadly ironic that, having whetted our appetites, Locke eventually abandons the project, on the general ground that real essences are inaccessible and incomprehensible:

> we, having but some few superficial *ideas* of things, discovered to us only by the senses from without or by the mind reflecting on what it experiments in itself within, have no knowledge beyond that, much less of the internal constitution and true nature of things, being destitute of faculties to attain it.[12]

He claims that we must be satisfied with nominal essences, and must concede that '*men make sorts of things*'.[13] Sometimes it seems as though his pessimism about our knowledge of real essences is due to a certain technological pessimism, to the thought that, since the real essences of things are typically hidden from us, and since they consist in certain properties of their insensible parts, we shall never have microscopes adequate to the task of observing them:

> The little bodies that compose that fluid we call *water* are so extremely small that I have never heard of anyone who by a microscope ... pretended to perceive their distinct bulk, figure or motion.[14]

But a more careful reading suggests that the pessimism is much more profound, and rests on two fundamental assumptions which surface again in Berkeley's and Hume's accounts of causation. One assumption is that, if we are to take real essences seriously, we must leave room for features that are not strictly observable, even with the aid of the most powerful scientific instruments imaginable. The other assumption is that we cannot comprehend the unobservable. Profound pessimism immediately follows. For example, with the aid of powerful instruments, we might see tiny objects cohering together or repelling one another, but strictly speaking we would not *see* the coherence or repulsion. Strictly we see groups of particles that are always in close proximity, or groups that are never in close proximity. Since the coherence and repulsion are not strictly observable, they are incomprehensible:

> He that could find the bonds, that tie these heaps of loose little bodies together so firmly, he that could make known the cement that makes them stick so fast to one another, would discover a great and yet unknown secret.[15]

Very much the same inaccessible secret would enable us to understand the connection between primary and secondary qualities:

the ideas of sensible secondary qualities, which we have in our minds, can by us be no way deduced from bodily causes, nor any correspondence or connexion be found between them and those primary qualities which (experience shows us) produce them in us.[16]

Like Hume, Locke concedes that, if we are to allow real essences, we must allow de re necessities in nature, and de re necessary connections between distinct existences. Like Hume, Locke despairs of understanding necessary connections, because he despairs of strictly observing them.

Locke never uses the expression 'natural kind'. The account that I have attributed to him is built around two distinctions. One is that between real and nominal essences. The other is that between substances and modes:

the *ideas* of *substances* are such combinations of simple *ideas* as are taken to represent distinct particular things subsisting by themselves ... *Modes* I call such complex *ideas* which, however compounded, contain not in them the supposition of subsisting by themselves, but are considered as dependences on, or affections of substances.[17]

This distinction has a decidedly Aristotelian ring to it, particularly when it is presented as a distinction between objects capable of 'subsisting by themselves' and objects that are merely 'dependences on, or affections of' others. I suggest that, if we are to produce a plausible account of natural kinds, we might be wise to go back to Aristotle. In this section I shall develop an account that is suggested by a sympathetic reading of Aristotle.

Both in the *Categories* and in the *Metaphysics*, Aristotle explores the suggestion that one group of entities has a special status. Although, broadly speaking, there are ten groups of entities, ten categories, one group, the category of substance, has a special status. And one aim of the *Metaphysics*, and especially of Books Z and H, is to show which things belong to the category of substance. Various candidates are rejected, such as matter, combinations of form and matter, and Platonic universals. The very best candidates, it seems, are medium-sized material objects, and in particular plants and animals. They qualify because they fulfil at least one crucial condition, namely that substances are what they are independently of other things, whereas non-substances are what they are in virtue of a relation to, or dependence upon, something else:

For of the categories none can exist independently, but only substance.[18]

That remark clearly recalls various remarks in the *Categories*:

if the primary substances did not exist it would be impossible for any of the other things to exist ... A *substance* ... is that which is neither said of a subject nor in a subject.[19]

So (to repeat) one aim of the *Metaphysics* is to show which things belong to the category of substance.

Another connected aim is to confront the very general question, What makes something the kind of thing it is? In Book H, chapter II, Aristotle argues that it is very difficult to give a clear and simple answer to that question, because there are so many different kinds of kind. There are, as his translators put it, so many different kinds of 'differentiae' which determine membership of kinds:

> some things are characterized by the mode of composition of their matter, e.g. the things formed by mixture, such as honey-water; and others by being bound together, e.g. a bundle; and others by being glued together, e.g. a book; and others by being nailed together, e.g. a casket; and others in more than one of these ways; and others by position, e.g. the threshold and the lintel (for these differ by being placed in a certain way); and others by time, e.g. dinner and breakfast; and others by place, e.g. the winds; and others by the affections proper to sensible things, e.g. hardness and softness, density and rarity, dryness and wetness.[20]

As we read on, however, we discover that this heterogeneous list of examples has a double purpose. On the one hand, they are together examples of the range of kinds of kind, and illustrate the range of possible answers to the question, What makes something the kind of thing it is? On the other hand, it appears, they all ultimately fail to fulfil Aristotle's conditions for substance:

> Now none of these differentiae is substance, even when coupled with matter, yet in each there is something analogous to substance.[21]

The reasons for the failure will prove to be instructive.

Now, there are many questions about the proper interpretation of Aristotle. One interesting question is whether his category of substance should include both kinds of individual (chimpanzees, tigers, humans) and kinds of stuff (gold, carbon, water). Another is whether the remarks about substance in Books Z and H of the *Metaphysics* can be made to sit comfortably with the account of the Prime Mover in Book Λ. Yet another is whether I can legitimately follow many commentators in moving from Aristotle's talk of 'substance' in the singular to talk of 'substances' in the plural. But I am not going to pursue any of those questions. Indeed, in the spirit of Kripke's account of Wittgenstein,[22] I have already implied that what follows is an account of natural kinds that was suggested to me by reading Aristotle. I want to pursue the thought that, if we are to have a useful notion of a natural kind, we should distinguish between things that are what they are independently of other things, and things that are what they are in virtue of a relation to, or dependence upon, something else. The first are, as such, members of natural kinds, and the second are, as such, members of non-natural kinds. Implicit in that thought is a distinction that I have already incorporated into the three general constraints on the search for natural kinds, that is, the distinction between intrinsic and relational properties.

So the Aristotelian thought is that some things are what they are in virtue of their intrinsic properties, others are what they are merely in virtue of relational properties. For example, something is a chimpanzee or a tiger or a stickleback in virtue of its intrinsic properties, and something is a table or a coin or a threshold in virtue of a relation to, or dependence upon, something else. If I was right to connect the notions of a natural kind, a real essence and an intrinsic property together, the story about intrinsic properties becomes a story about the real essences that lend themselves to scientific investigation. Chimpanzees, tigers and sticklebacks, as such, have real essences which lend themselves to scientific investigation, whereas tables, coins and thresholds do not. My main proposal, then, is that we should distinguish between 'natural' and 'dependent' kinds. One considerable advantage of the proposal is that it allows us to deal with a wide range of examples, and thereby to do justice to the various insights of those who have used the narrower distinctions between natural and conventional, or natural and artificial, or natural and culturally generated, or natural and nominal kinds.

But first I must say more about the crucial notion of dependence, which I touched on in the first chapter. Life is too short to list every possible kind of dependence, so I shall content myself with listing three. One is the kind of dependence I shall need for the rest of this discussion, and the other two are sufficiently close to it to require examination, so that we shall be able to distinguish between the two kinds of dependence that are not relevant, and the one kind that is. To help all of us to remember which is which, I shall flag each one with a suitable prefix. The first kind of dependence is that of constitution, or C-dependence: a whole C-depends for its existence on the existence of constituent parts. If I had no arms, legs, kidneys, heart, liver, brain, etc., I would not exist; if there were no ants, there would be no ant colony; if there were no soldiers, there would be no army; if there were no citizens, there would be no nation; and so on. It does not follow, and it is not true, that the *identity* of the whole C-depends on the *identity* of the constituent parts. I may donate a kidney to a sick relative without undermining either my or her identity; the loss or acquisition of one or two ants or soldiers or citizens in no way affects the identity of the colony or the army or the nation; and so on. So the existence of the whole C-depends on the existence of some suitable constituents, not on the existence of a set of particular constituents. It is perhaps important to note that, since we are talking about the constitution of wholes, the relation only runs one way. That is, although the existence of the whole C-depends on the existence of the constituents, the existence of the constituents does not C-depend on the existence of the whole. A dismantled human body, ant colony or nation leaves in its wake various organs and limbs, ants and human beings.

If we were very fussy, we might want to distinguish cases, because some wholes are *structured* arrangements of constituents, while some are not. If we are talking about humans, ant colonies, armies and nations, then structure is clearly important. If structure is lost, the whole is lost, and the existence of the whole therefore C-depends on the existence of organized or structured constituents. But there will be many 'objects' (if they are objects at all) which are more or less unstructured collections of constituents — heaps of sand, piles of rubbish, bundles of clothes. We may dig over the heap of sand, shake up the rubbish, or pick over the old clothes and tie them together again, and we still have the objects we started with. Here the whole consists of any more or less contiguous arrangement of the constituents. But, whether we are talking of structured wholes or unstructured wholes, the existence of the whole at a given time C-depends on the existence of the constituents.

The second kind of dependence I shall call property-dependence, or P-dependence. My properties, states, features, processes, etc., P-depend on me, for without me there could be no properties-of-me, states-of-me, features-of-me, processes-in-me. It seems characteristic of properties, states, features and processes that they logically require something to have the properties, to be in the states, to exhibit the features, to undergo the processes. The grin cannot exist without the Cheshire cat. However, unlike the first kind of dependence, this second kind seems to run both ways. Although a whole C-depends, at a given time, on the existence of constituents, the constituents can exist without the whole. In contrast, grins and Cheshire cats P-depend on each other. There would be something odd in a story about a grin without a cat, but there would be something equally odd in a story about a cat with no facial expression at all. More generally, there would be something odd in a story about an object with no determinate properties, in no determinate states, with no determinate features, undergoing no determinate processes. Such a story would lead directly to Lockean substrata.

It is not at all clear whether the existence of an object P-depends on the existence of quite specific properties, states or processes. For example, it is not clear whether my existence depends on my having quite specific physical or psychological features. In order to answer that question, we would need to settle general questions about identity. I shall have something to say about such questions in chapter 6, but for the moment I only need to insist that properties, states and processes P-depend on the existence of their bearers, and that the existence of the bearers P-depends on their having some determinate properties, being in some determinate states and undergoing some determinate processes. If we are to avoid a commitment to Lockean substrata, we need to recognize that the distinction between object and property, or object and state, or object and process, is at best a distinction between two ways of describing the world around us. Considerations about the ontological status of universals, and about the type-identity of properties and states and processes, may force us to concede that the language of objects is in some way more fundamental than the language of properties, states and processes, but it would be absurd to argue that the existence of one is P-independent of the existence of the other. As far as their existence is concerned, they seem to come into existence, and go out of existence, together.

The third kind of dependence I shall call relation-dependence or R-dependence, and will lie at the heart of my account of natural kinds. It differs from the other kinds of dependence in at least one important respect. Consider the standard examples of entities that are supposedly members of natural kinds. They include physical particles (protons, neutrons, electrons), chemical elements and compounds (carbon, hydrogen, water, nitric acid) and biological individuals (narcissi, sticklebacks, human beings). If we assume for the moment that both particles and quantities of chemical elements and compounds can count as objects or entities, we might reasonably argue that such entities have spatial and temporal position, and that A is a different entity from B if and only if they occupy different places at a given time. It is interesting to note that, since the existence of a whole C-depends on the existence of constituent parts, both it and the totality of its constituents at a given time occupy the same place at that time. Similarly (turning now to the second kind of dependence, P-dependence) an object is to be found in exactly the same place as its current states, properties, features and processes. But, in turning to R-dependence, we find a sense of 'dependence' in which the object depends on something which typically occupies a quite different place at a given time.

I shall now develop my account of natural kinds by exploiting this third sense of 'dependence'. The central thought is that certain things exist, as such, only in virtue of a relation to, or R-dependence upon, something else. In these cases, what makes something the kind of thing it is R-depends, not on its intrinsic properties, not on its constituents, not on its non-relational properties, states, features, processes, but on what is happening in the rest of the world. If the rest of the world were significantly different, then it would not be that kind of thing. It might continue to exist under some other description, because almost everything exists under a range of possible descriptions, but it would not be *that* kind of thing. The best way to illustrate that rather abstruse claim is with the aid of examples:

a)   Sometimes an object is what it is in virtue of a functional relation to something else, and the obvious examples are artefacts. Something is a table if it is moderately portable, and has a flat upper surface capable of supporting our books, cups and saucers, tools, ornaments, etc. Something is a vehicle if it can transport a small number of people by road under the control of a driver. To different beings, in different circumstances, tables could not be tables or vehicles vehicles. To beings much bigger than us, tables might be footstools, and to beings much smaller than us, they might be the frames of houses. In much stronger or much weaker gravitational fields, our tables and vehicles would be literally useless, and could not be properly described as tables or vehicles at all. It is important to note that the functional relation which determines membership of the kinds in this group does not have to be a functional relation to human beings. Something is a fuel pump because of a functional relation to an internal combustion engine, and something is a pillar because of its functional relation to a bridge or a roof. In other circumstances the fuel pump might be a water pump, and the pillar might be hardcore for a new road. There are many biological examples that belong to this group: a leaf is a leaf because of its functional role in manufacturing food for the whole plant, and a heart is a heart because of its functional role in pumping blood around the body. In different circumstances the leaf might be compost and the heart might be food. The only point that matters here is that all the examples are examples of objects that are what they are in virtue of a functional relation to something else.

b)   Sometimes an object is what it is because of a definite, though perhaps implicit, convention. Certain lumps of metal or pieces of paper are coins or banknotes because, according to a statute or statutory instrument, they can be used as a means of exchange. Certain acts count as murder because they are regarded, not just as killings, but as morally impermissible killings. A change in law or convention or moral attitude immediately affects the status of the thing in question. A lump of metal ceases to be legal tender, and so ceases to be a coin; an act ceases to be murder, but is regarded as political protest or the execution of a fatwa or manslaughter or acceptable self-defence, or whatever. If we were to treat clubs, societies and nations as genuine objects, they would probably belong in this group, for typically their existence depends on purely conventional rules, and on recognition of those rules by both members and non-members. A new nation might come into existence if a sufficient number of other nations recognize it (as Israel came into existence in 1948) and an old nation might disappear if a sufficient number of people stop treating it as a nation (as Yugoslavia disappeared some time in 1991 or 1992).

c) Sometimes, as Aristotle noticed, an object is what it is because of its spatial or temporal position. A lump of stone in one place is a lintel, in another a threshold, in another a coping stone, in another part of a pavement, in another simply a lump of stone. A mass of air moving in one direction is the north wind, in another the south wind, and so on. A quantity of water in one place is a tarn, in another a river, in another a glacier, in another a cloud. These are perhaps some of the most interesting examples, for, more than any others, they support my earlier claim that, if we are to have a satisfactory account of natural kinds, neither the distinction between the natural and the artificial, nor that between the natural and the conventional, nor that between the natural and the culturally generated, will quite give us what we want. Although some of the examples in group a) are members of artificial kinds, and all those in group b) are members of conventional kinds, and although many of the examples in both groups are members of culturally generated kinds, none of those in group c) are members of natural, or members of artificial, or members of conventional, or members of culturally generated kinds. Again I suggest that our main distinction should be between natural and R-dependent kinds.

Real but superficial kinds

Let us briefly review the state of play. I am trying to find an acceptable account of natural kinds. I have argued that the distinctions between natural and artificial, between natural and conventional, between natural and culturally generated, and between natural and nominal kinds, are not quite what we want, and that the important central distinction should be between natural and dependent kinds. Since there were at least three kinds of dependence in the offing, I tried to distinguish them, and tried to exploit the third kind of dependence, that of a relational dependence upon something else. Broadly, the distinction between natural and dependent kinds is a distinction between things that are what they are in virtue of their intrinsic properties, and things that are what they are in virtue of a relational dependence upon something else. I gave three groups of examples, three ways of qualifying for membership of a dependent kind.

I do not claim that my list of examples of dependent kinds (a) to c) above) is complete, and ingenious readers will no doubt be able to think of other cases. Nor do I claim that the three groups are mutually exclusive. For example, in certain quarters chamber pots, lead water tanks and earthenware sinks are prized as plant containers, so both their function (a)) and their place (c)) have changed with their transformation into plant containers. In this section I want to return to some of our awkward examples, to see if they can be accommodated with the aid of the broad distinction between natural and dependent kinds. Some of them are easily accommodated. A landmass would count as a valley in one environment, a mountain in another, and part of the sea bed in another. A quantity of liquid would be part of a volcano in one place, part of the Earth's core in another, and so on. That is, whether or not something is a valley or volcano depends, not on its intrinsic properties, but on its relation to something else. Similarly, a plant will be a perennial in one climate but an annual in another. Its being one or the other depends, not on its intrinsic properties, but on its ability to survive the winter in local climatic conditions. In one climate it will be an annual, and in another a perennial. So all these examples could be regarded as belonging to dependent kinds, in group c), that is, as belonging with lintels and thresholds, north winds and south winds, tarns and rivers.

Other examples remain obstinately awkward, however. Whether or not a plant is a tree or a shrub has nothing to do with its relational dependence upon something else. If it has a single woody stem and breaks into branches some feet above the ground, it is a tree, and if it is woody and breaks into many stems very close to the ground, it is a shrub. Similarly, any fairly small piece of rock with smooth round edges is a pebble, whatever its relation to other things. And any fairly concentrated but haphazard collection of things is a heap or a pile or a bundle, whatever its relation to other things. Interestingly, one of Aristotle's own examples will not fit the account that I have borrowed from him. Honey water is a mixture of honey and water,[23] and it is precisely that, independently of other things. Any mixture of honey and water is honey water in any possible world. Nor could I deal with this example by arguing that honey water is properly not an object at all, but a quantity of stuff, since I have already conceded that no serious consequences will follow from treating quantities of stuff as objects or entities. Since honey water is a mixture of stuffs, it does not belong to a natural kind. It is at best a mixture of members of natural kinds. Could I argue that it lacks the structure that is characteristic of many important entities and which is particularly characteristic of members of natural kinds? That it is in effect no more than a heap, or a bundle, which has constituent parts but no essential structure? Clearly not. Honey water has a minimal, though important structure, for its constituents must be fairly evenly mixed together!

How then are we to deal with these remaining awkward examples? I suggest that, in addition to natural kinds and dependent kinds, we must distinguish a third kind of kinds. In order to appreciate exactly what is required, we need to develop a number of points I have already made or hinted at. First, we should explore the notion of an intrinsic property, and the connected notion of a real essence. It is significant that in the passage from *Metaphysics*, H, II, that I quoted earlier, Aristotle argues that some things that fail ultimately to be substances are characterized 'by the affections proper to sensible things, e.g. hardness and softness, density and rarity, dryness and wetness' — in other words, by their superficial and directly observable properties, and in particular by what were later to be called their secondary qualities. It is also significant that Locke often described real essences as unobservable, unknowable, hidden, internal, inaccessible, in contrast to the superficial and observable nominal essences of things. But why should we value such a contrast? It might be argued that nothing I have so far said actually entails that membership of a natural kind must depend on internal and unobservable features. Quite the contrary. In chapter 1, I argued that entities can be individuated only relative to a certain level, and that general descriptive and explanatory patterns might emerge at comparatively high levels of size and complexity. I was therefore anxious to leave open the possibility that scientific prediction and explanation might on occasion be concerned with large macroscopic features that are plainly visible to the naked eye, rather than with features that are small, microscopic and invisible. Why then should the real essence of a tree not consist in its being a woody plant with a single straight stem, branching some feet above the ground? Why should the real essence of a pebble not consist in its being a small rounded lump of stone? And so on mutatis mutandis?

The answer will become clear, I hope, in what follows. In my introductory remarks about the notion of a natural kind I argued that, both historically and philosophically, three thoughts are particularly important. First, the notion of a natural kind must be connected to that of a real essence; second, members of natural kinds lend themselves to scientific investigation; and third, since scientists are concerned with the causal powers of things, and since causal powers are constituted or realized by intrinsic properties, the real essences of kinds will prove to be intrinsic properties. We can now combine those three thoughts into a single thought, namely that, when we identify something as a member of a natural kind, we are in principle able to explain a wide range of its properties, including the apparently superficial properties. The real essence of such a thing not only determines its proper de re classification (as an electron, proton or neutron; as carbon, hydrogen or nitric acid; as a tiger, elm, ash or stickleback), but also directly explains many of its properties. It is precisely because a narcissus has a certain genetic structure that it has green leaves, flowers in early spring, dies down in early summer, and so on. It is precisely because gold has the atomic number 79 that in normal atmospheric conditions it is malleable, fusible, soft and heavy.

But that in turn is why real essences are often hidden, internal, microscopic and invisible, rather than superficial, macroscopic and observable. Whereas the internal or microscopic properties directly explain the superficial or macroscopic, the converse is not true. The superficial properties of members of natural kinds have but a slight bearing on their other properties. Indeed, I have already used examples of plants and animals whose superficial properties are positively misleading. Marsupial tigers and wolves were not tigers and wolves, and *Hebe cupressoides* is not a cypress. Nor is a mountain ash an ash, an arum lily a lily, nor a flying squirrel a squirrel. One of many engaging examples is the Late Spider Orchid, which looks and smells just like the females of a local species of wasp: male wasps, whose everyday scientific work is extremely sloppy, and confined to the examination of purely superficial features, are persuaded to copulate with it, thereby spreading the orchid's pollen.

So, in thinking about the notion of a natural kind, and the associated notion of a real essence, we must tie both notions to a proper science, e.g. to a systematic taxonomy in biology, or to a physics and chemistry of the fine structures of things. No doubt some explanation and prediction is possible, even at a superficial level. Putnam claims that I can tell straight off that a rigid cube, with sides fifteen sixteenths of an inch square, will not pass through a circular hole, one inch in diameter, and that I need no knowledge of the fine structure of the cube.[24] Similarly, I can presumably predict that trees will be blown over by gales, will die from drought, will undermine my neighbour's foundations and will plunge his garden into shade, without even knowing their species. But, I would argue, any systematic explanatory and predictive work will involve penetrating beneath the surface, to the real essences of things. Pace Putnam, my assumption that the cube is rigid requires a quite complicated theory about the properties of materials over time, and my expectations about trees are rational only if I can appeal to laws about the transmission of light, the elasticity of strings of cellulose molecules, and so on. It follows, incidentally, that my attempt to leave open a certain possibility may ultimately prove to be vain. Since entities can only be individuated relative to a certain level, and since certain descriptive and explanatory patterns may emerge at comparatively high levels of size and complexity, I was anxious to leave open the possibility that, on occasion, scientific prediction and generalization might be concerned with large and macroscopic features. In particular, I was concerned not to prejudge certain questions about the status of the social sciences. Although I shall return to those questions in the next chapter, I seem already to have committed myself to the view that sociological kinds are superficial rather than natural.

Let us now return to our obstinately awkward examples, to the kinds *tree, shrub, pebble, cloud, honey water*, and the like. It seems clear that they are not natural kinds, because the features associated with each kind are superficial. They cannot be connected at all closely with features that would allow serious scientific prediction and explanation, for example, with the genetic features of certain plant species, or the molecular structure of certain kinds of stone, or the chemical composition of particular kinds of honey or particular samples of water. In order to explain and predict the behaviour of a tree or shrub, I need to know the species to which it belongs; in order to explain and predict the behaviour of a pebble, I need to know of what stony material it is made; and so on. On the other hand, the kinds *tree, shrub, pebble, cloud, honey water*, etc. are not dependent kinds either, for membership of each kind does not consist in a relational dependence on something else. Whatever else is going on in the universe, a plant with a single main woody stem is a tree, and one with many woody stems is a shrub; any concentrated mass of gas in the atmosphere is a cloud, and any small stony object with rounded edges is a pebble; and so on. So I propose to introduce a third kind of kinds, real but superficial kinds. They are *real* because the characteristic features of the kinds are not relationally dependent on anything else. In particular, they exist quite independently of any of our beliefs about them or interest in them. But they are *superficial* because their characteristic features, the features that determine membership of the kind, are not, and are not closely connected with, the real essences that would underpin serious scientific prediction and explanation.

Hybrid kinds, and a summary

If we were concerned to produce a complete list of kinds, we would be wise to borrow a point from Wiggins,[25] and distinguish a fourth kind of kinds, hybrid kinds. Wiggins argues that certain terms, though not strictly natural kind terms, work very much like them. For example, the kind *vegetable* is strictly not a natural kind, for it includes plants of different species, even of different genera and families, in a way that does not correspond even approximately to any formal taxonomy. Yet it excludes plants that are botanically very closely related to familiar vegetables: for example *Solanum crispum*, a popular garden plant, is not a vegetable, despite its very close relation to tomatoes and to the common potato. On the other hand, *vegetable* is in one respect rather like a natural kind, because one necessary condition of something's being a vegetable is that it belongs to one of a comparatively small number of plant species. Just as decoy ducks are not ducks, synthetic vegetables are not vegetables.

What then should we say about this kind of kind? One obvious move is not available to us. We cannot treat *vegetable* as a real but superficial kind, because vegetables are determined in part by their function, namely to tempt the palates and to satisfy the hunger of human beings. The neatest way of resolving the puzzle is to say that *vegetable* is a hybrid kind. It is neither a pure natural kind, nor a pure dependent kind, but a hybrid of both. Membership of the kind is determined in part by membership of a natural kind, and in part by a functional dependence on human appetite. Other examples of that sort of hybrid (a hybrid of natural and dependent kinds) are *fruit, pot plant, herb, bedding plant, pet* (i.e. *domestic animal*), *cattle, medicine*. In every case the object or stuff in question must be a member of a limited range of natural kinds, but in every case there is more than a hint of a functional dependence on human interest.

Note that in some cases the hybrid kinds will be highly specific. For example, farmers and greengrocers divide apples into the kinds *dessert, cooker* and *cider*, and butchers distinguish the kinds *ham, bacon* and *pork*. The first distinction is at best a distinction between levels of acidity, and has little botanical significance (particularly the distinction between dessert apples and cookers), and the second distinction reflects the different ways in which pig carcasses are cured. Both distinctions clearly reflect human purposes and interests. There are, however, other kinds in this group which are quite specific but which do not so clearly reflect human purposes or interests, such as the kinds *brother, sister, son, daughter, father, mother, grandmother*. Initially we might be tempted to treat these as natural kinds, determined by mechanisms of reproduction of interest to biologists. But on reflection we can see that they are not genuine natural kinds, for two reasons. One reason is that they are determined by a blood relation, rather than by any intrinsic property, and to that extent are dependent kinds. The second reason is that we consistently refuse to apply them in certain contexts where the same biological relation is to be found, and to that extent they depend on our interests, including perhaps our moral interests. The general names 'son', 'daughter', 'brother', 'sister', etc. are only applied to members of a comparatively small number of natural kinds, namely to humans or to animals that we think of as faintly human, as in some way close to our moral community. Although we sometimes refer to 'parent' plants, we never talk of the sons and daughters of plants and only talk cosily of the family life of fish and tortoises in the pages of children's books. In short, these kinds are best treated as hybrids of natural and dependent kinds.

There are also kinds that are hybrids of dependent and real but superficial kinds, for example, the kinds *ski slope, surfing beach, gravel pit, oasis, biennial*. The characteristic features of each kind are real but superficial in the sense I explained. That is, the objects in question exist quite independently of other things, and in particular quite independently of our beliefs and interests. Whatever else was going on in the world, there would be long inclines covered in deep snow or some synthetic analogue, quantities of sand or similar stuff sloping under the approaching sea in such a way as to cause high breaking waves; holes in the ground full of small stony particles; small and isolated areas in the desert where water is close to the surface and where plants grow throughout the year; plants that flower in the second season after germination. Yet they are not features that are sufficiently closely tied to the real essences of things to allow serious scientific description and explanation. To that extent the kinds are real but superficial. But the name of the kind often gives a definite hint of a certain sort of dependence, a connection with human interests, such as the desire to ski or surf, to use gravel for building, to refresh oneself on a desert journey, and so on. Perhaps no such hint is immediately evident in the name 'biennial', for a biennial is a plant which flowers in the second year after germination. But in horticultural practice there is a clear connection with human interest: the name is only ever applied to biennial plants whose flowers in the third and subsequent years are likely to be disappointing. So these are hybrid kinds, hybrids of dependent and real but superficial kinds.

To sum up, then, I have distinguished four kinds of kind:

(1) **Natural kinds**, which are characterized by real essences, by intrinsic properties that make the individuals or stuffs the kinds of things they are, and which lend themselves to detailed scientific investigation, e.g. the kinds *electron, proton, neutron*; *carbon, hydrogen, water, cellulose*; *chimpanzee, stickleback, narcissus*.

(2) **Dependent kinds**, whose members are what they are because of a relational dependence upon something else, e.g. the kinds *table, coin, lintel, threshold, cliff, glacier, north wind, perennial, annual*.

(3) **Real but superficial kinds**, which are characterized by real, non-relational but comparatively superficial similarities and differences between things, similarities that do not lend themselves to detailed scientific investigation, e.g. the kinds *tree, shrub, cloud, pebble, honey water*.

(4) **Hybrid kinds**, especially hybrids of (1) and (2), e.g. the kinds *vegetable, fruit, pot plant, cattle, medicine, ham, pork, bacon*; and hybrids of (2) and (3), e.g. the kinds *ski slope, surfing beach, gravelpit, oasis, biennial*.

I should add one footnote. For ease of exposition, I have consistently used plants and animals as examples of members of natural kinds. In doing so, I have resolutely ignored a very serious problem, which I shall address in chapter 5.

Notes

1   Aristotle, *Physics*, II, 1; 192b16-20.
2   See J.L. Mackie (1974), pp. 12-13.
3   See, for example, Roger Woolhouse's account of 'essentialism' and 'relativism' in his (1971), especially pp. 81, 104, 105.
4   See, for example, A.C. Grayling (1982), p. 183f.
5   See C.L. Elder (1989).
6   Locke (1690), III, v, 3.
7   Locke, op. cit., III, iii, 13.
8   Locke, op. cit., III, iii, 15 and III, vi, 2.
9   S. P. Schwartz (1980), p. 182.
10 J. L. Mackie (1976), p.104.
11 I commend the translation by Jonathan Bennett and Peter Remnant.
12 Locke, op. cit., II, xxiii, 32.
13 Locke, op. cit., III, vi, 35.
14 Locke, op. cit., II, xxiii, 26.
15 Locke, op. cit., ibid.
16 Locke, op. cit., IV, iii, 28.
17 Locke, op. cit., II, xii, 6 and 4.
18 Aristotle, *Metaphysics*, Z, I; 1028a34-5.
19 Aristotle, *Categories*, 2b5-6 and 2a13-14.
20 Aristotle, *Metaphysics*, H, II; 1042b15-23.
21 Aristotle, *Metaphysics*, H, II; 1043a3-5.
22 See S. Kripke (1982), p. 5.
23 I am grateful to Lari Sideris, who kindly told me about the constitution and uses of honey water.
24 H. Putnam, 'Philosophy and our Mental Life', in his (1975), pp. 295-7.
25 Cf. D. Wiggins (1980), pp.171-2.

3 Problems

Realism and essentialism

In the previous chapter, I outlined an account of natural kinds that was broadly Aristotelian, for it rested on a distinction between intrinsic and relational properties. It was the result of three general thoughts. The first was that natural kinds must be determined by real essences, properties necessary and sufficient for membership of each kind. But that thought led directly to a second, namely that, if the notion of a natural kind is to be at all interesting, the properties in question must be properties that lend themselves to scientific generalization. Third, since scientists are interested in the causal powers of things, and since causal powers are constituted or realized by intrinsic properties, it followed that the real essences of natural kinds would be intrinsic properties. These thoughts provided the three main conditions that an account of natural kinds would have to meet. I concluded that we needed a central distinction between natural kinds, whose membership was determined by certain intrinsic properties, and dependent kinds, whose membership was determined by a relational dependence on something else.

In the course of the discussion it emerged that, in saying that natural kinds are determined by properties necessary and sufficient for membership of the kind, I intended the expressions 'necessary' and 'sufficient' to be interpreted very strongly. That is, I committed myself to a non-Humean account of scientific laws in general and causal laws in particular. The notion of real essences at the heart of my account of natural kinds belongs firmly to the group of notions, such as necessary connection and generative power, that Hume found so difficult to accept. Moreover, it also became clear that I do not regard this commitment as in any way separate from the commitment to natural kinds, as an optional extra to the main package. Quite the contrary.

I believe that the commitment to natural kinds is a commitment to certain real essences that permit scientific generalization, and that scientific generalization consists in the articulation of de re necessary truths about the causal powers of things. In other words, scientific generalization is over causal powers, some of which are constituted or realized by the real essences that determine membership of natural kinds. So the properties that determine membership of natural kinds are precisely the properties that determine in general how individual members *must* behave in such and such circumstances.

But that general programme still requires further defence and explanation, in three connected areas. First, my account of natural kinds was an account of a programme, not a defence of it. I have yet to produce arguments in favour of adopting the programme, of talking about natural kinds in this 'interesting', 'strong' and decidedly non-Humean way. Or, to put the same point slightly differently, I have to prove that metaphysical realists must hope to find natural kinds in my sense of 'natural kind', and that they must expect to use a non-Humean notion of natural necessity. They cannot merely claim that there is a distinction between reality, on the one hand, and our beliefs and theories about it, on the other, but must suppose that reality includes members of natural kinds, in my strong sense of 'natural kind'. Second, I need to say more about the non-Humean notion of natural necessity. Third, so far I have only used examples of natural kinds from physics, chemistry and biology, and I have concentrated on examples of kinds of individual and kinds of stuff. It is now time to explore other possible examples, including examples from other disciplines, and in particular to consider whether we should expect to find natural kinds in the social sciences. Those three tasks will occupy us in this chapter.

So to the first task, that of explaining the connection between metaphysical realism and the version of essentialism I have outlined. As I explained in chapter 2, I have assumed the truth of metaphysical realism, that is, the view that there is a fundamental distinction between the world as it is in itself and our thoughts and beliefs about it. If all goes well, our thoughts and beliefs will correspond to reality, but the two are logically independent of one another. On the one hand, our beliefs and theories may be more or less false, and on the other, reality may well have features that we fail to discover or describe. As I have already said, I have not defended that assumption, and I have no intention of doing so. This book is not a defence of realism, but an exploration of one version of it, namely a version that involves a commitment to a certain doctrine about natural kinds, and in turn to decidedly non-Humean doctrines about real essences and causal powers. Nor am I in the least concerned to examine the theoretical and methodological reasons that might move a scientist to conclude that he or she had discovered certain real essences determining natural kinds, rather than purely superficial properties. The question that interests me is this. Does metaphysical realism actually *entail* essentialism of the kind I have defended? Does the distinction between reality and our thoughts about it commit us to a belief in natural kinds, in my sense of 'natural kind'?

Prima facie the answer is that it does not. That is, it seems clear that some metaphysical realists can reasonably refuse to accept that there are natural kinds in the sense I have explained. Perhaps we can imagine a world in which science never reveals the underlying real essences of things, because there are none to be discovered. It would be a world in which there are many real similarities and differences, but in which the similarities and differences are, without exception, superficial and quite incapable of supporting any but restricted and local inductive inference. The only general kinds would be dependent, real but superficial, and hybrids thereof. There would no doubt be some work for the explanatory liberal, but no comfort at all for the budding essentialist.

However, for Kantian reasons I do not believe that that answer will work. If we look both on and between the lines of *The Critique of Pure Reason*, we can find at least two interesting arguments for the view that metaphysical realism entails essentialism. It is undeniably odd for me to lean on Kant, since he was a metaphysical anti-realist (or, as he himself put it, a 'transcendental idealist') and, despite his Leibnizian background, he had remarkably little to say about natural necessity in the first *Critique*. But the two arguments that interest me do not depend crucially on their Kantian context. The first argument is quite specific, and is concerned with our conception of time. I shall ignore exegetical questions altogether, save to say that, if the argument exists at all in the first *Critique*, it can be found buried in the second and third Analogies of Experience, and in The Refutation of Idealism (A189-215/B232-262 and B274-9). Kant is concerned with a problem about our measurement of time. Time is not an individual, as Newtonians thought; nor are the temporal features of things in any sense open to direct sensory inspection. 'Time', as he frequently remarks, 'cannot by itself be perceived.' Furthermore, for reasons later celebrated in Wittgenstein's private language argument, our measurement of time must in some sense be a measurement of *objective* time, of the passage of time in the world, logically independent of us and our thoughts about it. The solution of the problem seems obvious: we should construct time in the preferred Leibnizian manner, as a set of temporal relations between objects.

But how in principle can we do that? How can we establish the temporal relations between objects? As Kant has already explained, the peculiar relational properties of temporal precedence, succession and coincidence do not reveal themselves, either directly or indirectly, in the content of my experience. Nothing in the content of my experience will show, for example, that the blossom appears before the fruit, and that the fruit starts to fall before the leaves fall. In order to have a working notion of temporal sequence, I must know something about the laws of nature. That is, I must know something about the underlying structure of things, about their behaviour and changes. For example I need to know something about the mechanism of reproduction in fruit trees, the fact that blossoms produce fruits, rather than the reverse, and that therefore fruits appear after blossom. So my notion of time is parasitic upon my understanding of the real causal connections between events. But how, if at all, does the notion of necessity arise? What, if anything, requires me to suppose that, in context, certain events or states of affairs happen necessarily? The answer is that I can only rationally establish when an event *does* happen if I know when in context it *must* happen. My knowledge of causal laws gives me a warrant for drawing rational conclusions about temporal sequences only if I know when one event *must* happen in relation to another. In other words, causal laws are necessary truths. For example, the causal laws which determine that fruits follow blossom are necessary truths, and determine that fruits *must* follow blossom, and that blossom *cannot* follow fruit. But necessary truths about the underlying structure, behaviour and changes of objects are in effect general truths about the real essences of natural kinds, those features that are necessary and sufficient for membership of the appropriate kinds, and which lend themselves to scientific generalization. For the causal powers of things are constituted or realized by their intrinsic properties, some of which will be the intrinsic properties that constitute the real essences of natural kinds.

A neat summary of this first argument might prove helpful:

(1) I need to measure objective time. (This is metaphysical realism about time.)
(2) But time cannot by itself be perceived.
(3) I must therefore represent time in terms of the temporal relations between objects.
(4) But in order to establish temporal relations between objects, I must discover the causal laws affecting their changes.
(5) But I can have a good reason to expect any event to happen at a particular time only if I can establish when it *must* happen.
(6) In other words, the causal laws governing the structure and behaviour of objects are necessary truths.
(7) But a commitment to necessary truths about the structure and behaviour of objects is a commitment to the real essences that determine natural kinds.
(8) So metaphysical realism about time entails a commitment to the real essences that determine natural kinds.

Hence anyone committed both to metaphysical realism, and to the view that it is possible in principle to make rational inductive projections, is committed to a belief in natural kinds, in the strong sense in which I am interested.

That argument, as I pointed out, is a specific argument about the measurement of time, but at a crucial point (step 5) it turns on important considerations about the possibility of rational inductive inference. The second argument is an attempt to generalize those considerations. Let us for a moment return to chapter 2, where, following Hume, I argued that rational inference is possible only if the laws of nature are necessary truths, which will prove to be necessary truths about the structure and behaviour of members of natural kinds. I claimed that I can have a good reason for expecting a particular outcome only if, given a certain initial state, the outcome *must* follow. Furthermore, I take it that the metaphysical realist's conception of the world as it is in itself is a completely empty one unless it makes sense for us to attempt to discover its properties, and to attempt rational prediction and retrodiction. It goes without saying that our attempts may not be entirely successful. Indeed, given that any sentient being will have only finite capacities, the world will almost certainly have features that no sentient being can discover or understand. But it must be a world whose features are in general available for inspection, and which allow the possibility of rational inductive inference.

Now let us explore the consequences of these thoughts. Suppose that there were no natural necessities and no natural kinds, determined by real essences, that is, by intrinsic properties directly affecting the structure and behaviour of their members. It follows that nothing would then show that one event must happen, rather than another. But if nothing would show that one event must happen, rather than another, rational inductive inference would then be impossible. In particular, I could not have a workable theory of perception, an account of laws of nature which govern the relation between me and the world, and which yield a distinction between perception and hallucination, between psychological states that are caused by the real world, and those that are mere psychological states. But if I have no scientific theory, and in particular no theory of perception, and if I therefore have no distinction between perception and hallucination, then I lose in turn the distinction between myself and the external or objective world. In other words, I give up metaphysical realism. At this point, card-carrying Kantians will press on to conclude that, if I lose the distinction between myself and the external world, I will inevitably lose all sense of my own identity as a sentient being, and consciousness itself will be impossible. But that conclusion is irrelevant for my purposes.

So the second argument can be summarized as follows:

(1) There is a distinction between the world as it is in itself and our thoughts and beliefs about it. (This is metaphysical realism.)

(2) If the world is genuinely independent of us, it must obey laws that are logically independent of our thoughts and beliefs.

(3) But if the realist conception of the world as it is in itself is to have any content, it must be possible, in principle, for us to discover the laws governing its structure and behaviour, and to employ our knowledge of those laws to make rational inductive inferences.

(4) We can discover those laws, and can make rational inductive inferences, only if the laws are necessary truths about the structure and behaviour of the basic entities of the world.

(5) But a commitment to necessary truths about the structure and behaviour of the basic entities of the world is precisely a commitment to the real essences that determine natural kinds.

(6) In short, metaphysical realism entails a commitment to the real essences that determine natural kinds.

I should perhaps add an explanatory remark about step (3), which is an essential part of the argument, but which may seem to some readers to be an odd version of metaphysical realism. My thought is simply this. For familiar reasons, anti-realism (including Kantian transcendental idealism), is profoundly implausible. It is profoundly implausible to argue that so-called reality fundamentally depends on our thoughts and beliefs about it. On the other hand, anti-realists would be right to be sceptical about a conception of reality that was, in principle, wholly inaccessible to any kind of scientific investigation. Sober metaphysical realists should surely insist on two things. First, they should insist that reality is logically independent of us and our theories, and that its intrinsic features would be exactly the same even if all sentient beings suddenly disappeared. Second, they should insist that it makes perfect sense for us to attempt to discover as many of the features as we can. Furthermore, the two claims are perfectly compatible. Successful discovery in no way undermines the general thought that the features discovered are logically distinct from the beliefs and thoughts of those who discovered them, and unsuccessful attempts at discovery (due, perhaps, to the limitations of the human intellect) in no way undermine the general notion of reality as it is in itself. Indeed, if anything, the talk of unsuccessful attempts at discovery positively entails thoughts about how the reality resisting discovery is in itself. And a natural, though optional, adjunct to this kind of sober metaphysical realism would be a version of externalism, which in this context amounts to the claim that, if we are to say anything coherent at all, then at least some of the kinds we distinguish (even if only at the level of folk physics and chemistry) must be natural kinds in the world as it is in itself. In other words, if we are to say anything coherent at all, some of our attempts at discovery must be successful.

I can imagine a number of objections to this attempt to connect realism and essentialism. One, which demands little attention, provided Hume's main reason for being sceptical about the notion of necessary connection, and rests on the thought that natural necessity (or generative power, or whatever we choose to call it) is unobservable. That is, I cannot in any sense literally observe that one event must in context follow another. We should therefore abandon all talk of natural necessity and be content with the sort of unambitious metaphysical realism offered by an explanatory liberal. The reply to the objection is obvious and straightforward: although, as good empiricists, we should claim that theory and observation must be intimately connected, it would be absurd to claim that every property mentioned in our theory must be literally observable. Hume's use of his principle that every idea must proceed from some preceding impression would make nonsense of modern natural science.

A second objection, however, requires more patient treatment. It is all very well to say that rational inductive inference must be based on knowledge of necessary truths, and that any scientist moved by a commitment to metaphysical realism is thereby committed to the real essences that determine natural kinds. But how, if at all, can we tell when our theories are successful? How, if at all, can we tell that our theoretical generalizations do indeed record natural necessities? As I have just conceded, necessity is not an observable feature of anything, and successful theoretical generalizations do not emerge with a special syntactic marker or footnote announcing their special status — and even if they did, we would have no special reason to believe that the marker or footnote had been properly attached. But if we cannot show that certain theoretical generalizations do indeed record natural necessities, the alleged commitment to the real essences that determine natural kinds is empty. Far from being a serious commitment to specific real essences and natural kinds, it amounts merely to a mixture of pious hope and profound pessimism. The pious hope will consist in the belief that one day we shall find the essences and the kinds, and the profound pessimism will arise from our realizing that we have no reason to suppose that anyone will notice when they have been found.

One reply, which I offer with very little confidence, might be found in externalism. Representations typically represent in virtue of their having the right sort of causal connection with things of the kind represented. A fortiori, theoretical remarks about the world around us typically have meaning only if they have the right sort of causal connection with their referents. If all that is true, total scientific muddle is impossible. We can allow that some of our theories are false, that some of our representations fail to represent, but at least some of our attempts to make sense of the world must be successful. It follows that the metaphysical realist's commitment to the real essences of natural kinds would be far from empty, for at least some of the kinds we distinguish must be real kinds.

That first reply offers us an a priori guarantee that at least some of our scientific theories are true. But although I find that sort of guarantee very pleasing, I confess that I have a strong suspicion that it is simply too good to be true. There may be something to be said for the view that some of my beliefs must be correctly grounded in features of the real world, but I am not convinced that externalism can provide a guarantee that my beliefs must be grounded in the features that constitute the real essences of natural kinds. That is, I am not convinced that externalism can rule out the possibility that my beliefs are grounded in entirely superficial features. Since I propose to discuss externalism in the next chapter, I shall move quickly to a second reply, which, in general outline, I borrow from a very interesting book by Harré and Madden.[1] In discussing Humean scepticism about induction, and in setting out their own essentialist alternative, they distinguish two problems of induction, the 'little' problem and the 'big' problem. The big problem can be put like this. Given the premiss that a certain state of affairs obtains at a certain time and place, what, if anything, warrants an inference to the conclusion that a numerically quite different state of affairs obtains, at another time or place? Presumably an inference is warranted only if the premiss in some way rules in certain possible outcomes, and rules out others. In other words, if I am rationally to infer that the second state of affairs *will* happen, I have to be assured that in context it *must*. If, as Hume believes, there are no necessary connections in nature, nothing warrants the inference. If on the other hand, as Harré and Madden believe, there are necessary connections in nature, then the inference is warranted. Since the basic furniture of the world consists of 'powerful particulars', which, given their intrinsic features, necessarily change and develop in certain ways and not others, the first state of affairs must in context generate the second. Given the intrinsic features of hydrogen, any application of a naked flame to the hydrogen in the presence of oxygen must produce ignition and water vapour. Hydrogen must ignite and produce water under certain conditions; if, per impossibile, it did not, it would not be hydrogen.

So the 'big' problem of induction is a problem about moving from the premiss of an inductive argument (for example a premiss about a given event or state of affairs) to the conclusion (for example a conclusion about a numerically different event or state of affairs). The 'little' problem of induction is merely that of assuring ourselves that the premiss of our inductive argument is indeed true, for example, that we are indeed confronted with hydrogen, and that the causal powers of hydrogen do indeed include its being highly inflammable. As Harré and Madden point out, the two problems are often confused, but Hume's challenge is addressed to the big problem rather than to the little problem. According to Hume, even if we had perfect knowledge of the state of the world at a given time and place, we would have no rational warrant for any inference to another state at another time or place. Furthermore, Hume's challenge ensures that the big problem is a big problem, and is soluble only by making sense of the notions of natural necessity or generative power that he rejects. The little problem is a little problem because it is only a special case of a general little problem about belief: how, in general, can I guarantee that my beliefs are true? The little answer to this little problem is that I can't, for it is the nature of beliefs to be true or false, and, whatever belief we consider, there can in principle be no guarantee that it is true.

We can now summarize the reply to the objection. The objection was that any realist commitment to the real essences that determine natural kinds is an empty commitment unless we have some guarantee that our scientific theories are, at least in part, true, some guarantee that we have discovered at least some natural kinds. The reply has two stages, neither of which is earth shattering. The first stage is to say that we always have some sort of guarantee that our scientific theories are true, if they obey the general constraints on rational acceptability — if, for example, they are consistent with observation, are comparatively simple and mathematically elegant, yield true predictions, generally get us from truth to truth, and minimize inexplicable coincidence. Not only can we be confident that a theory that passes such tests records natural necessities, but it would be absurd for us to ask for any further guarantee. There cannot be further, second-order, standards of rational acceptability that allow us to weigh our first-order standards of rational acceptability. The second stage of the reply is to say that the objection then collapses into the complaint that, whatever belief we consider, there can be no general guarantee that it is true. But that complaint can hardly be taken seriously, since, as I have already noted, it is the nature of beliefs to be true or false. A belief that could not be false would not be a belief at all. Indeed, as Wittgenstein argues in his private language argument, a necessary condition of using a language, of saying anything at all, is that it should be possible to make a mistake. The possibility of scientific mistake is a cause for congratulation, not complaint. I conclude that the objection fails and that the metaphysical realist is committed to believing in the existence of real essences that determine natural kinds. In short, metaphysical realism entails essentialism.

Natural necessity

We can now turn to our second problem. I have claimed that the real essences of natural kinds will consist in certain intrinsic properties, which govern the behaviour and development of individual members of the kinds. That is, they govern the respects in which the individuals can and cannot, must and must not, change. In the previous section I argued that metaphysical realists are committed to that kind of essentialism, and that they cannot dispense with the relevant modalities. But that is a commitment to natural necessity, to the thought that, in articulating the laws of physics, chemistry and biology, we are expressing generalizations about what *must* happen in nature, not what does happen. But what is natural necessity supposed to be? In claiming that the laws of physics, chemistry and biology are de re necessary truths, what exactly am I claiming? The obvious way to analyse natural necessity is in terms of truth in all possible worlds. That may not be the whole story, but it is the main part of the story: the true scientific generalizations that are to count as laws are necessary truths in the sense that they are true in all possible worlds. No doubt in some possible worlds some of our scientific laws will be but vacuously true, because those worlds do not contain the same range of elements as our own, or because their initial conditions were very different from the initial conditions of our own world. But that fussy technical point does not affect the central claim. True scientific generalizations are necessary truths in the sense that they are true in all possible worlds, and an inventory of the laws of physics, chemistry and biology in this world is also an inventory of the laws of physics, chemistry and biology in all possible worlds.

The notion of natural necessity has been notoriously unpopular since Hume's attack on rationalist accounts of causation in Book I of the *Treatise*, and I think that the discomfort that many philosophers feel about it can best be expressed in the form of three objections. The first is the objection I mentioned in the previous section, and is Hume's central objection: if there were such a thing as natural necessity, or generative power, or whatever special property we take ourselves to be talking about in this context, we should in principle be able to observe it. But we cannot observe it, so it does not exist — or, at least, it does not exist as a property of objects. The point of the final qualification is to allow the historical Hume to argue that natural necessity exists, in some sense, but only as a curious by-product of our psychological processes. Experience leads us to connect impressions or ideas of a given cause with impressions or ideas of its effect. This 'movement of the mind' is then projected back on to the world, and mistaken for a necessary connection in nature, a real connection between cause and effect.

This first objection does not deserve serious discussion. One reason is the reason I gave earlier: a crude empiricism, which demands that all objects and all properties must be literally observable, would make serious science, and especially serious twentieth-century science, impossible. But there is another, much more important and much more subtle, reason for rejecting the objection, namely that it rests on a confused assumption about the logical status of natural necessity. Hume claims that the terms *'efficacy, agency, power, force, energy, necessity, connexion and productive quality'* are all 'nearly synonimous'.[2] And, as the reference to a 'productive quality' makes plain, he talks as though, if there is to be natural necessity, it must be some kind of first-order feature, available to sensory inspection, on a par with colour, shape, weight, taste, and so on. Mackie seems to share his view, and refers to the properties that prompt Hume's scepticism as 'occult properties'.[3] Since Hume and Mackie think of natural necessity in that way, it is hardly surprising that they fail to find anything to do the trick. For, in talking about natural necessity, we are definitely *not* talking about another first-order property, whether overt or occult.[4] If it is a property of anything (and on balance I would prefer not to use the language of properties at all), it is either a property of properties, or a property of sentences. That is, it is *either* a property of the crucial properties that determine membership of natural kinds, since they are the properties that members of those kinds will have in all possible worlds; *or* it is a property of certain sentences, namely, true scientific generalizations about the members of those kinds, since those sentences will be true in all possible worlds. So any talk about natural necessity in the case of hydrogen, oxygen, carbon etc. should be understood *either* as a reminder that the real essences of those kinds make it necessary that their members behave in certain ways, and impossible that they behave in others; *or* as a claim that the sentences expressing the fundamental scientific truths about the behaviour of members of natural kinds are necessary truths.

A second objection is that my account of natural necessity is too weak. I have suggested that the central component of the notion of natural necessity is truth in all possible worlds, but that also seems to be the central component of the notion of logical necessity. Presumably 'Bachelors are unmarried' is a necessary truth if and only if it is true in all possible worlds. But I then seem to lose the distinction between logical and natural necessity, since both consist in truth in all possible worlds. My reply is to say that the objection is substantially true, but is not an objection. For I do not wish to enforce a distinction between logical and natural necessity. I am inclined rather to say that there is just one notion here, the notion of necessity, and that that notion should be analysed in terms of truth in all possible worlds. The supposed distinction between logical and natural necessity is not a distinction between two kinds of necessity, but is at most a distinction between a special case and the general case. A logically necessary truth is one in which a certain necessity is represented, more or less explicitly, in a natural language; the distinction between logical and natural necessity is a distinction between necessities explicitly represented in a language (the special case), and necessities that may or may not be so represented (the general case). Incidentally, the etymology of the word 'hydrogen' confirms my view that we should not wish to press the supposed distinction very hard.

The third objection takes us back to Hume. Scientific laws typically express, or can be paraphrased to express, functional relations between one event or state of affairs and another, for example between the state of the world at a given time, when quantities of free hydrogen and free oxygen are close to a flame, and a subsequent state, when the hydrogen combines with the oxygen to generate considerable heat and to produce a quantity of water. If we claim that scientific laws are necessary truths, we are in effect claiming that there are necessary connections between distinct existences. But, Hume insisted, that is absurd: no statement about the intrinsic properties of an object, event or state of affairs can show that there must be an entirely different object, event or state of affairs, with certain intrinsic properties. He refers scornfully to 'the tie' by which two objects are supposedly united.[5]

But once again, I think that Hume is guilty of muddle. In talking about necessary connections between distinct existences, he is supposing that natural necessity would have to be a special kind of relational property, rather like spatial or temporal relation, a special kind of 'tie' or metaphysical glue, which attaches a cause to its effect, and allows the cause to push the effect along, rigidly and inevitably. But that supposition is quite wrong. As I explained in my discussion of the first objection, necessity is not a property, either intrinsic or relational, of objects or events; nor is it any kind of tie or glue, either literal or metaphorical. If it is a property of anything, it is either a property of the properties determining membership of natural kinds, or a property of the true sentences describing the behaviour of their members. Once again, the central thought is that members of natural kinds have certain real essences, which not only determine membership of the kinds, but directly govern the behaviour of individual members. Members of a particular natural kind will have exactly the same real essence in every possible world, and they will therefore behave in exactly the same way in every possible world. Given that hydrogen is an element with a certain real essence (a certain atomic structure), it is a matter of necessity that samples of hydrogen behave in certain ways and not others. If, per impossibile, they behaved quite differently (for example, formed the stable molecules HO_2 or HO_7), then they would not be samples of hydrogen.

Perhaps I should add one defensive comment. At some point in discussions of causation, we can normally expect the class bore to lean forward complacently and to drone on about quantum mechanics. Furthermore, on almost every occasion, it soon becomes clear that any differences between Newtonian and quantum mechanics have no bearing on the philosophical issues. This discussion is no exception. I have talked interchangeably of causal laws and of the laws of physics, chemistry and biology, but my central point about natural necessity remains exactly the same, even if we argue that the laws of physics, chemistry and biology are strictly probabilistic, rather than deterministic. I have claimed that scientific laws are necessary truths, in the sense that they are true in all possible worlds. Given the obvious concession to quantum physicists, that amounts to the claim that the probabilistic laws that govern objects in this world are true in all possible worlds. If the probability in this world of a certain outcome, given a certain initial state, is p, then the probability in all possible worlds of that outcome, given that initial state, is p. Those who are puzzled by the suggestion that statistical laws are necessary truths are precisely those who think of necessary connection as a curious kind of natural property, or tie, or glue, binding initial state to outcome. Once we free ourselves of that thought, we shall have no further difficulties with the notion of natural necessity.

More examples, and the social sciences

So far in this discussion of natural kinds, I have dealt with a fairly limited range of examples. I have only considered kinds of particle (*electron, proton, neutron*), kinds of individual (*chimpanzee, stickleback, narcissus*) and kinds of stuff (*gold, water, cellulose*), and I have only considered natural kinds that are likely to be of interest to natural scientists, the kinds of physics, chemistry and biology. In this section I want to broaden the discussion, first, by considering examples of natural kinds that are neither kinds of particle nor kinds of individual nor kinds of stuff, and second, by considering whether the notion of a natural kind has application in the social sciences. On my general account of natural kinds, which ties the notion of a natural kind to that of a real essence and in turn to a view about the proper scope of science, the second part of the discussion will in effect be a discussion of the status of the social sciences.

First, then, some more examples of members of natural kinds. So far I have not mentioned natural kinds of state, or event, or condition, or process, or property. Since, on my account, a natural kind is determined by a real essence, a feature that is both necessary and sufficient for membership of the kind, and which underpins scientific description, explanation and prediction, it would seem obvious that there are many natural kinds that are kinds of state, event, condition or process. Physics is a rich sort of examples, since physicists routinely talk about waves, fields, forces and strings, and have a complex vocabulary for describing the features of elementary particles. I can see no objection to my general project in allowing that there are natural kinds of wave, field, force, string and elementary particle, each with an appropriate real essence. Indeed, in enlarging the range of examples in that way, I am implicitly doing justice to two important claims. The first is the claim that, although folk scientists tend to talk only of kinds of particle, kinds of individual and kinds of stuff, and are therefore wedded to something like an Aristotelian language of persisting substances, formal physics requires a much richer range of entities, and has little or no use for the notion of a persisting substance. And the second important claim is that there may be different levels of natural kinds.

Another discipline that should encourage us to broaden the range of examples is medicine, for many diseases are determined by a real essence, but are neither kinds of particle, nor kinds of individual, nor kinds of stuff. They consist rather in kinds of event or state or condition or process. For example the real essence of diseases may consist in the presence of a specific virus or bacterium, or the failure of a specific organ, or the blockage of a blood vessel, or an imbalance of a specific chemical. I am not qualified to work patiently through a list of possible examples, but will be content to point out one or two general philosophical difficulties that would have to be confronted by anyone who might wish to produce such a list. One difficulty is that certain diseases are described as 'syndromes', that is, collections of concurrent and supposedly related symptoms. In some cases it may prove impossible to isolate any single underlying real essence, any single property or set of properties responsible for the syndrome, and those are probably best regarded as real but superficial kinds, as belonging with kinds such as *pebble, cloud, tree, shrub*. In other cases, however, notably the case of AIDS, syndromes are due to very definite single causes: most available evidence suggests that AIDS is caused by a specific virus, HIV. We should treat these as cases of natural kinds, where each natural kind is determined by the causal origin and development of the disease. There are also cases where a syndromic disease turns out to be a group of quite separate diseases with similar symptoms, which are united only by superficial properties. Perhaps the group of diseases known popularly as 'cancer' might be an example: cancerous tumours are united by a superficial property, namely, rapid and uncontrolled cell division, but different tumours, in different parts of the body, are caused, and develop, in different ways. These are also examples of what, in chapter 4, I shall call botched shots at natural kind classification. That is, they illustrate our tendency, when trying to classify natural kinds, to rely heavily on symptoms, on Lockean nominal essences, which may mislead us. We collect together objects (or diseases) that are superficially similar but profoundly different, and fail to collect together objects (or diseases) that are profoundly similar, but superficially different.

A second difficulty concerns psychiatric diseases. Often they are defined solely in terms of symptoms or collections of symptoms. Sometimes, as in the case of manic depression, it seems that the disease can be initially associated with, and then identified with, a certain chemical disorder. Often that is not so, and we are left simply with symptoms or collections of symptoms, as in the case of many other depressive illnesses. In the first kind of case we can regard the disease as a natural kind, but at the cost of reducing psychiatry to neurophysiology, and in the second kind of case we can treat the disease as a real but superficial kind, but at the potential cost of casting doubt on psychiatry as a serious scientific discipline.

A third difficulty (or perhaps I should say, complication) is that natural kinds are relative to a level, in the sense of level I sketched in chapter 1. A simple example rests on the distinction between genera and species: what counts as the same kind at the level of genera (e.g. the kind *Geranium*) will count as a different kind at the level of species (e.g. the kinds *Geranium sanguineum* and *Geranium phaeum*). Unfortunately, as we shall see in chapter 5, there are serious problems involved in treating standard taxonomic categories as natural kinds, so it might be wise to take another example, this time from chemistry. At one level various compounds are of the same natural kind, because they are all proton donors, but at another level they are of different kinds, because their chemical composition is different — H_2SO_4, NH_3, etc. Similarly, in thinking about diseases, and in wondering whether they form natural kinds, we need to think about levels of explanation. At a rather high level of explanation we might treat cancer as a natural kind, on the ground that it consists of abnormal and rapid cell division, but at a lower level it might become clear that the exact mechanisms involved in different kinds of cancer, in different parts of the body, are very different.

I now turn to the social sciences, to the status of families, nations, banks, rates of unemployment, and of course to beliefs, desires and intentions. Since I have tied the notions of a natural kind, a real essence, and scientific explanation very firmly together, I am in effect asking whether the social sciences are proper sciences at all. Before saying directly what I have to say, I want to get certain bad arguments out of the way. One bad argument, which attempts to exploit work by Hegel, Weber, Dilthey, Croce, Collingwood, Wittgenstein and many others, might go like like this. There are fundamental differences between the natural and the social sciences, and the differences are so profound that the notion of a natural kind can have no application in the social sciences. Natural scientists are concerned to give an objective account of the world as it is in itself, quite independently of our beliefs and theories about it. They are positively required to stand back from their subject matter and to describe it from a spectator's or third-person point of view. In contrast, social scientists are and must be part of their own subject matter. In order to make sense of the social scheme of things, they have to be part of it, for they must understand it from the inside. They must share the basic beliefs and attitudes of their experimental subjects if they are to make the imaginative leap that is required for proper understanding. Without Weberian *Verstehen* the social sciences are impossible. If I am to explain religious practices, I must share some basic empathetic understanding of religious matters; if I am to explain human (or bat) psychology, I must share the human (or bat) point of view, and so on. In a sense, therefore, the findings of the social scientist must always be expressed in the first person, or from a first-person point of view, and will be imbued with the beliefs and attitudes of both observer and observed. It follows that there can be no natural kinds in the social sciences, for all the phenomena described and explained will have a relational dependence on the beliefs and attitudes of the society in question, including the beliefs and attitudes of the social scientist. It will be irredeemably an account of the world from a particular point of view.

I have to say that this familiar kind of argument is extremely foggy. Fortunately we do not have to penetrate very much of the fog, for we can simply concentrate on the move from premiss to conclusion. The premiss is that social scientists must have a certain imaginative ability or empathy to do any work at all (Weberian *Verstehen*), and that that ability or empathy rests on a framework of beliefs and attitudes that they share with their subjects. The conclusion is that there are no natural kinds in the social sciences. I wish to argue that the conclusion does not follow. According to my account of natural kinds, a natural kind is determined by a real essence, that is, an intrinsic property which permits scientific generalization. The premiss of the argument above could be paraphrased as follows: if social scientists are to discover the real sociological essences of things, they must themselves share those essences. Failure to share them would guarantee a complete failure of understanding, and social science would grind to a halt. But then it is clear that the conclusion does not follow. That is, nothing has ruled out the possibility that social scientists, who themselves have certain intrinsic sociological features, and are members of sociological natural kinds, may discover intrinsic sociological features, shared by themselves and by others. The important methodological constraint, that experimenter and subject must have something in common, in no way entails that the features discovered in experimenter and subject are non-natural.

Let us therefore move quickly to another bad argument. The central thought is that in a discussion of natural kinds, we positively need not and should not say anything about the social sciences, because the notion of a natural kind can only have application in science and the social sciences are not sciences. They fail to achieve that elevated status because they fail to fulfil two conditions. First, any scientific generalization must be testable in principle under closed or artificial conditions. Second, a scientific generalization is logically universal, whatever its superficial grammatical form may be. It states, or purports to state, what would occur if certain conditions were to obtain. It therefore implies counterfactuals, and does not merely record that certain events have occurred, from time to time, in certain rather peculiar local conditions. Moreover, these two important conditions are closely connected. It is precisely because scientific generalizations are logically universal, and imply counterfactuals, that we expect to be able to repeat crucial experiments under closed conditions.

Now (the argument goes on) the social sciences fail both tests. First, it is impossible to test the generalizations of the social sciences under proper experimental conditions. We cannot, for example, isolate the factors we are interested in, by setting up an experiment in the laboratory. For all sorts of obvious reasons, social life relentlessly trundles on in its complex entirety, and no proper part of it can be sliced off for examination in the laboratory. Nor can we set up certain experimental groups, altering a crucial variable in each case, and keeping a control group throughout for comparison. No doubt social scientists describe their work in the language of experiment and observation, and set great store by what they call 'control groups', but they deceive themselves. Nothing in the social sciences approximates, even roughly, to the totally isolated experimental environment of the natural scientist's laboratory. Indeed, the whole idea of isolating certain factors in laboratory conditions makes no sense in a social context, because so many of the features of interest to social scientists are relational, are determined by a social context. To isolate a citizen, or a family, or a firm, or a consumer, entails that it is no longer a citizen, a family, a firm or a consumer. Moreover, social scientists are themselves part of the social fabric being examined, and the process of gathering information and of making predictions inevitably infects the experiment. To take a simple example: in examining people's voting intentions the psephologist is bound to affect their behaviour, even if the results of the survey are not published before the poll. The very fact that I am asked to reveal my intentions is apt to affect them in some way.

Second, although the language of the social sciences is superficially universal, it is logically singular. Science is concerned with the universal, with the repeatable-in-principle, and scientific generalizations entail counterfactual conditionals. Nothing of significance is repeated or even repeatable in the social sciences. Although we may discern similarities between one historical period and another, or between one society and another, they are never close enough to allow us to draw universal conclusions about the nature of social reality. Whatever the superficial features of our descriptions of social reality (the apparent use of variables, the absence of proper names and other singular terms, and so on), the descriptions are logically singular, descriptions of one very complicated historical sequence.

Unfortunately this argument will not do, because the suggested constraints on serious science are too strong, even when applied to the natural sciences. If we regard the two conditions as necessary conditions of a serious science, then a number of historically important scientific disciplines will no longer be such. For example (to take the first condition), if we insist that a scientist must be able to make experiments under closed conditions, must be able to isolate the variables in which he is interested, then we must regard astronomy and cosmology as unscientific. Nothing whatever would enable us to check our astronomical and cosmological theories by isolating astronomical and cosmological phenomena in the laboratory, under closed conditions. No doubt there is *some* connection between astronomy and cosmology, on the one hand, and laboratory experiments, on the other, but the connection is loose and remote, and social scientists can reasonably claim that their own experiments have the same kind of loose and remote connection with theory. Furthermore (moving to the second condition) it is no good to argue that scientific phenomena are typically repeatable and that sociological phenomena are not; that scientific generalizations are logically universal and that social scientific generalizations are not. On the one hand, as history makes plain, many features of the human condition are repeated to a degree that is thoroughly depressing. Human vanity, cruelty and stupidity seem to produce exactly similar results over and over again, and one is bound to draw dispiriting counterfactual conclusions. On the other hand, many scientific disciplines are concerned with unique sequences of events. Two rich sources of examples have already been mentioned, namely astronomy and cosmology. A third is evolutionary biology. The history of the universe is unique, yet we reasonably take the theories of astronomers, cosmologists and evolutionary to be logically universal, as articulating connections between conditions *of a certain kind* and other conditions *of a certain kind*, and as entailing counterfactual conditionals.

I am therefore still content in principle to regard the social sciences as sciences, and to accept at least some social scientific kinds as natural kinds. Moreover, I have already mentioned an argument dear to the heart of my explanatory liberal, which would make such contentment even more contented. The argument is that patterns of description and explanation may be entirely invisible at one level, but emerge clearly at a higher level. The patterns of interest to a biologist may not be obvious to a chemist, nor those of interest to a chemist be obvious to a physicist. Even within physics itself, we need to distinguish patterns at different levels: Brownian motion is visible only at the level of groups of atoms, not at the level of the individual atom. At the very much higher level of psychology, sociology, economics, history, political science, we should not be surprised to discover descriptions, explanations and predictions that are irreducible to those at some lower level. In a perfectly harmless way, and in a perfectly harmless sense of 'emerge', new properties and new explanatory concepts are bound to emerge at each new level of explanation. A further point worth mentioning is that at least some of the social sciences use sophisticated quantitative methods, and quantitative methods are typical of the natural sciences. Perhaps the best example is economics, where very sophisticated mathematical models of economic behaviour are now available, and where economists do seem to be capable of making quite definite predictions about the course of economic events.

Pessimism about the social sciences

However, although I am prepared in philosophical principle to allow that there might be social scientific kinds that are natural kinds in the sense I have defined, I have to say that in philosophical practice I do not expect to find any. I want to leave the possibility open, but in a pessimistic frame of mind. My best guess is that we should treat social scientific kinds either as dependent kinds or as real superficial kinds. I have two main reasons for pessimism. First, and most obviously, many social scientific kinds are clearly dependent kinds, that is, membership of the kind is determined by a relational dependence upon something else. In some cases it depends upon human laws, conventions, interests, moral attitudes, etc. For example, the kinds *nation, club, society, firm, bank, building society, contract,* are all determined by certain moral or legal conventions and interests. Had the conventions and interests been different, there would not have been the same nations, clubs, banks, etc. In psychology many kinds are determined by context, at least, according to those of us who embrace some version of externalism. At its most general, externalism is the view that representations represent only if they have the right kind of causal connection with objects of the kind represented. It follows that psychological representations, such as beliefs, thoughts and intentions, are determined, not by the intrinsic features of the people concerned, but by a complex relation between them and the rest of the world.

That objection only works, however, if my account of natural kinds is correct. For a central feature of my account is the distinction between natural and dependent kinds, and the associated claim that natural kinds are determined by intrinsic, rather than by relational, properties. On any account of natural kinds that allows real essences to be relational properties, social scientific kinds might well prove to be natural kinds. So it is fortunate that I have a second objection, as follows. On any remotely interesting account of natural kinds, even a fairly weak account, a natural kind is determined by a real essence, a property or set of properties necessary and sufficient for membership of the kind. A fortiori, if there were natural kinds in the social sciences, there would have to be real essences to determine the kinds. But it is very difficult to see what the essences would be. For example what is a nation? We might suppose that a nation is determined by political and geographical criteria, but the Jews thought of themselves as a single scattered nation for two thousand years, and the aspirations of Poles, Kurds and Basques are still not neatly catered for by political institutions and geographical boundaries. Or, to take another example, what is a family? There are nuclear families, extended families, families with children, families without children. Sometimes friends and partners qualify as aunts and uncles, sometimes not, and so on. Indeed social kinds seem to be excellent examples of kinds determined by Wittgensteinian family resemblances, by a complex and open-ended network of overlapping and criss-crossing similarities. If there were real essences which determined social scientific kinds, they would in each case be single properties or sets of properties, but a family resemblance is precisely not a single property or set of properties. It is not even a closed disjunctive set of properties.

Moreover, although I have so far made as many concessions to the explanatory liberal as I decently can — in arguing, for example, that the general patterns that yield explanatory laws may only appear at comparatively high levels — we need to think harder about the features that actually underlie such laws and make them explanatory. It may well be true that the patterns detectable by a social scientist are detectable only at the level of individual human beings and groups of human beings, and are invisible further down, but if such patterns are to permit rational explanation and prediction, they must be grounded in some features, and particularly in the causal powers, of the individuals or groups of individuals in question. I think that a proper understanding of social scientific laws requires us to retreat to a lower level. For example, whatever the success of mathematical techniques in making sense of whole economies, what happens in a whole economy is the direct (if exceedingly complicated) result of the decisions of individual agents. Social patterns are the direct (if complicated) result of patterns in individuals. And those patterns in individuals will in turn require explanation in terms of the features that determine membership of that kind of individual, for example in terms of the psychological and biological features of human beings. Human sociologists or economists rest their disciplines on an account of human beings, and so in turn on psychology, and psychologists rest their discipline, at least in part, on a biological account of the genetically determined peculiarities of human beings. Martian sociologists and economists, though possibly devoted to discovering very similar sociological and economic patterns on Mars, will rest such patterns on an account of individual Martians, which in turn will rest on an account of the fine (silica-based?) structure of Martians.

Those who have read too much Hegel, or who have misunderstood Hollis,[6] might talk about the Cunning of Reason. They might claim that certain patterns emerge at the level of whole social groups that cannot be reduced to patterns at a lower level (e.g. the level of individuals), so cannot be explained in terms of those lower level patterns, for individual decisions may have all sorts of consequences at the level of the group that are impossible to predict at the level of the individual. But such a response would be beside the point. It is of course true, as Hollis and others are at pains to explain, that a rational decision by an individual, added to other rational decisions by other individuals, might have consequences that none of them either expect or approve. Indeed, in the imperfect market of life, that result is more likely than not. It may also be true that the remarks about the higher level patterns cannot be translated neatly into remarks about the lower level patterns. Both those claims could reasonably be regarded as reasonable concessions to a doctrine about the Cunning of Reason: Reason may produce consequences for the group that are a) neither wanted nor intended by the individuals, and b) logically expressible only in terms of concepts that apply to the group, not the individual. But none of that undermines my original claim, namely that the sociological and economic explanations of the features of the group are truly explanatory only if the features of the group are in some way constituted or realized by features of its individual.

To take a simple example, consider what Hollis calls the Hobbesian trap.[7] I may be contemplating something uplifting and ambitious, such as partnership in the social contract, or something much less uplifting and much less ambitious, such as helping old ladies across the road or taking my litter home. Other rational agents, we may suppose, are confronting the same decision, and we are all aware that we are all confronting the same decision. I cannot force the best result for myself, though I can avoid the worst. Everyone thinks the same thought, and the inevitable result is that we all do moderately badly: the Social Contract gives us something but not very much, old ladies are run down and the town is full of litter. The features of the whole group (including facts about social arrangements, the fate of old ladies and the incidence of litter) are traceable directly to the decisions of

individuals. Patterns at a high level have explanatory significance only if
they are constituted or realized by facts at some lower level. The relevant
causal powers are the causal powers of the individuals, not those of the
group.

It might appear that I am now committed to giving a special status to
psychology. For, if the causal powers of social groups are to be explained
ultimately in terms of the causal powers of individuals, it might seem that
the discipline dealing with the causal powers of individuals, namely
psychology, has a special status. In John Stuart Mill's rousing words,

> The laws of the phenomena of society are, and can be, nothing but the laws
> of the actions and passions of human beings united together in the social state
> ... Human beings in society have no properties but those which are derived
> from, and may be resolved into, the laws of nature of individual man.[8]

Furthermore, since throughout this book I shall connect the notions of a
natural kind, a real essence and a causal power very closely together, I now
seem ready to claim that there could in principle be psychological natural
kinds. But that important trinity — natural kind, real essence and causal
power — forces us to the opposite conclusion, for three connected reasons.
First, as I hinted earlier, there is good reason to think that sociological
properties in general, and psychological properties in particular, are
examples of cluster or family resemblance properties. That is, even when we
confine our attention to the fairly high level at which psychological
properties are visible, and leave on one side any consideration of their
physical realization at some lower level, a careful philosophical analysis of
them reveals either a group of properties clustering together, or an open-
ended set of overlapping and criss-crossing similarities. Over and over again,
we discover with Ryle that there is no definite 'nuclear activity' crucially
associated with each psychological property.[9] That means that we could not
sensibly refuse to extend our psychological vocabulary to beings whose
properties are only a proper sub-set of our local human cluster, or which
overlap with the cluster, or which only form a narrow or peripheral or
overlapping part of the family. It also means that, even at the psychological
level, there is not the slightest chance of isolating a property or set of
properties necessary and sufficient for membership of the psychological kind.
That possibility is closed off as soon as we start talking about cluster or
family resemblance properties.

Second, as functionalists are fond of reminding us, psychological features
are, or could be, multiply realized, that is, may be constituted or realized by
a range of physical features. Even if we concentrate on human beings, we
can see that one and the same belief, or one and the same intention, or one
and the same desire, is almost certainly associated with a very wide range
of specific neurophysiological states. And if we leave open the possibility

that other animals, and other beings, are capable of having, quite literally, psychological features similar to ours, then there is no sort of close fit between a specific psychological property and a specific physical property. Each psychological property will be constituted or realized by a range (perhaps even an open-ended range) of physical properties. But a natural kind is determined by a real essence, a property or set of properties necessary and sufficient for membership of the kind. A property that is capable of multiple realization, a property that might be constituted or realized by a range of physical properties, is precisely a property that is not determined by a real essence in that sense of 'real essence'. So psychological kinds are not natural kinds.

Third, a few pages ago I committed myself to externalism, to the view that representations (including desires, intentions and beliefs) represent only if they have the right sort of causal connection with objects of the kind represented. That view, which I accept, entails that many psychological states are individuated, not in virtue of any intrinsic features of the agent (for example, in virtue of physical, chemical and biological features) but in virtue of complex relational features. I and my Doppelgänger on Twin Earth may have the same intrinsic features without sharing the same psychological features, because we are in quite different causal contexts. Conversely, I and some other sentient being may have very different intrinsic features but share similar desires, intentions and beliefs, because we are in very similar causal contexts. But the causal powers of a thing are grounded firmly in its intrinsic features, not in its relational features: the next state of the universe depends solely on its present intrinsic physical, chemical and biological state. A fortiori, the causal powers of psychological states turn out to be the causal powers of the physical, chemical and biological entities that realize or constitute them. Since natural kinds are determined by real essences, which are intimately connected with the causal powers of things, and in turn with their intrinsic properties, it follows that psychological kinds (which are determined by relational properties) cannot be natural kinds (which are determined by intrinsic properties).[10]

What then should we say about the kinds of the social sciences? I suggest we should return to remarks I made in chapter 2, in the course of a discussion of agriculture, horticulture, geology, geography and meteorology. I argued that many of the kinds that feature in those disciplines are not natural kinds, because they do not have real essences and do not lend themselves to scientific generalization. I suggested that their explanatory apparatus is perpetually provisional, and is constantly being reduced to, or connected with, or supplanted by, the explanatory apparatus of physics, chemistry and biology. Geology and geography would be impossible if there were no physics and chemistry of the elements and compounds that constitute our planet; meteorology would be impossible if there were no science of gases, of electricity, of the behaviour of massive bodies in gravitational fields; and so on. Moreover, all these 'provisional' sciences involve the application of physics, chemistry and biology to specific cases, and especially to cases where conditions are comparatively stable and constant. Indeed the conspicuous success of statistical methods in, say, meteorology depends on the constancy and stability of terrestrial conditions. It would be impossible to use terrestrial agriculture, horticulture, geology, geography and meteorology to explain and predict the behaviour of objects whose constitution and local conditions were very different from those on Earth. It was therefore no surprise when we eventually discovered that the kinds *glacier, cliff, cloud, thunderstorm, tree, shrub, perennial*, etc. were either dependent, or real but superficial.

I suggest that we should treat the social sciences in exactly the same way. In one sense of course social scientists are doing important scientific work. But their subject matter, the human being, is made of a quite specific range of materials, and is to be found in a very limited range of conditions. Any explanations or predictions are perpetually provisional, and must be reduced to, or connected with, or supplanted by, the explanatory apparatus of physics, chemistry and biology, for the fundamental causal powers of human beings are the causal powers of interest to physicists, chemists and biologists. We could not sensibly extend our sociological predictions and explanations to beings made of very different materials and living in very different local conditions. It should therefore be no surprise that the kinds distinguished by social scientists are either dependent, or real but superficial.

An objection: function and realization

Those who do not share my pessimism about the social sciences may at this point make an important objection. On a number of occasions I have alluded, with apparent approval, to the distinction between function and realization, and to its importance in making intelligible certain kinds of high-level description and explanation. For in many disciplines we have to recognize that one and the same function may be realized in many different ways: there may be many different pieces of machinery all doing the same job. The objection to my pessimism about the social sciences rests on the thought that I have simply ignored an important consequence of the distinction between function and realization.

The crucial points, it will be said, are these. In many disciplines, and particularly in psychology and other social sciences, we find ourselves interested in patterns, features and functions that are only visible at a comparatively high level of explanation, and are totally invisible at lower levels. Indeed, when the pattern, feature or function is capable of many quite different realizations, it is hardly surprising that it is invisible at lower levels, and equally it is clear why our explanatory apparatus focuses on the level of pattern, feature or function, rather than the level of realization. The psychologist gets on very well if he thinks about the explanatory role of the psychological function; if he even attempts to think hard about the many possible realizations of the function, he will soon be in wandering mazes lost. Moreover, his colleague the neurophysiologist, who has been working on the realization, will only be able to apply his experimental discoveries to other beings with brains and nervous systems. The psychologist, however, will be able to apply his results to absolutely any being functionally equivalent to a human being. Mutatis mutandis, exactly the same point will apply to economists, sociologists and political scientists, who detect patterns, features and functions at a very high level, and can — indeed must — safely ignore differences in realization. Multiple realization, same function. And there can be no objection to our finding natural kinds determined by a single property at the level of the function, but associated with many different properties at the level of realization.

At the risk of being thought unfashionable, I have to say that this breezy way of talking about function and realization is extremely dangerous. Anyone who attempts to describe and explain phenomena at the level of function ignores the realization at their peril. Quite often it is just not true that there can be multiple realizations of the same function, even if we concentrate on comparatively simple pieces of machinery. For differences in the realization are apt to produce differences in function. Consider washing machines, which sometimes feature in functionalist explanations of the distinction between function and realization. The claim is that there are top-loading machines, front-loading machines, single- and double-drum machines, women bashing clothes on river banks, and so on; and that these multiple realizations may be functionally equivalent. That, I suggest, is nonsense. Even small differences in the realization, in the physical structure of the machine, are likely to produce differences in function. Some machines produce cleaner clothes, some spin more or less efficiently, some consume less electricity or water, some vibrate less or make less noise, and so on. The suggestion that there could, as it were, be a science of washing machines, without constant reference to details of the realization, is quite absurd.

Similarly, there can be no science of psychology, economics, politics or sociology, no confident generalization or prediction at the high level of function, for here we are dealing with far more complicated pieces of machinery. The possibility of multiple realization is likely to undermine all but the roughest and least ambitious explanatory remarks. Success is possible only in cases where all the realizations are fundamentally rather similar, for example where all the sentient machines in question are powered by human brains and nervous systems. But then the explanatory success of the high-level disciplines (e.g. the social sciences) depends entirely on the explanatory success of those at the lowest levels, those dealing with the realization (e.g. physics, chemistry and biology). And we can continue to rely on those at the lowest levels (e.g. physics, chemistry and biology) precisely because, with one notable exception that will occupy me in chapter 5, they have little or no use for the distinction between function and realization. There is absolutely no reason to suppose that the specific biological or chemical properties of things could be multiply realized: biological features are tied very closely to specific chemical features, and chemical to physical. For example, the properties of genes are directly determined (or, as some might prefer to say, encoded) by the distribution of two matching pairs of bases on the strings of DNA, adenine and guanine, and thymine and cytosine. The chemical properties of elements and compounds are directly determined by the physical structure of their atomic constituents. Even the structural properties of a molecule will be directly determined by the structure of its atomic components. It does not follow, and it is not true, that chemistry and biology can be reduced to, or replaced by, physics, for all sorts of familiar reasons. But the crucial point is that we can safely accommodate higher levels of explanation only when we are confident that relevant high level functions are not multiply realized, when the functional property at the higher level is directly determined by the properties of the realization. We can therefore continue to treat chemistry and biology as sciences, and to talk comfortably about chemical and biological natural kinds. But we must continue to be very pessimistic about our chances of finding natural kinds in the social sciences, where multiple realization is the norm.

But doesn't that reply backfire? If very specific psychological features are tied to quite specific features of their realization, psychological kinds are natural kinds. Indeed the sentence 'very specific psychological features are tied to quite specific features of their realization' seems to mean 'psychological kinds are determined by real essences, properties (of the various realizations) necessary and sufficient for members of the kinds'! But I don't think that I am forced to that conclusion. I wish merely to warn against too free a use of the distinction between function and realization, and to stress that successful explanatory reference to psychological function requires a constant weather eye on specific features of the realization. Confident use of higher level psychological explanation is possible only if we lean heavily on the lower level explanations of neurophysiology. But since I do not want to rule out the possibility of multiple realization of the same psychological function, I am committed to the pessimistic conclusion that psychological kinds are not natural kinds.

Brief review

In this chapter and the previous chapter, I have tried to clarify the notion of a natural kind. I have tied it very closely to the notion of a real essence, a property necessary and sufficient for membership of a natural kind; I have also put it at the centre of scientific explanation; and I have argued that real essences must be intrinsic rather than relational properties. Moreover, I have committed myself to a non-Humean view of scientific laws, as de re necessary truths capable of supporting counterfactuals. These rather strong constraints on the enquiry appear to entail that the social sciences are not sciences within the meaning of the act, and that even sciences such as agriculture, meteorology and geology are wholly parasitic on physics, chemistry and biology. If all that is true, we now have a reply to explanatory liberalism. For although there are many different kinds of entity, and many different kinds of description and explanation, some have a special status, because some entities are members of natural kinds, and therefore lend themselves to serious scientific investigation.

Many other questions will now arise, but I am just going to concentrate on three of them. The first question arises in the theory of meaning: how are the names of natural kinds invented and used in natural languages? And should we give a very different account of our use of the names of non-natural kinds? The second question concerns the notion of a real essence: I have argued that natural kinds are determined by real essences, but are there any real essences of kinds? That is, is it possible to sustain the claim that each natural kind is determined by an intrinsic property necessary and sufficient for membership of the kind? Many of my examples have been members of biological species, and defenders of accounts of natural kinds have apparently supposed that species are excellent examples. But, as we shall see, it is far from clear that species are natural kinds. I need to consider the status of species. The third question is an invitation to think about the essences of individuals: does my account of the essences of kinds imply, or does it give me the materials to construct, an account of the essences of individuals? These three questions will be the topics of my three remaining chapters.

Notes

1   R. Harré and E.H. Madden (1975), especially ch. 4.
2   Hume (1739), I, iii, 14; Selby Bigge, p. 157.
3   J.L. Mackie (1974), p. 60.
4   After completing this book, I discovered an interesting article by Antony Flew, in which he argues that we do have experience of natural necessity and impossibility: it lies in 'our abundant and ever repeated experience of activity as creatures of flesh and blood operating in a mind-independent world: experience, that is, of trying to push or to pull things about, and of succeeding in pushing or pulling some but not others'. See A.G.N. Flew (1990), especially p. 256.
5   Hume (1739), I, iii, 14; Selby-Bigge, p. 162.
6   See M. Hollis (1987).
7   M. Hollis, op. cit., especially the early chapters.
8   J.S. Mill (1843), VI, vii, 1.
9   See G. Ryle (1949), passim.
10   For further arguments against treating psychological kinds as natural kinds, see C. McGinn (1991), chs. V and VI.

4 The names of kinds

The names of natural kinds

So far I have presented the doctrine of natural kinds as a metaphysical thesis, as a view about what the world contains and how it works. It involves talking about natural kinds and real essences, and does not involve asking, for example, how the *names* of natural kinds function in natural languages. Some philosophers will consider that omission a very serious one, and will argue that a sane account of natural kinds must rest upon an understanding of the way in which we learn and use general names, and natural kind names in particular. I am not at all sure that I agree, and if I were reading this book, I would be inclined to press on swiftly to the beginning of chapter 5. But for the sake of those who do not share that inclination, I propose to devote this chapter to the semantics of general names. One very influential account of general names can be found in a number of papers by Putnam,[1] and in this section I want to consider whether the account applies to the names of natural kinds, that is, to names such as 'tiger', 'lemon', 'gold' and 'water'. In the following section I shall consider the names of non-natural kinds. In discussing the names of natural kinds, I will tend to concentrate on the names of biological kinds, for reasons that will become clear in due course. So, although Putnam has a great deal to say about such names as 'gold' and 'water', and although my own account of the names of natural kinds is supposed to apply to them, I shall be mainly interested in what he has to say about such names as 'tiger' and 'lemon'. (I shall make nothing of the trivial fact that it is lemon trees, rather than lemons, that might reasonably count as members of natural kinds.) I want to discuss an important objection to his account and, although I broadly agree with Putnam, I shall disagree over many important details.

In the papers that form the focus of our discussion, Putnam develops the general outlines of a view since dubbed 'externalism', that is, the view that representations represent only if they have the right sort of causal connection with objects of the kind represented. In particular, he argues, words do not get their meaning in virtue of our being in certain special psychological states 'narrowly' conceived, that is, in certain psychological states thought of in complete abstraction from their relation to the rest of the world. 'Meanings ain't in the head.' Words get their meaning rather because their use is causally connected in an appropriate way with objects of the kind referred to. When I use a word like 'tiger', I may well have certain thoughts or ideas going through my mind ('narrowly' conceived), but it really doesn't matter very much what they are. I may for example have thoughts of striped, feline, fierce Indian quadrupeds going through my mind — thoughts about a set of properties that Locke would have called the 'nominal essence' of the animals in question — but such thoughts ('narrowly' conceived) do not determine the *meaning* of the word 'tiger'. The crucial (though not perhaps the only) consideration is that my use of the word 'tiger' should have the right sort of causal connection with tigers. The 'right sort of causal connection' might be fairly direct, and consist in my perceiving and taming tigers, or it might be indirect, and consist in discussions with others who have direct access to tigers, or who have access to those who have access to tigers ... , and so on.

How then are general names, and particularly names of natural kinds, introduced? According to Putnam, we are blessed with a curious mixture of confidence and ignorance. We naturally find ourselves focusing on a group of objects that are superficially similar in colour, shape, habit, geographical position, etc., and we begin to think of certain objects as typical of the whole group. The general name is introduced originally as an indexical, as an expression which allows us to *point*, literally or metaphorically, to objects in the group. So, for example, we focus on a group of animals that are large, striped, fierce felines from India, and we introduce the word 'tiger' to point to one of *those*, in other words, to one of the typical tigers. Not only can we confidently apply the general name to any one of a number of these objects, but with equal confidence we can list the properties of tigers: they are large, striped, fierce felines from India. But (and this is a crucial point) according to Putnam, those properties do not determine membership of the kind, and the list is not a list of defining properties of tigers, in any relevantly formal sense of 'definition'. They merely help us, in Kripke's words, to 'fix the reference' of the word 'tiger'.[2] That is, they merely help us to determine which individuals are being referred to. Indeed, such properties could not determine membership of the kind, because some members are abnormal and will lack one or more of them: there are albino tigers, toothless tigers, tigers that are mild and amiable, three legged, or native to Regent's Park. At best, the properties define a tiger 'stereotype', and in practice our readiness to classify something as a tiger will depend on the extent to which it approximates to the stereotype.

Confidence may now give way to ignorance. We confidently apply the word 'tiger', literally or metaphorically pointing to certain typical tigers, but may not have the faintest idea what actually determines membership of the kind. In introducing the name, we suppose that there is some underlying property common to all the animals in question, and not merely to any stereotypical animals, a property that, in nature, determines membership of the kind. Moreover, in introducing the word 'tiger', we have committed ourselves to applying it to anything that has that underlying property, that has the relevant sameness relation to our original, and largely stereotypical, tigers. But we may not know what the underlying property is, and quite often will not know what it is, since comparatively few of us have any knowledge of physics, chemistry and biology, and no-one had any such knowledge until comparatively recently. At this point, Putnam argues, most of us are compelled to exploit the 'division of linguistic labour'. We wait upon the revelations of experts, who will discover the underlying property that supports our use of 'tiger', and, mutatis mutandis, all the underlying properties that support our use of other names for natural kinds.

Two implicit assumptions now need to be brought to the surface. First, Putnam never says explicitly how we are supposed to connect his account with a formal taxonomy, but if we read between the lines, I think it is quite clear that he regards the names of biological kinds as names of *species*, and supposes that the underlying properties determining natural kinds are the genetic properties that determine species. Second, I don't think that it would be at all unfair to characterize Putnam's account as quasi-historical. Indeed, he introduces his remarks about the division of linguistic labour as a 'socio-linguistic hypothesis'.[3] I would not put too much weight on the word 'historical', any more than, when thinking about social contract theories of political obligation, I would search diligently for historical evidence. But Putnam does seem to be offering some kind of psycholinguistic rational reconstruction of the way in which general names, and especially natural kind names, are invented, introduced and passed on to others. He is therefore committed to an empirical theory about the way in which general names, and especially natural kind names, are used in natural languages such as English. If Putnam is right, we should expect to find that English names of biological kinds normally refer to species, and that their use is supported by underlying genetic properties that determine membership of species. Or, to adopt the language that I have used in previous chapters, we should expect to find that their use is supported by genetic real essences that determine membership of species. We should also expect to find that we wait upon the experts to tell us what those genetic real essences are.

At this point we must examine an important objection, namely that ordinary language classification (hereafter OLC) does not fit Putnam's model: English names of biological kinds do not pick out species, they are not supported by genetic real essences that determine membership of the species, and we do not wait upon the revelations of biological experts. John Dupré has produced a large number of interesting counter-examples,[4] which I shall borrow with gratitude, mixing in a few of my own as we go. First, Putnam thinks of biological names as picking out species, but many OLC names pick out kinds of a higher level than the species. For example, 'oak', 'beech', 'elm', 'willow', 'rose', 'iris', 'cypress', 'rhododendron', 'narcissus' pick out genera; 'duck', 'wren', 'woodpecker' pick out families; 'gull' and 'tern' pick out sub-families; 'owl' and 'pigeon' pick out orders. Second, some OLC names fail to pick out any formal taxonomic kinds at all. For example, Dupré tells us, Americans easily distinguish between prickly pears and chollas, but the distinction corresponds to no taxonomic division. The same point applies to the very general and very familiar OLC kinds *tree, shrub, perennial, weed, vegetable* and *fruit*, which have no taxonomic significance. Third, some OLC names collect very different and unrelated species together, for example, 'wren', 'lily', 'daisy', 'orchid' and 'wolf'. Fourth, some OLC names have different uses in different idiolects: according to Dupré, 'robin' collects one species in North America, another in Britain, and a genus of flycatchers in Australia.

What follows from all these examples? They might seem to throw some doubt on Putnam's account of natural kind names, if it is regarded as a quasi-historical account of the development of our ordinary language classifications, but does anything else follow? For example do Dupré's examples have any bearing on general attempts, such as my own, to defend an account of natural kinds? Dupré believes that they do. For his careful analysis of OLC names is a central part of his argument against the doctrine of natural kinds, and in favour of a view that he calls 'promiscuous realism'. Those who defend a doctrine of natural kinds claim that, although there are many similarities and differences between things, one set of similarities is privileged, because they are the real essences which determine membership of natural kinds. In contrast, the promiscuous realist argues that there are many different kinds of classification, each concerned with rather different groups of similarities; no classification, and no group of similarities, is privileged. Each group of similarities is important only relative to a particular concern. As far as biological individuals are concerned, a formal taxonomic classification will be of interest to biologists, horticultural and agricultural classifications will be of interest to gardeners and farmers, gastronomic classifications to cooks and gourmets, taxidermal classifications to taxidermists, floral classifications to florists, and everyday classifications will serve many of us very well for ordinary non-specialist purposes.

This view is a version of realism, because the similarities and differences that underpin each system of classification are independent of our beliefs and theories, but the realism is promiscuous, because there will be an indefinitely large number of possible systems of classification, each one reflecting a different interest and concern. Moreover, the various classifications may overlap and run across each other. For example, we would expect to find a considerable overlap between formal taxonomic classifications and the classifications of gardeners, farmers and zoo keepers. But we would also expect to find that the different classifications tend to run across one another: a zoo keeper needs, among other things, to distinguish between dangerous and safe animals, between those that can tolerate low temperatures and those that cannot, and between those that swim and those that do not. But those distinctions run across formal taxonomic categories. (Dupré might have mentioned a short story by R.K. Narayan, in which the narrator's gardener has only two kind names. One is an example of a name for what I have dubbed a hybrid kind, and the other is a very high level natural kind name: '"This, Sir, is a weed." "And that?" "That, Sir, is a flowering plant."').

I shall return to promiscuous realism in chapter 5, and for the moment I will be content to wonder whether Dupré's examples, though important and interesting, seriously undermine Putnam's account of the meaning of natural kind names. Prima facie, Putnam's position looks secure. He claims that I introduce a natural kind name by pointing, literally or metaphorically, to apparently typical examples of the kind, examples which share various properties that are associated with, but do not strictly define, the kind name. And I suppose that the kind is determined by some property common both to the original, and largely stereotypical, individuals and to other members of the kind, though I may not know what the property is, and will usually need to call on experts to tell me.

But Dupré helps us to see that there are at least two important omissions in this account. The first omission consists in a failure to recognize that many of our OLC classifications were never intended to pick out natural kinds in the strong sense of 'natural kind' that interests me and Putnam. For example, florists and managers of garden centres are quite consciously interested in merely superficial features, and have no interest in the underlying real essences that inspire formal taxonomies. They want to know which plants have dramatic flowers or foliage, which plants flower at particular seasons, which are capable of resisting dry conditions, which are tall and which are fastigiate, and so on. The classification is no doubt concerned with natural kinds in the very weak sense of 'natural' I distinguished at the beginning of chapter 2, since even superficial properties are a part of the natural world and are quite independent of our thoughts and beliefs about them. But florists do not expect or intend the classification to be supported by underlying real essences of the kind that are at the centre of my account of natural kinds and of Putnam's account of general names.

The second omission consists in failing to pursue the consequences of certain kinds of scientific mistake. Putnam does attempt to remedy the failure, but in a very half-hearted and cursory fashion.[5] He does not acknowledge sufficiently strongly that many of our attempts to invent new natural kind names misfire, because our assumption that there is some underlying property common to all the members of the supposed kind, some property that will count as the real essence of the kind, may prove to be false. Our language has a long memory, and is littered with the débris of numerous botched shots at natural kind classification. We collect various stereotypical animals or plants together, and use their superficial features to fix the reference of 'wolf' or 'wren' or 'lily' or 'daisy' or 'orchid', not realizing that we are collecting different species together. Or our popular names for species suggest close relationships where none in fact exist (consider 'ash' and 'mountain ash'; or 'lily' and 'arum lily'; or 'squirrel' and 'flying squirrel'). Or, in an attempt to collect species, we collect genera (*oak, beech, elm, willow*), or kinds that correspond to no taxonomic categories at all (*prickly pear, cholla*). At the limit, we even introduce natural kind names that turn out to refer to nothing at all, such as 'ether' or 'animalcule' or 'phlogiston' or 'the Missing Link'.[6]

Such failures are not surprising. Until fairly recently, we have had neither the scientific expertise nor the necessary technology to discover the real essences that determine physical, chemical and biological natural kinds. We have had to lean heavily, even exclusively, on superficial features, on Lockean nominal essences, for they were the only features accessible to our primitive experimental instruments, our five senses. For example, in attempting to classify plants and animals, we have had to concentrate solely on gross morphological and physiological features, and have inevitably been misled by them. I suppose Dupré might try to argue that the *survival* of antiquated systems of classification is highly significant, and might invite us to wonder why we pay so little attention to the received wisdom of the experts: the thought would be that, whatever Putnam may say, we often display no interest at all in the scientific knowledge of experts. But again I cannot see that the survival of scientifically discredited systems of classification is either surprising or significant. As Scott Altran has pointed out, even when a name has originally been introduced as a supposed natural kind name, whose use is underpinned by some underlying but unknown property, it may survive the discovery that our supposition is incorrect. For we may have such a strong special interest in the objects in question, and the interest may be reflected so perfectly in our mistaken classification, that we are not in the least concerned to classify anew with the help of experts:

> the 'phenomenological concept' may persist *as an underlying trait* term regardless of science's opinion on the matter. 'Hawk' and 'sparrow' persist as underlying trait terms because their usual denotations are readily perceived to be components of local nature.[7]

Furthermore, even when we have the scientific expertise and the necessary technology, we cannot guarantee that we will produce the right answers, will routinely uncover the real essences of things. So my initial response to Dupré's examples is to remedy the two omissions in Putnam's account. In other words, Putnam should formally concede, first, that many of the supposed counter-examples belong to classifications that were only ever intended to be classifications of superficial properties, and second, that many simply commemorate unsuccessful attempts at a natural kind classification.

The thought that many OLC names were only ever intended to pick out superficial properties, and the thought that many commemorate failed attempts at natural kind classification, tend to get lost in Putnam's zealous flight from intension. And it might seem that he can happily make suitable concessions, by slightly changing the emphasis here and there. That is, instead of saying that I introduce a name by pointing at a group of objects, which share some underlying property that determines membership of the kind, perhaps he should say, first, that I sometimes introduce a name merely to pick out a superficial property, and suppose that the objects to which I point are united only by that superficial property; and second, that sometimes, when I try to introduce a name to pick out objects that I suppose to be united by some underlying property, my supposition is false. Perhaps he could borrow a useful word from lawyers, and argue that many of the crucial assumptions made by inventors of natural kind names are 'defeasible', and may well be defeated by new scientific discoveries. But on reflection, I am not at all sure that the second part of the response will work. Representations, we are told, represent only if their use has the right sort of causal connection with objects of the kind represented. 'Meanings ain't in the head.' But what does that slogan mean? How strong is Putnam's externalism? If he concedes that some attempts to introduce natural kinds misfire, because there is no underlying property uniting members of the supposed kind, then presumably the use of the name does not have the right sort of causal connection with objects of the kind represented. And when there is a bad misfire, when the classification does not even approximately reflect real similarities and differences in nature, the only place for meanings to be is in the head.

In order to answer these questions, we must explore the distinction between 'narrow' and 'broad' content a little further. The narrow content of psychological states consists of those relevant intrinsic features of agents, considered quite independently of their relation to the rest of the world — crudely, whatever is 'in their heads'. The broad content consists of the conjunction of the narrow content and all the relevant relational features that connect agents to the external world. So, for example, the broad content of my thoughts about water will include, not merely what is 'in my head', but also the complicated relation, via perception and behaviour, between me and quantities of H_2O. According to a classical Cartesian or Lockean theory of meaning, psychological states are individuated by their narrow content. The historical Descartes therefore saw nothing problematic in provisionally isolating himself from the rest of the world, and thinking interesting thoughts. According to an externalist such as Putnam, however, psychological states are individuated by their broad content: I and my Doppelgänger on Twin Earth might share narrow content, might share exactly similar features 'in our heads', but our thoughts would be different, since my head is related to H_2O and his is related to XYZ. And if we were both wholly isolated from the two worlds, in the spirit of the first Meditation, we would think nothing at all.

Now to our problem. Despite the compelling arguments in favour of individuating psychological states by their broad content, meanings do seem to be in the head, in all sorts of obvious ways. And that is particularly obvious when we consider examples of scientific ignorance, muddle and misfire. It is we who must decide what we want to say, and we are often in the best position to say whether we mean what we say. Our knowledge of what we mean may not be incorrigible, but we are often the best authorities on what we mean. We must decide which systems of classification to use, and it is we who are sometimes blissfully ignorant of the sorry lack of fit between our theories and the world. We certainly know what we *mean* when we collect plants or animals that belong to heterogeneous taxonomic categories, or when we claim to have observed the traces of the ether or animalcules or phlogiston or the Missing Link, but our thoughts and our sentences certainly do not have the right kind of causal connection with objects of the kind represented. Indeed, in many cases there are no objects of the kind represented. Either we mean nothing at all, or meanings are in our muddled heads.

There are several possible responses. One is to say that externalism only requires meaning to be anchored in *some* features of the objects referred to. When all goes well, and our classifications are more or less as nature intended (in the strong sense of 'nature' that Putnam and I are concerned with), meaning is anchored in the real essences that, in nature, determine membership of the kind. So the meaning of 'water' is anchored in the underlying combination of hydrogen and oxygen in stable water molecules.

But, for at least two reasons, the meaning of certain general names will be anchored in purely superficial features. The first reason, as I pointed out above, is that some general names were only ever intended to pick out objects united by superficial features. Perhaps when the words 'tree', 'shrub' and 'weed' were invented, no-one seriously supposed that they marked distinctions of profound botanical significance. The second reason is that things may go very badly, and our scientific work may be blighted by muddle and misfire. For example, the meaning of 'prickly pear', 'wren', 'daisy' or 'lily' cannot rest on relevant real essences determining the kind, for there are none, but rests on the gross and superficial features naturally captured by the untutored eye. And had we been mistaken in our supposition that all samples of water share an underlying real essence, the meaning of 'water' would inevitably have been anchored in purely superficial properties, in merely nominal essences:

> It could have turned out that the bits of liquid we call 'water' had *no* important common physical characteristics *except* the superficial ones. In that case the necessary and sufficient condition for being 'water' would have been possession of sufficiently many of the superficial characteristics.[8]

Unfortunately that response will not cater for all the difficult examples. It will help us to deal with our deliberately superficial or unintentionally muddled classification of objects that actually exist — with shrubs and trees, with prickly pears and chollas, with wrens and lilies — but it is powerless to deal with the disastrous misfires involved in talking about the ether, phlogiston, animalcules or the Missing Link. Such things do not exist at all, under any description, and there are therefore no superficial properties to anchor the relevant names. If broad content is to be construed as a complex relation between representations and objects of the kind represented, then thoughts about the ether, animalcules, phlogiston and the Missing Link have no broad content. It would be ridiculous, I think, to draw the conclusion that they are not thoughts at all, and that the sentences used to express them are meaningless. Scientific mistakes, even on a large scale, are typically just that: mistakes. They are cases of falsehood, not of babble.

That suggests that externalists would be wise to retreat to a slightly weaker position, where the general spirit of externalism is preserved without any fierce letter. It may be significant that the difficult examples under discussion are all examples of theoretical terms, that is, terms invented and introduced in an attempt to make systematic sense of the world around us. They are introduced as names of fundamental (and possibly unobservable) physical and chemical entities, or of taxonomic kinds. They are not part of the central and persisting folk scientific core of our language, which names and classifies objects mainly according to their observable and superficial properties. Externalists are surely right to insist that Cartesian attempts to explain meaning wholly in terms of narrow content are incoherent: someone wholly isolated from the external world is logically incapable of having psychological states, and in particular of meaning and understanding anything. But it does not follow, and it is not true, that *every* representation must have the right sort of causal connection with objects of the kind represented. The truth lies somewhere in between. I suggest that what I called the folk scientific core of our language must have the right sort of causal connection with objects of the kinds represented. But the theoretical shell makes sense, not in virtue of a similar causal connection with the real essences of things (though, if all goes well, there will be such a connection), but in virtue of its being an attempt to make systematic sense of the folk scientific core. There may be an argument for the view that at least *part* of the theoretical shell must have the right sort of causal connection with objects of the kind represented, but I don't know what the argument would be. In chapter 3, I argued that realism entails essentialism, that a belief in a world quite independent of us and our beliefs about it entails a belief in the existence of natural kinds, in my strong sense of 'natural kind'. But strictly that argument does not entail that we are ever successful in our attempts to discover in detail what natural kinds there are. In any event, however strong or weak that argument may be, we are left with a rather paler version of externalism than we started with: at least a few meanings ain't in the head.

The names of other kinds

In an attempt to sharpen our understanding of the semantics of natural kind names, I want now to consider names of other kinds, that is, names of dependent, real but superficial, and hybrid kinds. (Attentive readers will notice that I am heavily indebted in this section to an interesting paper by Crawford Elder.[9]) It has not generally been noticed that Putnam offers his account as an account of most, if not all, general names, and he explicitly argues that his remarks about natural kind names such as 'tiger' can be extended to cover other general names such as 'pencil' or 'paediatrician':

> So far we have only used natural-kind words as examples; but the points we have made apply to many other kinds of words as well. They apply to the great majority of all nouns, and to other parts of speech as well ... 'pencil' is not *synonymous* with any description — not even loosely synonymous with a *loose* description. When we use the word 'pencil', we intend to refer to whatever has the same *nature* as the normal examples of the local pencils in the actual world. 'Pencil' is just as *indexical* as 'water' or 'gold'.[10]

As it stands, that claim is patently false. In one crucial respect, words such as 'pencil' (which picks out a dependent kind) and 'paediatrician' (which picks out a hybrid kind) work quite differently from natural kind names, because pencils and paediatricians (and, more generally, all members of non-natural kinds) do not have 'natures', underlying intrinsic properties or real essences that make them the kind of thing they are. Their membership of the relevant kinds is determined by a relational dependence on something else, or by comparatively superficial properties, which resist ambitious scientific generalization, or by both.

Students of philosophical pathology might wish to pause at this point, and wonder why Putnam is anxious to commit himself to such an apparently odd view, to extend his account of natural kind names to all general names. Putnam is the best person to answer that question, but in his absence I offer a diagnosis. As I pointed out earlier, his account of natural kind names is a central part of an externalist account of meaning. That is, it is a central part of an attempt to show that words get their meaning only if their use has the right kind of causal connection with objects of the kind referred to. If their use is not appropriately related to real objects out there, they fail to be words at all. It would seem natural to go on to say that, in a sense, meaning is therefore determined by the real world, not by us, since we cannot simply stipulate that the appropriate causal connections do or do not obtain. A fortiori, meaning is not determined by any set of descriptions that may be in our heads, or by any Lockean nominal essences. Finally, if we are too impressed by the special case of natural kind names, it is tempting to go further and to say that the extension of a general name is determined by a certain intrinsic real property of things out there, that is, by the 'real essence' of the kind, which is precisely the property of interest to serious scientists.

There are a number of quite separate claims buried in that loose but compelling train of thought. If we distinguish them, we get a very interesting result. For we see that there are many striking similarities between our use of natural kind names and our use of the names of other kinds. Putnam's principal mistake, clearly revealed in the passage above, is to overlook the one crucial difference. Let us begin by listing the main general features of our use of natural kind names:

(1) *They are indexical expressions.* They enable us to point, literally or metaphorically, to members of kinds, and successful reference is achieved typically by that pointing, rather than by an appeal to a battery of suitable descriptions.

(2) *Their meaning is not analysable in terms of a set of descriptions, or, for example, in terms of Lockean nominal essences.* Indeed, many of the properties we commonly associate with the natural kind name will not be shared by all the members of the kind. There will, for example, be abnormal

cases. Furthermore, such properties may not be peculiar to the members of the kind: to borrow one of Putnam's examples, we may be quite unable to produce a description of beeches that distinguishes them from elms.

(3) *Their meaning is not determined by what is in the heads of native speakers ('narrowly' conceived), but by a complex causal relation, via perception and behaviour, between native speakers and members of the kinds.* That is merely to apply the general externalist thought that representations represent only if they have the right sort of causal connection with things of the kind represented, and is subject to the qualifications I made in the previous section, when talking about serious scientific muddle and misfire.

(4) *Our beliefs about members of natural kinds are corrigible, and we have to discover what determines the extension of each name.* In one way, of course, this claim is trivial, for we have to learn natural kind names from our parents and teachers. But even when we count as fluent native speakers, there is scope for at least two kinds of discovery and, by the same token, for at least two kinds of mistake. First, I can discover, perhaps with surprise, which objects belong to which kinds: for example, I can discover that apples and roses belong to the same family of plants, and that hardy geraniums and bedding geraniums are not even of the same genus. So I can use the names successfully even before the discoveries are made, even though I hold incomplete or false beliefs about the underlying properties that unite or separate members of the kinds in question. Second, I can discover their properties, including the underlying and typically 'hidden' properties that determine their membership of the kinds: I can discover the 'real essences' of true *Geranium* species. It is at this point that we exploit the division of linguistic labour, since most of our discoveries will be at second hand, and will wait upon the work of experts.

(5) *The extension of each name is determined by the real features of objects, not by human thought, belief or decision.* In other words, the commitment to natural kinds is a special case of a general commitment to metaphysical realism, to the view that there is a distinction between reality, on the one hand, and our thoughts and beliefs about it, on the other. Once a natural kind name has been introduced, its extension depends on nature, on the real distribution of relevant similarities and differences, not on us.

(6) *The extension of each name is determined by an intrinsic 'real essence' or 'nature', a property or set of properties which is necessary and sufficient for membership of the kind, and which permits scientific generalization.* The real essence permits scientific generalization for two connected reasons. One is that it underlies many of the properties of the members of the kind, and

features centrally in explanations of their behaviour. The other reason is that the expressions 'essence' and 'nature' are to be interpreted very strongly, so that the scientific generalizations linking real essence or nature to kind are metaphysically necessary truths, true in all possible worlds.

We should note in passing that (5) and (6) are different claims, and an argument is needed to get from one to the other. Claim (5) is merely the claim that the meaning of natural kind names is grounded in real similarities and differences between things, and leaves open the possibility that such similarities and differences are purely superficial. Equally, it leaves open the possibility that the only natural kinds are natural in what I have called a weak sense of 'natural'. Claim (6) is designed to close off those possibilities, and to show that our use of natural kind names is ultimately grounded in underlying real essences, and that the sense of 'natural' in question is a very strong one. As far as I can tell, Putnam has no explicit argument to show that (5) implies (6). Indeed, it is only on rare occasions, such as in the passage about water that I quoted earlier, that he seems to be sensitive to the difference between the two claims. Most of the time, he seems to talk as though a commitment to metaphysical realism and to externalism is automatically a commitment to a strong account of natural kinds, and to the view that kinds are determined by non-superficial 'underlying' real essences. If the arguments I produced towards the beginning of chapter 3 were successful, we can remedy the omission, since those arguments were supposed to show that realism entails essentialism, that is, that claim (5) leads eventually and inevitably to claim (6).

Now let us compare and contrast the names of non-natural kinds. How many of those general claims, (1) to (6), are true of names of non-natural kinds — of expressions such as 'tree', 'shrub', 'table', 'pencil', 'coin', 'vegetable', 'cattle', and so on? The first claim seems to apply without serious qualification. That is, (1) the names of non-natural kinds are indexical expressions and are typically introduced, taught and used by native speakers as tools for pointing to something. Quite often inventors, teachers and ordinary users of the words will be able to say little more than that a table is one of *those*, that *that* is an Irish coin, that *these* are fruits and *those* vegetables, and so on. Indeed, this point about indexicality is worth making only because philosophers have failed to appreciate the extent to which we use sentences to point to objects in the geographical or conversational vicinity. A conspicuous and influential exception is Keith Donnellan, who argues that in context I may refer to something successfully by using an entirely inappropriate description. He distinguishes between the 'referential' use of a general term (where I am simply trying to draw attention to something) and the 'attributive' use (where I am attempting to ascribe a property to something), and argues that it is only in attributive uses where the criterion of success is that there should be a descriptive fit between general term and object.[11] In referential uses we may use the description successfully even when it does not strictly apply to the referent at all. For example, in the course of a conversation, we might refer consistently and successfully to 'the man drinking a martini', even though his glass contains water (and perhaps the person in question is a female transvestite). The referring phrase is used merely as a device for picking out a referent, for focusing attention. I would merely add that that kind of case, where we successfully refer by using a totally inappropriate description, is extremely common, and suggests that some uses of language are little more than sophisticated shouts, attempts to direct attention. Even when the description is appropriate, when the object is indeed a table, or a coin, or a fruit, or a vegetable, or a man drinking a martini, reference is typically achieved by the shout, as it were, rather than by use of an appropriate description. Compare Wittgenstein: 'meaning something is like going up to someone'.[12]

So claim (1), that the names of non-natural kinds are indexical, appears to be correct. It is natural, though not absolutely inevitable, to go on to argue (2) that the meaning of the names of non-natural kinds cannot be analysed in terms of a set of descriptions, or, for example, in terms of Lockean nominal essences. One reason, as I have just hinted, is that those who introduce, teach and use the names may have no very clear idea of the properties of the things in question, but manage quite happily on an unreflective ability to recognize them when they see them. Another reason is that the names will often refer to cluster properties, that is, to sets of properties that tend to cluster together, but resist easy analysis in terms of necessary and sufficient conditions. Even when introducers, teachers and ordinary users have reached a high level of reflective competence in their use of the names of non-natural kinds, the meanings of the names will not be analysable in terms of sets of descriptions, for example in terms of Lockean nominal essences, for there can be no such descriptions, even in principle. There is no non-trivial property or set of properties necessary and sufficient for being a table, or a chair, or a tree, or a shrub, or a vegetable, or a fruit. There are at best cluster properties. However, there are important exceptions, particularly where the kind is dependent upon an explicit convention or an explicit definition. For example, in any advanced or codified legal system, many crucial expressions will be defined in terms of necessary and sufficient conditions: 'mens rea', 'citizen of the United Kingdom', 'third degree homicide', 'registered practitioner'. In many academic disciplines, important technical terms will be defined quite explicitly: 'marginal cost', 'gross domestic product', 'balance of payments'.

The existence of these exceptions forces us to make similar qualifications when applying the next three claims to the names of non-natural kinds. In one sense it is true (3) that their meaning is not determined by whatever is in the heads of native speakers (narrowly conceived), but by a complex causal relation, via perception and behaviour, between native speakers and members of the kinds. We must insist that representation does not work by magic, and that the use of 'tree', 'coin' and 'vegetable' must be connected to real trees, real coins and real vegetables, via perception and behaviour, just as the use of 'tiger', 'water' and 'gold' is connected to real tigers, real water and real gold, via perception and behaviour. Equally, it is in one sense true (4) that our beliefs about members of non-natural kinds are corrigible, and that we have to discover what determines the extension of each name. Trivially, I must learn names such as 'table', 'coin' and 'vegetable' from parents and teachers. Less trivially, even when I am a fluent native speaker, there is scope for at least two kinds of discovery and therefore for at least two kinds of mistake. First, I can discover which objects belong to which kinds. In the early days of television there was an archaeological quiz, 'Animal, Vegetable, Mineral?', which involved identifying — and often in practice misidentifying — artefacts from other historical periods or other civilizations. The existence of the quiz demonstrated that a fluent command of the language of non-natural kinds does not guarantee successful identification of the corresponding objects. Second, I can discover the properties of the objects. I can discover that trees have a cambium layer under the bark, that coins are made of various alloys, that citizens of the United Kingdom are not yet required to carry an identity card, and so on.

But in certain cases, namely, where the kind is directly determined by an explicit decision by some suitably qualified body, or by an explicit definition by a conscientious academic, those two claims need to be qualified. That is, it is not always true that the meaning of the names of non-natural kinds is determined by a complex causal relation between native speakers and members of the kinds, and it is not always true that our beliefs about members of non-natural kinds are corrigible. There will be no kinds until the statute is passed, the decree is issued, or the definition is made known. In an obvious sense, in these cases meaning is very much in the head of the person who legislates or who issues the decree, and the beliefs of that person are incorrigible. 'Citizen of the United Kingdom' means precisely what that person or body thinks it means, because he or she or it has just decided what it will mean. The only possible room for self-correction would be yielded by the unrealistic case in which the legislators are so hopelessly muddled that they issue a decree that is completely meaningless, and therefore fail to determine a new kind at all. Perfect legislators would of course follow the Popes' example, and take the precaution of declaring themselves infallible in advance. All of their beliefs about the relevant non-natural kinds would then be incorrigible.

Someone might try to defend claim (3) by replying that there is still an appropriate connection under some description between the person who has issued the decree or formulated the definition and members of the kind. There are plenty of people related to me under the description 'person' before I attempt to classify them as citizens of the United Kingdom. So I am merely introducing a distinction to sit on top of one I already use. It would follow that what is in the head of the person who issued the decree or definition is not meaning narrowly conceived. But that reply will not work, for there may be no members of the kind either before or after the decree or definition. For example, in a spirit of gratuitous but conscientious endeavour, I might write a constitution for Mars, and carefully distinguish citizens from different Martian provinces. Since I have no idea whether there are any Martians, under any description, my newly invented kinds cannot be made to sit on top of one I already use. So once again we must qualify our externalism, to allow a certain kind of misfit between native speaker and world.

What of the next claim? Is it true (5) that the extension of each non-natural kind name is determined by the real features of objects, and not by human belief, thought and decision? I want to argue that it is indeed true. Some readers will be very surprised, but I suggest that their surprise is due in part to confusion, and in part to their failing to draw the distinction between natural and non-natural kinds in the right place. In chapter 2, I argued that we should not use a distinction between natural and artificial, or natural and conventional, or natural and culturally generated, or even between natural and nominal kinds. And I went on to claim that there are several distinct kinds of non-natural kinds. There are dependent kinds, whose membership is determined by a relational dependence of its members on other things. Sometimes the dependence is upon human needs and interests (as with the kinds *table* or *coat*) or upon human convention (as with the kinds *coin* or *nation*), but in many cases the dependence proves to have nothing to do with the concerns of sentient beings of any kind (as with the kinds *glacier*, *perennial* and *north wind*). There are also real but superficial kinds, whose membership is determined by properties that are non-relational but too superficial to support serious scientific generalization: for example I mentioned the kinds *tree*, *shrub*, *cloud* and *pebble*. Finally I distinguished hybrid kinds, that is, kinds that are not strictly natural, nor dependent, nor real and superficial, but hybrids of at least two of those kinds.

Now, I want to say that the extension of all the names of non-natural kinds is determined by the real features of objects, not by human thought, belief or decision. That is obvious in the case of real but superficial kinds, such as *tree* or *perennial*, for their defining features are clearly features of the world, not of us. It is equally obvious in the case of dependent kinds when the dependence does not consist on human interests or conventions. A glacier or a north wind would still be a glacier or a north wind even if there were no sentient beings to appreciate the fact. Moreover, it is obvious that we should be realists about the properties of trees, perennials, glaciers and north winds, and expect the painful process of mistake and muddle that inevitably accompanies our attempts to discover what they are. But I want to insist on realism even with respect to dependent kinds whose membership is determined by a relation to human interests or convention. It is just true, 'really' true, that some objects perform a certain function, for example that they have flat surfaces suitable for supporting our possessions or a shape that makes them perfect portable seats for one. It is just true, 'really' true, that some groups of people have a certain national identity, and are recognized as such by other similar groups, and so on. Of course it is true that membership of the kind in each case depends on a relation to human interest or convention, for a relation logically requires (at least) two relata. But the fact that that relation obtains does not depend on human thought, belief, interest or convention: it is simply true that there are two relata so related.

Notice incidentally that here we do not have to make an exception for the case of kinds determined by explicit decree or decision. If I am king, and I decree that certain named individuals are to be Knights of the Round Table, then their being Knights logically depends on my issuing the decree. That is, the property of being a Knight is a relational property. But the fact that that relation obtains does not depend on me or on anyone else. If the decree has been issued, then it is true, 'really' true, that the relation obtains; if not, not.

So far, we have found that the names of non-natural kinds function in very much in the same way as the names of natural kinds. But in turning to the final claim we find an enormous difference. It is not true (6) that the extension of each name of a non-natural kind is determined by a 'real essence' or 'nature'. For members of non-natural kinds do not have real essences or natures, that is, intrinsic or non-relational properties which are necessary and sufficient for membership of the respective kinds, and which permit scientific generalization. As we saw in chapter 2, in some cases the determining properties are relational rather than intrinsic, and so determine dependent kinds; in others they are non-relational, but are literally or metaphorically superficial, and quite unable to support the kind of scientific generalization that is characteristic of our thought about natural kinds. Furthermore, the properties that determine non-natural kinds are typically cluster properties, and the properties that cluster are often superficial. They therefore cannot be defined in terms of a closed set of necessary and sufficient conditions, and they cannot support scientific generalization.

Putnam, paediatricians and pencils

We can now return briefly to Putnam's implausible remarks about the natures of paediatricians and pencils. Consider these passages:

> Couldn't it turn out that paediatricians aren't doctors but Martian spies? Answer 'yes', and you have abandoned the synonymy of 'paediatrician' and 'doctor specializing in the care of children'. It seems that there is a strong tendency for words which are introduced as 'one-criterion' words to develop a 'natural kind' sense, with all the concomitant rigidity and indexicality ... The extension of our terms depends upon the actual nature of the particular things that serve as paradigms, and this actual nature is not, in general, fully known to the speaker.[13]

Much of that is unexceptionable. Names such as 'paediatrician' and 'pencil' are indexical; their meaning is not analysable in terms of a set of descriptions (e.g. by reference to Lockean nominal essences), or by what is in the heads of native speakers (narrowly conceived); our beliefs about paediatricians and pencils are corrigible, and we have to discover, perhaps with surprise, what determines the extension of the names; finally, their extension is determined by the real features of members of the kind (including their relational features), not by human thought, belief or decision.

But Putnam's account has two weaknesses. First, his whole account concentrates on our use of general names as grammatical subjects. If we consider their use as grammatical predicates, we see that his example cannot force us to abandon the synonymy of 'paediatrician' and 'doctor specializing in the care of children'. Imagine someone in Putnam's story relating her discovery: 'You're not going to believe this, but paediatricians aren't paediatricians after all'. That sentence clearly makes sense. But if it is to make sense, the first occurrence of 'paediatrician', in the subject position, must be construed as an indexical, or, in Donnellan's words, as an example of a purely 'referential' use; and the second, in the predicate position, must be construed as a description, as an example of an 'attributive' use. The second clause means '*Those* things are not doctors specializing in the care of children'. This curious difference between subject and predicate position is also evident in our efforts to display muddle in our use of natural kind terms: 'Arum lilies are not lilies; a mountain ash is not an ash; bedding geraniums are not geraniums'; flying squirrels are not squirrels; marsupial wolves are not wolves'. All the sentences make sense, but only because the first occurrence of the general name is indexical (or 'referential'), and the second is descriptive (or 'attributive').

With appropriate acknowledgements to Donnellan, I therefore add a general footnote to everything I have said in this chapter.[14] When a general name is used 'referentially', it typically functions as an indexical, and loses any close connection it might have had with descriptions. But when it functions 'attributively', the connection with descriptions is re-established. We cannot of course insist on too close a connection, and nothing in this general footnote should give lasting comfort to those who hope to analyse all general words in terms of complete and exhaustive sets of descriptions. Even when we exploit some set of descriptions to construe a general name used attributively, we cannot guarantee that it will uniquely identify the objects in question. We cannot entirely rule out the possibility that the descriptions fail to collect abnormal cases, or that they collect one or two members of other kinds. In the case of natural kinds, the main reason is that the descriptions to which we appeal will usually name Lockean nominal essences, rather than the real essences that determine the kinds. In the case of non-natural kinds, the main reason is that the descriptions to which we appeal will often prove to name cluster properties.

The second, and much more serious, weakness of Putnam's account concerns claim (6). Although our use of the names of non-natural kinds must be anchored in real features of the world, in real features available for discovery, we should not suppose that such features count as 'natures', at least in the strong sense of 'nature' that has informed my account of natural kinds. As good externalists, we must acknowledge that meaning is determined (at any rate normally or typically or most of the time) by a complex causal relation, via perception and behaviour, between native speakers and members of the kinds. But we must also acknowledge that the features of objects that engage in that causal relation are 'natures' in the relevant sense only in the case of natural kinds. That is, they are underlying intrinsic real essences, necessary and sufficient for membership of the respective kinds, and capable of supporting scientific generalization. In the case of non-natural kinds, the properties uniting members of the kind are merely relational or superficial features, which are at best cluster properties, and which are quite incapable of supporting scientific generalization.

Notes

1   See 'Is Semantics Possible?', 'Explanation and Reference' and 'The Meaning of "Meaning"', collected as chapters 8, 11 and 12 of Putnam (1975).
2   S. Kripke (1980), passim, and especially pp. 134-9.
3   See H. Putnam, op. cit., p. 227.
4   See J. Dupré (1981), passim.
5   See H. Putnam, op. cit., pp. 240-1.

6   If I read him correctly, Kripke denies that there can be the limiting case, where the supposed natural kind name turns out to refer to nothing at all. Cf. S. Kripke (1980), p. 135n. Talking of gold, he says: 'We know in advance, a priori, that it is not the case that the items are *typically* fool's gold'. But that seems an odd view. In a sense we have discovered that all our samples are samples of fool's phlogiston, or fool's ether, or fool's Missing Links!

7   S. Altran (1987), pp. 51-2.

8   H. Putnam, op. cit., p. 241.

9   C.L. Elder (1989).

10 See H. Putnam, op. cit., pp. 242 and 243.

11 See K.S. Donnellan (1966), passim.

12 L. Wittgenstein (1953), Pt. I, §457.

13 H. Putnam, op. cit., pp. 244 and 245.

14 See K.S. Donnellan, op. cit.

5 Species and kinds

The case against biological essences

In chapter 2, I attempted to clarify the notion of a natural kind. Central to my account was the notion of a real essence: something is a member of a natural kind if and only if it has a certain real essence, that is, an intrinsic property or set of properties that is both necessary and sufficient for its being a member of that kind. The word 'real' crept in, not just as a historical reminder of Locke's distinction between real and nominal essences, but as a philosophical reminder that we are here concerned with essences that are de re, not de dicto, essences that lie in the things themselves and not in our beliefs, thoughts, theories or remarks about them. In chapter 3, I argued that a general commitment to metaphysical realism is inevitably also a commitment to natural kinds in the sense in which I was interested.

The success of that account of natural kinds rests firmly on the success of an account of real essences. If the notion of a real essence makes no sense, then the notion of a natural kind, at least in the strong form that I have explored, will make no sense. In this chapter, I shall attempt to defend an account of real essences against a fairly familiar and powerful objection. In this first section, I shall set out the case against real essences, and I shall concentrate on biological kinds. There are of course many other examples of natural kinds, such as kinds of particle (*electron, proton, neutron*), kinds of element (*carbon, hydrogen, oxygen*), kinds of chemical compound (*water, cellulose, kerosene*). But there are good reasons for concentrating on biological kinds. One reason is that, in the literature, they are often taken as typically excellent examples of natural kinds. Aristotle argued that the best candidates for membership of the category of substance are plants and animals and, as we saw in chapter 4, Putnam talks at length about tigers and lemon trees. Another reason for concentrating on biological kinds is that there are no serious difficulties in principle in discovering the real essences of physical and chemical kinds.

It has sometimes been argued that we should agonize about chemical isotopes, that is, different forms of the same element, with the same atomic number but different atomic weight. The thought is that in the case of isotopes it is impossible to say what counts as the respective real essences of the kinds, and it is therefore impossible to say how many natural kinds there are. If we regard atomic number as the real essence, we will have just as many chemical kinds as there are elements; if we regard atomic weight as the real essence, we will have far more chemical kinds than there are elements. I am afraid that I cannot persuade myself that there is a serious difficulty here. Throughout this discussion I have constantly referred to different explanatory levels, and have quite deliberately left open the possibility that two objects might belong to the same kind at a higher level and to different kinds at a lower level. Indeed, if the distinction between function and realization is ever to have application to members of natural kinds, we would be foolish not to leave that possibility open. As far as chemistry is concerned, we would be foolish to deny that there are kinds of element and kinds of compound, and that there can be different isotopes of one and the same element. In other words, we would be foolish to deny that there are natural kinds at the sub-atomic level, and at the level of elements, and at the level of molecules, and at the level of molecular compounds. The case of chemical isotopes seems a particularly striking example of the need to distinguish natural kinds at different levels. Since chemical properties are determined by atomic number, there is a good reason for supposing that different isotopes of the same element belong to the same natural kind at the level of elements. On the other hand, since a difference in atomic weight produces a difference in physical properties, there is a good reason for supposing that different isotopes belong to different kinds at the sub-atomic level. We can quite consistently both lump with the chemists and split with the physicists.

However, there are undoubtedly serious difficulties in attempting to discover biological kinds. According to the story I told in chapter 2, a biological individual belongs to a certain species (or genus, or family, or order) in virtue of its having the property (the real essence) that determines membership of that species (or genus or family or order). For simplicity, I breezily and parenthetically suggested that the essence in each case might be a genetic feature. I was merely following many other philosophers, and it is interesting to recall Putnam's general strategy, which I discussed in chapter 4. In attempting to show that the properties that are typical of members of a given natural kind will not yield analytic truths defining the kind, he has a great deal to say about normal and abnormal cases. His point is that a tiger cannot be analytically defined, for example, as a fierce striped feline quadruped with whiskers and a tail, because abnormal tigers may lack one or more of those properties. Some have three legs, some have no tail, some have lost teeth and whiskers, some are albinos, and so on. But he clearly supposes that both normal and abnormal tigers share a certain property, a real essence determining membership of the kind, and it is equally clear that he supposes it to be some genetic property. But the sceptic about real essences will argue both that there are a number of possible candidates for the role of real essence, and that none of the candidates are ultimately convincing. If we look at the practice of working biologists, for example, we find that the boundaries of species are drawn in at least four different ways: by reference to descent, to the capacity to interbreed and/or to produce fertile offspring, to more or less gross morphological features, and to genetic constitution. In brief, the case against real essences will be that none of these criteria give us a wholly satisfactory way of classifying biological kinds — at any rate, within the very strong constraints that I have placed upon the notion of a natural kind.

So we must first consider these four criteria very carefully. First let us consider descent. In the penetrating words of Anon, a cat is the offspring of two cats. More generally, two individuals are members of the same species if and only if they share a comparatively recent ancestor or ancestral population. We can in principle imagine an evolutionary family tree for all species (though, as Stephen Jay Gould has argued, we must be very careful in constructing and using such images[1]). If Darwin is right, all biological individuals have a common ancestor or ancestral population, albeit many hundreds of millions of years ago, and we can think of evolution as the successive appearance of more and more branches on the family tree, as different species evolve. Each branch represents a species and each node, or branching point, represents the division of species or the emergence of a new species. However superficially similar two individuals may be, they count as members of the same species if and only if they share a comparatively recent ancestor or ancestral population, that is, if and only if they find themselves on the same part of the same branch.

But there are at least three difficulties in taking the real essence of a species as the relational property of descent from a recent common ancestor. One is the purely practical difficulty that in many cases biologists have not the slightest idea what is descended from what. The fossil evidence is scanty, and vast numbers of intermediate ancestral species have disappeared without leaving any discernible trace. Any story about descent is in practice secondary: we first find some way of distinguishing one species from another, and then infer that two members of the same species have more or less recent common ancestors.

A second difficulty is that sometimes evolution occurs, and sometimes it doesn't. More formally, possession of a fairly recent common ancestor is neither sufficient nor necessary for membership of the same species. It is not sufficient, because individuals of one species can give rise, within a few generations, to individuals of a quite different species. Dupré illustrates this point dramatically, if unrealistically. He wonders what we would or should say if a chicken suddenly started to lay walnuts, which germinated and grew into a walnut grove.[2] I shall resist the urge to say that the example makes no sense, and argue instead that we should *not* say that chickens occasionally produce groves of walnuts, but rather that old species sometimes produce new ones by evolutionary change. And possession of a fairly recent common ancestor is not necessary for membership of the same species, because some species survive happily for considerable periods: consider, for example, the crocodile or the dawn redwood, *Metasequoia glyptostroboides*. We need to explain why certain recent ancestry seems to imply identity of species, while other recent ancestry does not. For example, by the standards of crocodiles and dawn redwoods, humans and chimpanzees have a comparatively recent common ancestor or ancestral population, but are of different species. Nor can we stiffen the word 'recent', argue that 'recent' means 'very recent', and claim that very recent common ancestry implies identity of species. Many plant species (including hybrid species) have been bred in recent years and are rightly treated as new species. The criterion of descent is not just secondary in practice (as I argued above). It is secondary in principle, for, even when we know which populations are descended from which, we can only determine where the branches of the evolutionary tree divide if we already have some other criterion for identifying species. Once we have an account of the various real essences of different species, we can construct an evolutionary tree, marking each node on a branch, or ancestral line, as the emergence of a new species. In doing so, we will notice with interest that some branches have divided very little in the course of their history.

The third difficulty about the criterion of descent is that we can imagine a kind of parallel evolution, in which initially different ancestral lines converge and produce species whose members are, from every relevant point of view, exactly similar. The notion of parallel evolution is a familiar one, and there are many examples of unrelated plants or animals that have evolved similar characteristics: birds, bats and insects have all developed wings, and pandas have developed an extra 'thumb' from one of the bones in the wrist.[3] I want to take that very familiar and realistic thought and extend it in imagination. I suggest that we can for example imagine that, after a series of mutations, gorillas and humans might evolve into animals that are very similar — as similar as, say, modern Europeans and modern Chinese. Some of the animals would be descended from gorillas, some from humans, yet it is far from obvious that we should regard them as belonging to different species. Those who prefer philosophical fables about Twin Earth can construct a similar story. Imagine that evolutionary history on Twin Earth was quite different from evolutionary history on Earth, but eventually produced a very similar range of plants and animals. Perhaps on Twin Earth life began on the land and spread to the sea, whereas on Earth life began in the sea and spread to the land, but both evolutionary histories eventually produced beings exactly similar to terrestrial humans. Philosophers sent to Twin Earth for research purposes on the spaceship 'Putnam' find that they can interbreed with the natives. The two groups of humans have an entirely different, and unrelated, origin, but it is far from obvious that we should treat them as of different species.

Indeed, we do not need to resort to stories about Twin Earth. Biologists specifically allow quite separate populations to count as belonging to the same biological kind, whatever their recent ancestry. For example, the most general botanical division of all, between angiosperms (Narayan's 'flowering plants') and gymnosperms, cannot be drawn by reference to ancestry, since it is likely that the flowering habit developed quite independently in different groups of plants, in different places. Strictly the example is irrelevant, because I shall argue that there is no hope of treating biological categories higher than the level of species as natural kinds, but even if we confine our attention to species, the same point applies. For example, in recent years there has been considerable discussion of the exact geographical origins of our own species, *Homo sapiens*. Some have argued that all modern humans are descended from a single (and probably African) ancestral population, while others have claimed that the various varieties of humans collected under the same species name are descended from a number of geographically quite separate populations. For our purposes it doesn't in the least matter who is right. The important point is that the claim that geographically distinct populations might belong to the same species is taken seriously, and is not immediately dismissed as flatly contradictory. The very existence of the dispute shows that we cannot insist on common descent as a central criterion for the identity of species.

Let us therefore move to a second possible criterion for identifying species, namely that two individuals are of the same species if and only if they can interbreed, or if and only if they can produce offspring, or if and only if they can produce fertile offspring. Despite the obvious danger of muddle, I offer different formulations quite deliberately, because different formulations are available. But there is no pressing reason to be more precise, since the criterion faces serious difficulties, however it is formulated. It clearly does not yield a necessary condition of the identity of species. One reason is that, although the criterion clearly does justice to sexual differentiation and to the vital role of sexual differentiation in evolution, it actually fails to do so in an obvious way. Two female members of a species, or two male members of a species, cannot interbreed. Another reason is that in some species, and especially in many plant species, members of one variety of the species cannot interbreed with members of another variety of the same species. They may simply be barren, because of congenital abnormality, disease or accident. Or, as happens for example with certain varieties of apples and pears, some varieties are said to be 'incompatible' with others. In certain, fairly rare, cases it is even impossible to graft the incompatible varieties on to each other. Here there is not even a remote horticultural analogue of interbreeding!

So the interbreeding criterion is at best a sufficient condition of the identity of a species. Unfortunately, it is not even a sufficient condition, for there are many hybrid individuals (think for example of the thousands of rose hybrids), and many hybrid species, for example, mules and zebroids. Hybrids are the offspring of members of two distinct species. Admittedly hybrid animal species are typically infertile, but it is clear that such infertility is not a matter of absolute de re necessity, because many hybrid plant species can reproduce themselves, to the delight of seedsmen selling F1 hybrids. No doubt when such fertile hybrids produce offspring, future generations of the line tend to 'revert', that is, to lose the characteristics of their parents and display characteristics of ancestral species. But again that seems to be a purely contingent matter, for many species must have been the result of hybridization that eventually settled down into consistently 'true' (and novel) breeding. I am merely inviting us to imagine hybridization that immediately produces offspring similar to the first generation hybrids. Imagine, therefore, a world in which hybrids such as mules and zebroids typically reproduce replicas of themselves. That would surely not imply that the parents of the hybrid (a particular horse and a particular donkey, for example) were members of the same species, any more than the appearance of yet another hybrid rose variety implies that the parent plants are members of the same species. Both in that imagined world and in the real world, parents of hybrids produce fertile offspring, but are not of the same species.

In setting out all those difficulties, I have concentrated on species which reproduce, or can reproduce, sexually. But the final, and in many ways the most serious, difficulty in applying the interbreeding criterion is that there are many species which do not reproduce sexually at all, or do not consistently reproduce sexually, or whose sexual reproduction does not involve a sexual relation between two individuals. In all those cases a criterion which rests on the ability to interbreed, the ability of two individuals to produce offspring, or fertile offspring, will not work. For example many insects, such as aphids and vine weevils, are capable of producing many successive generations by parthenogenesis: after initial fertilization, females produce females, which produce females, ... , and so on, without any further assistance from male aphids or male vine weevils.

The plant kingdom is full of interesting counter examples. Many primitive plants did not reproduce sexually at all, but by spores. Many of their direct descendants, such as ferns and mosses, reproduce sexually in one generation, and asexually in the next: one generation is a gametophyte, produced by a combination of a male and a female cell, and the next is a sporophyte, produced by a male, or by a female, cell. Indeed, even in modern flowering plants, or angiosperms, the atavistic alternation of reproductive mechanisms is reflected quite clearly in the two-stage process that leads from the fertilization of pistil by stamen to the germination of the seed and the appearance of a new plant. There are also many hermaphrodite individuals and members of so-called 'self-fertile' species or varieties, which reproduce sexually, but by fertilizing themselves. So their sexual reproductive cycle does not involve any *inter*-breeding between two individuals of the same species. Perhaps it is also worth pointing out some of the practical benefits and philosophical embarrassments of ancient and modern horticultural technology. That is, vegetative reproduction, by budding, grafting, layering, the taking of suckers and cuttings and, very recently, by micropropagation, clearly does not involve the production of offspring by two individuals. Of course we have an excellent reason for assigning the new plants and the parent plant to the same species, for the new plants are clones of the original, and genetically exactly similar to it. But our having that reason makes the interbreeding criterion simply irrelevant.

Before leaving the first two criteria, the criterion of descent and the interbreeding criterion, I should add a very important general comment. Both criteria were formulated in terms of relational properties. The first criterion turned on a relation to ancestors, the second on a reproductive relation to other members of the species. For that reason alone, both the criteria were contrary to the general spirit and letter of my account of natural kinds, for I have argued throughout that membership of a natural kind is determined by intrinsic rather than relational properties. Indeed, I specifically distinguished dependent from natural kinds, and argued that membership of dependent kinds is determined by a relational dependence on something else. I therefore approach the third and fourth criteria with much more optimism, because they are both concerned with intrinsic properties of some kind. The third invites us to consider morphological features, and the fourth to consider genetic features.

The third criterion for the identity of species brings us more closely to the practical concerns of field biologists, palaeontologists and evolutionary biologists. They need to have a battery of tests which, in the field or in the palaeontological laboratory, will enable them to distinguish individuals of one species from individuals of another. For purely practical reasons, genetic testing is almost always out of the question, and they must usually rely on a detailed analysis of morphological features. For example, in the case of plants, they must rely on the size, shape and structure of leaves, fruits, seeds or bark, on the general growth habit of the plant, its response to seasonal and other climatic changes, and so on. There is no doubt that the results of such a procedure are very impressive, and there are numerous historical examples of a successful classification or reclassification that was due to a careful analysis of morphological features.[4] However, this criterion can be rejected quite quickly, for a reason I gave in chapter 2. Both in theory and in practice, morphological features can be very misleading, because individuals of related species may have very different morphological features, and individuals with very similar morphological features may be quite unrelated. For example many extinct marsupial mammals were very similar in appearance and habit to later groups of mammals in other parts of the world, and filled the corresponding ecological niches, but they were only very remotely related to them. So, although this criterion must play a central role in the everyday work of practising biologists, it cannot be regarded as the determining criterion for membership of a species. In Lockean language we can say that nominal essences are but a poor guide to the real essences of things.

Someone might reply that I am misrepresenting and underestimating the skills of evolutionary biologists. Furthermore, in talking of 'gross' morphological features, I have given the definite impression that any technique for assigning individuals to species in virtue of morphological features will inevitably prove to be a pretty blunt instrument. But evolutionary biologists are not only aware of the dangers of such a crude technique: they are constantly refining it, by distinguishing, for example, between primitive and derived characters. For example, they are unlikely to be led astray by gross morphological features into thinking that there is a close relationship between tigers and marsupial tigers, or between wolves and marsupial wolves, since the primitive characters of each group — and in particular, the features of their reproductive organs — indicate quite clearly that there is no such relationship. But, although it is important to realize the sophistication of morphological analysis, we should still reject the third criterion. For we must ask how, in principle, it is possible to distinguish between primitive and derived characters. Nothing about the characters themselves shows them to be primitive or derived. In order to make the distinction, we need to have a general idea of the relationship between various groups of animals. For example, we need to know, on some other grounds, that marsupial animals are not closely related to tigers and wolves, and that many of their characteristics are therefore derived, rather than primitive. So the objection to the morphological criterion becomes disjunctive. *Either* we concentrate on gross morphological features, and risk being seriously misled; *or* we use a more sophisticated analysis of morphological features, but such an analysis presupposes some other method of establishing relationships between groups of animals, and cannot be used as the primary criterion.

The fourth and final criterion is perhaps the most obvious and superficially most promising. And it is at this point that I must confront a difficulty that I have so far scrupulously avoided. In setting out my account of natural kinds, I have used biological kinds as illustrative examples. Moreover, I have been concerned to distinguish kinds that are genera (e.g. the kind *Homo*) from kinds that are species (e.g. the kind *Homo sapiens*). Indeed, in talking about 'levels' of explanation, I might have given the very definite impression that explanation by reference to a taxonomic hierarchy might prove to be an interesting example of explanation at different levels. It is now time to test those remarks by examining the genetic criterion, and the prospects, I fear, are bleak. If a real essence is to be an intrinsic property, then it might seem obvious that the real essences of biological kinds are genetic, that humans are humans, chimpanzees chimpanzees, narcissi narcissi, etc., in virtue of their distinctive and peculiar genetic constitutions. But this suggestion is open to a very serious objection, namely, that there is typically enormous genetic variation between members of the same biological kind. The point is well beyond the bounds of controversy at the level of genera, families and orders, and there is not the slightest chance of defining any taxonomic categories higher than the level of species by reference to genetic features. We must either define genera, families and orders in some other way, or recognize that they are not natural kinds in the strong sense that interests me. I suggest that we should take the second alternative, and confine our attention to species as the most promising examples of natural kinds. But even if we confine our attention to species, and take those as the proper biological examples of natural kinds, the genetic criterion will not do, for genetic real essences of species, genetic features necessary and sufficient for membership of each species, do not exist.

Consider examples. I and my parents are certainly members of the same species, but, since I only inherited half of my genes from my mother and half from my father, I am genetically different from both of them. Any gardener will be aware of the enormous variation between different varieties of the same species. No doubt the variations can be explained by reference to genetic features, but there are no genetic features that unite all the members of the species, all the individual examples of the many varieties. There may not even be a genetic feature to unite all parts of the same individual, for, particularly in plants, different parts of the individual may be genetically different. Many variegated plants are genetically different in differently coloured sections of the plant. Gardeners who notice genetic variation in a new stem call it a 'sport', cut it off and propagate it, in the hope that it will prove to be novel and decorative, or even commercially successful. Someone might reply that the genetic feature we are looking for is a structural feature of the genetic material, for example, the number of chromosomes peculiar to each species. Despite the wide genetic variation between individual humans, it will be said, they all have twenty-three pairs of chromosomes. Sadly, they don't! On the one hand, a particular number of chromosomes may be characteristic of many different species. For example, diploid members of all species in the genera *Pinus* and *Quercus* typically have twenty-four chromosomes. Indeed, since the number of species is very large, and since the number of chromosomes in any cell must be comparatively small, it is impossible for particular numbers of chromosomes to be peculiar to particular species. There aren't enough small numbers to go round! On the other hand, different members of the same species may have different numbers of chromosomes. Down's syndrome, for example, is due to an extra chromosome, and human hermaphrodites have an extra sex chromosome. In plants polyploidy is very common. In other words, as the result of an irregular division of genetic material in ancestors, many plants have chromosomes arranged in sets of three or more, rather than in the paired sets characteristic of diploids. In some cases different varieties of the same species will have different numbers of chromosomes: in apples, for example, a few self-fertile species are haploid, with seventeen chromosomes, many are diploid, with thirty-four, some (such as Bramley's Seedling) are triploid, with fifty-one, some tetraploid, with sixty-eight, and so on.

Although I am not qualified to judge, it would seem that more sophisticated attempts to isolate genetic real essences — for example, by measuring the length, size and shape of whole chromosomes, or of fragments of chromosomes — are also doomed to failure. The more we attempt to isolate the genetic features that determine biological species, the more hopeless the task becomes. And perhaps those of us who have tended to think of species as good examples of natural kinds have unconsciously been driven by a misleading picture of the boundaries of natural kinds as clearly drawn by nature, rather in the way in which the boundaries between pigeonholes are clearly marked. But Darwin demolished that picture for ever. It is not just that the work of evolutionary biologists has revealed many more boundaries than had ever been imagined — more species, more intermediate and hybrid species — but the conception of *boundaries* is a thoroughly misguided one. If we are properly to understand evolution and genetic variation, and if we must have some picture to help us, then the picture must somehow reflect the fluidity of species, the way in which they may change through time, and in which they may merge, almost imperceptibly, into each other. Boundaries are no doubt helpful for field biologists, gardeners and zoo keepers, but they do not exist in nature. John Dupré makes this suggestion:

> The existence of species ... may be seen as consisting in the following fact. If it were possible to map individual organisms on a multidimensional quality space, we would find numerous clusters or bumps. In some parts of biology these clusters will be almost entirely discrete. In other areas there will be a continuum of individuals between the peaks. It can then be seen as the business of taxonomy to identify these peaks.[5]

The biologist Stephen Jay Gould also favours the language of continua, rather than that of discrete items separated by boundaries:

> Islands of form exist, to be sure: cats do not flow together in a sea of continuity, but rather come to us as lions, tigers, lynxes, tabbies, and so forth. Still, although species may be discrete, they have no immutable essence. Variation is the raw material of evolutionary change. It represents the fundamental reality of nature, not an accident about a created norm ... Antiessentialist thinking forces us to view the world differently. We must accept shadings and continua as fundamental.[6]

Gould's readers will notice that he wishes to draw certain liberal moral and political conclusions but, although those conclusions are appealing, they are irrelevant for my purposes here. I merely wish to explore his, and Dupré's, suggestion that species should be thought of as forming continua, rather than as separated like pigeonholes.

Incidentally, we should note in passing that the claim that there are no genetic real essences, and the claim that species should be thought of as forming continua, are distinct claims. The second claim probably implies the first. That is, if species are arranged in a continuum, it is very difficult to argue that each species is determined by a peculiar real essence. Each supposedly 'essential' feature determining one point on the continuum will be very similar to 'essential' features determining adjacent points on the continuum, and there will be no good reason to split the continuum in certain places rather than in others. But the first claim certainly does not imply the second. That is, if there are no genetic real essences, it does not follow that there are no discrete species. To contrapose: even if each species were discrete, and qualitatively quite distinct from every other, it would not follow that it was determined by a single property or set of properties necessary and sufficient for membership of that species. Both Dupré and Gould are anti-essentialist, and both insist that members of different species often turn out to be very similar, and that members of the same species often turn out to be very different. But they concede that there are, quite obviously, many different species. Again compare Dupré:

> the existence of discrete species is one of the most striking and least disputable of biological data. If one examines the trees or birds in a particular area, it is apparent that these fall into a number of classes that differ from one another in numerous respects. But the essentialist conclusion that one might be tempted to draw from this fact is dissipated first by more careful study, which reveals that these distinguishing characteristics are by no means constant within the classes, and second by extending the scope of the investigation in both space and time, whereupon the limitations both of intraspecific similarity and interspecific difference will become increasingly apparent.[7]

A bad reply: family resemblances

Let us see where we are. I argued that each natural kind is determined by a real essence, that is, by an intrinsic property or set of properties that is necessary and sufficient for membership of the kind. Biological species seemed to be the most obvious examples of natural kinds, but it has proved to be extremely difficult to say what, in general, would count as the real essences of species. There are apparently insuperable objections to our accepting any of the suggested criteria: descent, interbreeding, morphological features (whether gross or finer-grained), or genetic constitution. What is to be done? Let me say straightaway that I intend to abandon the first three criteria, for the reasons I have given, but, with astonishing heroism, I will attempt to defend a version of the genetic criterion. Such heroism will be supported by a long, and at times fruitless, discussion.

First I shall consider a reply that must surely have occurred to everyone. Perhaps I have made my task far more difficult than it needs to be, by characterizing real essences too strongly. So far I have said that a real essence is a property or set of properties that is necessary and sufficient for membership of the kind in question. Moreover, the expressions 'necessary' and 'sufficient' are to be interpreted very strongly, so that natural kinds can be identified across possible worlds and from Earth to Twin Earth. As I explained in chapter 3, my commitment to natural kinds is also a commitment to natural necessity, and I take the central part of the notion of natural necessity to be truth in all possible worlds. The real essences that determine membership of natural kinds are precisely the properties underlying the causal powers of the objects in question; they will feature in any account of the laws of nature; and those laws will obtain in all possible worlds. Finally, given my general account of natural kinds, I have insisted that the property or set of properties that constitute a real essence is intrinsic rather than relational. My remarks in the previous section about morphological features and about genetic variation seem to show that there are no such intrinsic properties necessary and sufficient for membership of species, so there are no real essences, so understood.

But could I not weaken the notion of a real essence, borrow Wittgenstein's notion of a family resemblance, and argue that the real essences that determine membership of species are family resemblances? After all, Wittgenstein never argued that classification determined by family resemblances (which, incidentally, for him meant *all* classification) was frivolous, unmotivated or arbitrary. He insisted that we can explain in detail which properties determine membership of the kind *game*, or *number*, or *use of language*, or whatever. He was anxious only to stress that no single property or set of properties — even a disjunctive set — was necessary or sufficient for membership of the kind; that at best, the feature that unites games, or numbers, or uses of language, or whatever, is a family resemblance. Why should I not therefore continue to say that natural kinds are determined by real essences, but claim that the real essences in question are family resemblances? Nature draws the boundaries, but she draws them with the aid of family resemblances.

In order to judge this proposal, we need to look in detail at Wittgenstein's original account. Until Baker and Hacker started their very important work on Wittgenstein, it had not generally been noticed that his account has at least two distinct layers, and that, as far as Wittgenstein himself is concerned, the first layer rests squarely upon the second.[8] The first layer consists in the claim I have just mentioned, namely that general names do not pick out single properties or sets of properties that are both necessary and sufficient for membership of the relevant kinds, but rather pick out family resemblances. For example, there are no properties or sets of properties necessary and sufficient for being a game: some games involve competition, some do not; some are played on a board, some are not; some are intended to amuse, some are deadly serious; some have endings or victories, some do not; some have very clear and definite rules, some allow the players to do almost anything; and so on. There is something that unites all the cases, just as there is something that allows us to talk of the Churchill face. But, just as there may be no feature common to and peculiar to all those who have the Churchill face, so there will be no feature common to and peculiar to all games. And it is no good to insist that there *must* be some relevant single determining property or set of properties:

> *look and see* whether there is anything common to them all. — For if you look at them you will not see something that is common to *all*, but similarities, relationships, and a whole series of them at that ... we see a complicated network of similarities overlapping and criss-crossing: sometimes

overall similarities, sometimes similarities of detail ... I can think of no better
expression to characterize these similarities than "family resemblances".[9]

Nor, incidentally, would it be useful to list all the criss-crossing and
overlapping similarities as a single disjunctive set: 'a game involves either
amusement or competition or victory or definite rules or ...'. For the
disjunction would, in principle, have to be open. However ingenious we may
be in making provision for odd and forgotten examples, the disjunctive list
of properties will, as it were, peter out eventually with a row of dots, to
allow us to add on any new cases that seem to us to belong naturally with
existing games. No definition can make provision for all the cases that
someone, somewhere, might wish to count as games, or numbers, or uses
of language, or whatever.

But that seems to leave us with a problem. If general kinds are not
determined by single properties or sets of properties that are both necessary
and sufficient for membership of the relevant kinds, if they are determined
by family resemblances, and if any attempt to characterize a family
resemblance disjunctively cannot, even in principle, be completed, nothing
prevents our classifications from being completely arbitrary. Just as I can
move from professional football to children's games of pretence, via a series
of different criss-crossing similarities, so I can move on to, say, writing a
paper on natural kinds. Football and games of pretence are both games;
games of pretence and writing papers on natural kinds are both good ways
of passing a wet afternoon; so I shall call writing a paper on natural kinds
'playing a game'! Indeed, since any two things are similar in some respect,
there is no particularly pressing reason for me to stop there. Writing papers
on natural kinds and being bored rigid by faculty meetings are both
unavoidable parts of the academic life, so I should regard being bored rigid
at faculty meetings as yet another example of playing a game. With mild and
comparable ingenuity I can in principle collect absolutely anything as a
game.

Wittgenstein of course responds, and here we move to the second layer of
his account of family resemblances. In a sense his response is scattered all
over the *Philosophical Investigations*, and as commentators we should note
that his account of family resemblances is not merely a contribution to
discussion of the problem of universals, but is an integral part of his later
philosophy. Consider this question: What counts as the right response when
I follow the rules governing the English word 'game'? How can I justify my
inclination to collect football and children's games of pretence, but not to
collect writing papers on natural kinds or being bored rigid at faculty
meetings? I can certainly offer justification, for example by listing examples
of games, by giving my reasons for including football but excluding writing
papers, by rehearsing some of the ground rules for anthropologists in the

field who classify games, and so on. For example I can start to justify my inclination by saying that writing papers on natural kinds is not rule-governed, that there are no players, no winning or losing, and that it involves very little in the way of fun.

But after a point, Wittgenstein would say, there is nothing more I can sensibly say. For my rule following rests on fundamental inclinations, which are intimately connected with my 'form of life', and which neither yield nor demand further justification. If I am faced with someone whose classifications are apparently systematic but eccentric, for example, someone who, quite deliberately, collects both writing papers on natural kinds and being bored rigid at faculty meetings as games, I cannot appeal to anything that might show that my classification is better or more accurate than hers. All I can say is that I find it natural to do one thing, and she apparently finds it natural to do something else. In extreme cases (where for example she is an 'odd adder'), I may be quite unable to understand what she is doing, and she may be quite unable to understand what I am doing:

> If I have exhausted the justifications I have reached bedrock, and my spade is turned. Then I am inclined to say: "This is simply what I do." ... I should have said: *This is how it strikes me* ... When I obey a rule, I do not choose. I obey the rule *blindly*.
> "So you are saying that human agreement decides what is true and what is false?" — It is what human beings *say* that is true and false; and they agree in the *language* they use. That is not agreement in opinions but in form of life.[10]

So, Wittgenstein would say, in a perfectly clear sense our classifications are not at all arbitrary or unmotivated, and there is not the slightest reason to suppose that we could intelligibly extend our use of words like 'game' without limit. For ultimately those classifications are underpinned by our natural inclinations, and their boundaries are fixed by what we find it natural to say. We should not be dispirited or puzzled by the thought that there could be beings whose classifications are very different from ours, and that we would find their languages more or less incomprehensible, because their natural histories and natural inclinations are very different from ours. We should always resist the urge to ask which classifications are correct, and should content ourselves with saying merely that this is what *we* do.

We can now return to my problem. I was exploring the view that there are natural kinds, that is, kinds whose boundaries are fixed by nature, quite independently of our beliefs or theories. I suggested that each natural kind is determined by a real essence, an intrinsic property or set of properties that is necessary and sufficient for membership of the kind in question. Biological species seemed to be good candidates for the role of natural kinds, but unfortunately we could not find suitable real essences to determine them. I wondered whether I might escape from my difficulties, while still defending a doctrine of natural kinds, by borrowing Wittgenstein's account of family resemblances, and by arguing that biological real essences are family resemblances. But it should now be clear that I cannot do so, for two reasons. First, a family resemblance is precisely *not* a single property or set of properties that is necessary and sufficient for membership of a kind. It cannot even be sensibly characterized as a disjunctive set, for any suitable disjunction will be open ended. Second, the general thrust of Wittgenstein's later philosophy is anti-realist. That is, he is committed to a version of the view that the properties we attribute to the world are in a sense not properties of the world, but properties of us. It turns out that our systems of classification do not reflect the way things are in themselves, but rather the way in which we find it natural to classify them. Indeed, the whole project of searching for real natural kinds, of asking how things are in themselves, is entirely incoherent on Wittgenstein's view, for ultimately we can attach no sense to the thought that one system of classification is the correct one, that it marks the joints of nature. All we can say is 'This is what we do'. Boundaries are not fixed by nature, but by us. In short, Wittgenstein's philosophical views, and in particular his account of family resemblances, are flatly inconsistent with mine, and if I am to defend a doctrine of natural kinds, I would be wise to have nothing to do with him.

However, someone might reply that we are under no obligation to accept Wittgenstein's philosophical views in a single package, and that we are entitled to use the first layer of his account of family-resemblances without committing ourselves to the second layer. That is, we are entitled to argue that biological kinds are not determined by real essences, by properties or sets of properties that are necessary and sufficient for membership of the kinds, but by family resemblances, by overlapping and criss-crossing similarities. We are not forced to accept the second claim, that ultimately the boundaries between family resemblances are determined by our natural inclinations and instincts, by what we find it natural to say. So we are not forced to follow Wittgenstein into embracing anti-realism. Briefly, the family resemblances in question are *real* in the sense dear to every metaphysical realist: it is just a brute fact of nature that there are certain family resemblances (perhaps genetic family resemblances) between members of the same species, and the resemblances and differences do not depend on us, or on our thoughts and beliefs about them.

Unfortunately, I do not think that the reply will work. It is, after all, impossible to separate the two layers of Wittgenstein's thought, for the reason I gave earlier: the second, or anti-realist layer, offers the only reasonable explanation for an important feature of family resemblances, namely that they are in principle open-ended. It is impossible to characterize a family resemblance in terms of a long disjunctive set of properties, since, according to Wittgenstein, the set will have to be open-ended, to allow the possibility of our collecting new cases, without, however, any clearly statable prior understanding of how exactly they should be collected. Of course, the fact that there is an open end does not in practice undermine the role of family resemblance concepts in our attempts to pick out non-arbitrary similarities and differences in nature. But, given that family resemblance concepts are open-ended, our attempts to pick out real similarities and differences must rest ultimately on the fact that we find certain distinctions natural, and others unnatural. So the suggestion that we can exploit the first layer of Wittgenstein's account of family resemblances, while rejecting the second, is bound to fail. One crucial feature of a family resemblance, namely that it is open-ended, inevitably implies that an account of the world in terms of family resemblances will be anti-realist.

However, before moving on, we should consider another closely related suggestion. In chapter 4, I suggested, almost in passing, that many non-natural kinds are determined by clusters of properties, that is, sets of properties that do not strictly determine the kind in terms of necessary and sufficient conditions, but nonetheless tend to cluster together. For example we might find it impossible to give an account of tables in terms of necessary and sufficient conditions, but there is no doubt that certain properties cluster together: having a flat surface, having a small number of legs, having legs at each corner, having corners, being within a certain range of heights, widths and depths, being made of a certain range of materials, and so on. Moreover, the set of properties that form the cluster is not an open-ended set, and the concept of a table does not ultimately rest on what we find it natural to say. It is just a brute fact that certain objects perform a function for normal human beings. Perhaps, in a similar way, we could solve our problem by arguing that the properties that determine species are cluster properties. Furthermore, genetic properties might seem to be particularly good examples of cluster properties. That is, they are properties that a) consistently cluster together in nature; but b) do not, even in principle, yield an analysis of species in terms of necessary and sufficient conditions; and c) do not form a set that is open-ended, and whose completion waits upon an inevitably local story about the natural inclinations of one community of sentient beings.

So the general thought would be this. There are many genetic properties, both of a fairly macroscopic kind (e.g. having forty-six chromosomes, or having an X chromosome) and of a microscopic kind (e.g. having a particular sequence of bases on some section of some chromosome), but none of the properties, and no relevant disjunctive set of the properties, will determine a given species in terms of necessary and sufficient conditions.

But it is clearly no accident that the properties cluster together in nature, and anyone interested in the structural features of a phenotype would, in principle, have to investigate the genetic properties of the phenotype. Should we not therefore draw the conclusion that species are determined by cluster-properties?

Unfortunately, I think not — or at least, I think that we should resist any attempt to give an account of biological natural kinds in terms of cluster properties. I have two reasons for saying so. First, there is, as it were, a matter of pride. I have now almost completed a book on natural kinds, in which I try to defend the view that a natural kind is determined by a real essence, that is, by a property or a set of properties necessary and sufficient for membership of the kind. If I allow that biological natural kinds are determined by cluster-properties, I shall abandon any hope of applying the general programme to biological kinds. The second reason has more to do with philosophy than with pride. Only a few lines above, I said that it is no accident that cluster properties cluster, and in particular, that the genetic properties that determine many of the features of a phenotype tend in nature to cluster together. We should never regard the fact of clustering as just a brute fact, as something that allows no further explanation. After careful analysis we may decide that the fact is indeed brute. For example, after careful reflection on the concept of a table we may conclude that it picks out a cluster property, and that there is no more to be said. But, at the risk of a certain kind of philosophical prudery, I want to say that we have not yet finished our careful analysis, and that there *is* more to be said about the genetic cluster properties that determine species, but I cannot say it now. I shall say it later in the chapter, when I set out my preferred solution of our problem. My solution will attempt to do justice to the important thought that genes are the basic engines of structure and change, and will attempt to develop that thought within the constraints of an account of natural kinds that has at its centre the notion of a real essence.

Another bad reply: promiscuous realism

Since I shall not redeem those impressive promises until much later in the chapter, we are still left with the original problem. If natural kinds are determined by real essences, and if species are not determined by real essences, then species are not, after all, good examples of natural kinds. Furthermore, realists of a nervous and pessimistic disposition might fear that realism will have to be given up altogether, and that we shall have to endure some kind of anti-realism, some version of the view that the features we attribute to the world are strictly features of ourselves and our systems of belief, and cannot coherently be regarded as features of the world as it is in itself. But that pessimism is too hasty. Even if we were eventually forced to abandon essentialism (and I hope to salvage it later in the chapter), there would be at least one other version of realism available, namely Dupré's 'promiscuous realism', which I touched on in chapter 4.

In the course of criticizing Putnam's account of the names of natural kinds, Dupré is struck by the range of purposes served by our ordinary language (or OLC) classifications. Some names are borrowed from biologists or are relics of discarded biological classifications; some reflect the interests of farmers; others those of cooks and gourmets, or timber merchants, or flower arrangers, or gardeners, or furriers, or hunters, or zoo keepers ... ; and so on. Each classification is admirable for its purposes, and typically reflects them. One classification may be entirely useless for other purposes: cooks and gardeners insist on a strong distinction between onions, garlic and ornamental *Allium* species, but biologists do not; zoo keepers' questions about the habits of animals cut right across taxidermists' questions about their suitability for stuffing and embalming. Each classification focuses on certain similarities and differences, but none of the similarities or differences are privileged or especially significant in themselves. A range of similarities and differences is significant only relative to a special interest, e.g. the interests of farmers, or gardeners, or cooks, etc.

So, in contrast to the essentialist such as Putnam,[11] who argues that the similarities and differences of interest to biologists are privileged, and somehow mark the real joints of nature, Dupré offers us 'promiscuous realism':

> The realism derives from the fact that there are many sameness relations that serve to distinguish classes of organisms in ways that are relevant to various concerns; the promiscuity derives from the fact that none of these relations is privileged.[12]

At the risk of being tediously repetitive, I should stress that promiscuous realism is a version of *realism*. I say that, because so often in philosophical discussion the claim that some concept reflects our interests quickly degenerates into the claim that it *merely* reflects our interests, and anti-realism is never far behind. But that is not Dupré's view. He wants to say that the features that interest, say, farmers or gardeners or cooks or taxidermists are *real* features of the world. It is just a fact about the world, not a fact about us, that some animals produce milk, that some plants survive the British winter, that some plants are edible, and so on. The only relevant fact about us is that if we are farmers, we will concentrate on one set of real features; if we are gardeners, we will concentrate on a rather different set; if we are zoo keepers, we will concentrate on yet another set; and so on.

It is pleasing to be offered different versions of realism, but I want to reject promiscuous realism, for two main reasons. Both reasons turn on the general thought that the promiscuous realist leaves too much unexplained. I concede straightaway that there are many different, but often overlapping, ordinary language classifications, and that typically each classification reflects the peculiar interests of, say, farmers or gardeners or cooks or gourmets or flower arrangers or taxidermists or zoo keepers, or of course of professional biologists. But my first worry concerns the reference to the interests and purposes of each group. The word 'interest' is ambiguous, and I suggest that Dupré's argument trades on the ambiguity. Sometimes when we say that someone has an interest in something, we mean merely that they think a lot about it, devote their leisure hours to it, easily focus their attention on it, and so on. The football fan is interested in football, the philatelist in stamps. Sometimes, however, when we say that someone has an interest in something, we mean that they they have some practical benefit in view. Despite the sad, and probably terminal, decline of the English word 'disinterested', we still manage to mark the distinction by distinguishing two different kinds of failure of interest: someone may be uninterested, or disinterested. If the legal dispute is nothing to do with me, but is full of juicy and scandalous detail, I will be interested but disinterested. If my name is Jarndyce, and I am heartily sick of the whole thing, I may be uninterested but have an interest.

There are related ambiguities in such words as 'anthropocentric' and 'anthropomorphic', which also occur in Dupré's comparison of ordinary language classifications (OLC) and scientific taxonomy (TC):

> The functions of OLC, unsurprisingly enough, are overwhelmingly anthropocentric. A group of organisms may be distinguished in ordinary language ... because it is economically or sociologically important ... because its members are intellectually intriguing ... furry and empathetic ... or just very noticeable.
> TC, hopefully, avoids this anthropocentric viewpoint. The number of species names is here intended to reflect the number of species that exist. Nonetheless, even here there is an anthropomorphic aspect. For an adequate taxonomy ... should ... be practically usable.[13]

But several different senses are being muddled together here. When I say that a classification is anthropocentric, I might mean that it is *logically* anthropocentric, that any analysis of the classification would involve essential reference to an actual or possible person. For example, as I argued in chapter 2, and again in chapter 4, our names for artefacts are typically *logically* anthropocentric, for they refer, explicitly or implicitly, to an actual or possible person. A table is something with a flat surface capable of supporting the portable goods of a normal human being, a house provides shelter for human beings, a coin is a small metal disc conventionally recognized as a means of exchange, and so on. Narayan's gardener uses a classification that is, in part, logically anthropocentric, for a weed is precisely a plant that human gardeners typically do not want in the garden. But sometimes when I say that a classification is anthropocentric, I mean that there is a direct *causal* connection between our use of the classification and some practical human interest or concern. Taxidermists classify skins and carcasses in a particular way because they want to find skins that survive preservation and stuffing; cooks are looking for things good to eat; zoo keepers want to entertain visitors and preserve threatened species; timber merchants hope to sell wood at a profit; and so on. And finally, sometimes when I say that a classification is anthropocentric, I may mean very little. I may be trying in vain to make something of the obvious and dreary fact that classifications are invented and used by classifiers.

I can now make my first point against promiscuous realism. I suggest that there is an important difference between many ordinary language classifications and scientific taxonomies, between OLC and TC. Much of our work with OLC is overwhelmingly connected with some purely practical interest. (I say 'much' rather than 'all' because, as I explained in chapter 4, some OLC names are the débris from one or other failed attempt at TC.) It arises from, and is stimulated by, a wish to make money, or eat agreeable food, or satisfy a desire to grow the pretty and the profitable, and would have very little point in the absence of such practical interest. Moreover, many (but by no means all) OLC names are anthropocentric in the two most interesting senses I distinguished. That is, they are logically anthropocentric, and implicitly make essential reference to human beings ('weed', 'houseplant', 'cattle', 'pet'); or they are causally anthropocentric, and their introduction and use causally depends on someone's desires and practical interests ('shrub', 'ground cover', 'guard dog', 'poultry'); or, of course, both.

In contrast, TC is neither logically nor causally anthropocentric. It neither refers implicitly but essentially to the desires and practical interests of human beings, nor causally depends on those practical interests. No doubt serious taxonomy would grind to a halt if there were no-one with a consuming professional or amateur passion for such things, but the classification would still have some point, for it would, at least in intention, record the important distinctions in nature. Indeed, it is very difficult to say what the 'practical interests' of biologists might be. Every answer seems fatuously circular ('their practical interest is in biological classification'), trivial ('they are interested in producing a classification that is usable'), or cynical to the point of obstinate irrelevance ('they want to gain honours, astonish the crowd and humiliate their colleagues').

My second point against promiscuous realism is a point about causation and explanation, and has been made already on several occasions. One central scientific concern is to explain the world around us and to predict how it will behave. But that requires an interest in the causal powers of things. At the risk of hyperbole, we might say that the scientist is concerned to expose the causal structure of reality. Now, as I argued in chapter 2, many of the kinds we distinguish do not lend themselves to serious scientific investigation, because they are not systematically connected with the causal powers of things. There can be no science of tables and chairs, as such, or even of trees, shrubs, glaciers and clouds, as such, because the classifications in question do not explicitly or implicitly classify causal powers. Of course tables, chairs, trees, shrubs, glaciers and clouds obey causal laws, but only relative to another, quite different system of classification, namely classification of natural kinds. So the causal powers of my table are determined by its being made of cellulose, not by its being a table; those of my tree by its being an *Acer palmatum atropurpureum*, not by its being a tree; those of the glacier by its being frozen H_2O in a certain gravitational field, not by its being a glacier; and so on. So my second point against promiscuous realism is that it overlooks an important difference between OLC (or ordinary language classifications) and TC (or formal taxonomy): typically only TC is intended as a classification that explicitly or implicitly reveals the causal powers of things. And that is why natural kinds, unlike many of the kinds we find in OLC, lend themselves to serious scientific investigation. Once again I make the obvious concession, namely that cooks, gourmets, taxidermists, farmers, gardeners and other users of OLC have a profound interest in cause and effect. If not, they could not guarantee that they cooked the meat, preserved the skin, fed the cattle and germinated the seeds. But my claim is that such guarantees are possible only if tacitly they move from the rather superficial concerns of OLC and lean heavily on the causal stories systematically interwoven with TC.

Before leaving promiscuous realism, I should perhaps add a brief comment. In discussing promiscuous realism I have concentrated entirely on biological classification, since that is the topic of Dupré's paper, but exactly similar points can be made, on both sides, about physical and chemical classifications. Consider for example the physics and chemistry of metals. The promiscuous realist will point out that there are many classifications available, each reflecting a special interest. In addition to academic physicists and chemists there are bridge builders, who are looking for cheap materials capable of withstanding loads and resisting attack by the weather; makers of pianos and other percussion instruments, who are concerned to produce arresting noises; electricians, who want good conductors; sculptors, goldsmiths, silversmiths and workers in wrought iron, who are variously interested in certain striking aesthetic effects; and so on. The classifications are thoroughly realistic, but they run across one another, and no interest is privileged. We use, and should use, whichever classification is appropriate for the purpose in hand.

But my reply is the same as before. First, we should not be mesmerized by the constant reference to interest, for, on inspection, such reference proves to be singularly fruitless. Second, all the classifications, save for those of the academic physicist and chemist, are concerned with superficial features which do not lend themselves to serious scientific generalization. Of course it is true that bridge builders, makers of pianos, electricians and others make successful predictions about the objects dear to their professional hearts, but success depends squarely on the success of physics and chemistry. Such inductive lore as is available to the bridge builders, makers of pianos, et al., is either borrowed from physics and chemistry, or is parasitic upon them. The classifications of physicists and chemists are privileged, because they are concerned explicitly or implicitly with the underlying causal powers of things.

The best reply

We should therefore reject promiscuous realism, and I shall continue to argue that, among the various overlapping systems of biological classification available to us, one (namely TC) is privileged, and the similarities and differences it records are privileged, because, at least in intention, it reveals the kinds determined by nature. But we are now faced once again with our original problem. Originally it seemed that biological species are excellent examples of natural kinds, given that each natural kind is determined by an intrinsic property or set of properties necessary and sufficient for membership of the kind. But there are typically no intrinsic properties or sets of properties necessary and sufficient for membership of species. The only candidate that looks remotely plausible, genetic structure, fails to do the trick, because in the real world there is considerable interspecific genetic similarity and intraspecific genetic variation. It seems to follow, in Gould's and Dupré's words, that we should think of species as forming continua, albeit with occasional bumps and clusters, rather than as forming quite separate, discrete islands of form.

In this section I shall offer my own solution of this problem, by exploiting a number of important points that have emerged from the discussion so far. One general point is that an account of natural kinds arises from an interest in causal explanation and prediction, and that the interest cannot be served by a promiscuous realism which gives equal weight to any useful system of classification. Some features are literally or metaphorically superficial, and have little to do with the causal powers of the object that has them. Other features, however, are directly connected with those causal powers. A second point is that, although typically it is impossible to find genetic features that uniquely determine each species, there can be no doubt that an interest in causal explanation inevitably generates an interest in genetic explanations. As I have pointed out on several occasions, there is a striking asymmetry between the gross macroscopic features of plants and animals and their microscopic — and especially their genetic — features. The microscopic features do not causally depend upon the macroscopic, but the macroscopic features do causally depend upon the microscopic. Anyone seriously interested in explaining and predicting the behaviour of plants and animals would be foolish to concentrate on, for example, purely morphological features. The fundamental engines of structure and change are genetic.

A third point can now be brought into the open. Causal explanations are implicitly or explicitly general. I may be trying to explain a particular event or state of affairs, but I am committed to offering the same explanation of all relevantly similar events or states of affairs. One common way of making the point is to appeal to the notion of a subjunctive or counterfactual conditional, and to claim that genuine causal explanations imply suitable general subjunctive or counterfactual conditionals. I may say for example that the chlorotic yellowing of the leaves in *this* plant was caused by the relative alkalinity of *this* soil, but I imply, among many other things, that any other plant of a relevantly similar kind *would* suffer from chlorosis if it *were* growing in a relevantly similar alkaline soil. Even when the event to be explained is historically unique, the explanation is implicitly general, and implies an appropriate general subjunctive or counterfactual conditional.

So to our problem. How can I continue to defend a doctrine of natural kinds, while conceding that species are not determined by genetic real essences? The simple (some might say, the wildly heroic) answer is that we should preserve our interest in genetic structure, but abandon the assumption that species are excellent examples of natural kinds. There are natural kinds, kinds determined by properties necessary and sufficient for membership of the respective kinds, but the kinds are typically not species. Indeed, in many cases the kind will be very much narrower than the species, and may only have one member. My line of thought is as follows. Let us return for a moment to Gould's remarks about continua:

> We must accept shadings and continua as fundamental ... The taxonomic essentialist scoops up a handful of fossil snails in a single species, tries to abstract an essence, and rates his snails by their match to this average. The antiessentialist sees something entirely different in his hand — a range of irreducible variation defining the species, some variants more frequent than others, but all perfectly good snails.[14]

So species are not ordered discretely, but in continua. But of what are the continua continua? Fairly obviously we have continua of individuals, where, on each continuum, two adjacent individuals share many similarities but are distinguished by at least one significant difference. But clearly we also have continua of *kinds*. Even in a species characterized by considerable genetic variation, where some individuals are genetically unique in all interesting respects, there will be a continuum of kinds. For explanation of the features of each unique individual requires generalization, and that requires the causal dependence of certain features *of a kind* on certain other features *of a kind*. The real essence which in part determines the behaviour of the genetically unique individual is the essence of the *kind* of which the unique individual is the only member.

To sum up, then, my view is this. There are natural kinds. Each natural kind is determined by a real essence, a property or set of properties necessary and sufficient for membership of the kind. The real essence in turn determines the causal powers of individual members of the kind. Biological natural kinds are determined by genetic real essences which causally affect the structure and behaviour of individual members of the kind. But, since there is considerable interspecific genetic similarity and intraspecific genetic variation, there are far more biological natural kinds than species.

In the interests of clarity, perhaps I should add two further explanatory comments (though I suspect that some readers will prefer to regard the comments as objections to my view). The first comment is this. I have stressed the role of genetic structure in causal explanations and have argued that, even when explaining the behaviour of an individual, I am implicitly explaining the behaviour of individuals of a *kind*. I have also stressed the range of interspecific genetic similarity and intraspecific genetic variation. But presumably any genetic feature may in principle have a causal role, and any genetic difference between two individuals is capable, in appropriate circumstances, of producing a difference in their behaviour. Since I want to say that natural kinds are determined by real essences, and that real essences underlie causal powers, I am forced to leave open the very definite possibility that there will be as many kinds as individuals. Isn't that absurd?

I think not. Given that all causal explanation, even of unique individuals, is implicitly general, I would not be particularly worried if we finished up with as many individuals as natural kinds. But, for two reasons, I think that such an odd result is very unlikely. One reason is that many genetic features are causally inert. Only a small fraction of the information carried in strings of DNA has any role in causally affecting the overall structure and behaviour of the individual concerned. At best, the inert sections of genetic strings only have the somewhat empty causal role of ensuring that the strings are complete. So we should not exaggerate the importance of genetic difference:

many of the differences are of no significance. The second reason is that there is a great deal of fog surrounding the expression 'genetic feature'. If I may help myself to the distinction between function and realization, which is normally prominent in a very different context, the point can be put like this. When I say that genetic features causally affect the structure and behaviour of the individual concerned, are the genetic features to be characterized in terms of their *realization* (e.g. as strings of adenine, guanine, cytosine and thymine, consisting in turn of atoms of hydrogen, oxygen, carbon, etc.), or in terms of their *functional role* (e.g. in terms of their anatomical and physiological effects)? Certainly, if we characterize them in terms of their realization, we may well be committed to as many kinds as individuals. But if we characterize genetic features in terms of their functional role, in terms of their causal role in influencing the structural features of the phenotype, then we can take advantage of the fact that there may be different realizations of the same genetic feature, and in turn will be able to regard two individuals that are strictly different at the level of realization as belonging to the same natural kind.

Now there is a good reason for characterizing genetic features in terms of their functional role. The crucial consideration is that the concept of a gene is itself a functional concept. That is, a gene is precisely a structure that directly affects the anatomical and physiological features of the whole organism. Moreover, the causal powers of a gene are the causal powers of a whole genetic sequence, not the causal powers of each section of its microscopic realization. As with any other object or structure in which we can distinguish function from realization, it doesn't matter what it is made of, or how it is constructed, as long as the causal powers of the whole object or structure remain the same. The various pencils on my desk, or the different washing machines in the shop, will be different at the level of realization, but at the functional level — qua pencils or washing machines — will have the same causal powers. Similarly, there may be different realizations of the same gene, different arrangements of atoms which at the level of the whole genetic sequence have exactly similar causal powers. So if biological natural kinds are determined by genetic structure, and if genetic structure is to be characterized functionally, that is, in terms of the causal powers of the whole gene or genetic sequence, we should not expect there to be as many kinds as individuals.

However, readers with keen memories will point to one potential problem. In chapter 3, I cast serious doubt on the philosophical usefulness of the distinction between function and realization. I pointed out that, even in comparatively simple pieces of machinery, small differences in realization are apt to produce differences in function. For example, small differences in the components and structure of washing machines are apt to produce differences in their power to produce clean clothes, their noise level, their consumption of electricity, and so on. If we now turn to comparatively complex pieces of machinery, such as genes, it is very unlikely that genes that are different at the level of realization could be functionally exactly equivalent, particularly if we ignore all the genetic material that is causally inert, and concentrate on the comparatively small amount of material that is causally significant. Equally it is unlikely that whole organisms that are different at some suitable level of genetic realization (and not merely with respect to the causally inert material) are functionally equivalent. Indeed, in my discussion in chapter 3, I mentioned biological machines as one important group of examples of the very tight fit between function and realization. If that is so, and genetic function is tied very closely to genetic realization, my attempt to distinguish biological natural kinds will almost certainly imply that there are as many kinds as individuals. I will then have to retreat to my initial response, which is to say that there is nothing fundamentally absurd in the thought that there are as many kinds as individuals, as long as we remember that any explanation that makes the behaviour of one individual intelligible is implicitly general, and implies suitably general subjunctive or counterfactual conditionals.

The second comment takes me briefly back to Putnam, whose account of natural kind names I discussed in chapter 4. Even if I manage to exploit a distinction between genetic function and genetic realization, I am still committed to far more natural kinds than species, for typically any species contains individuals genetically different from one another in ways that significantly affect their structure and behaviour. But such differences are not reflected in our names for natural kinds. Indeed, compared with the number of natural kinds as I conceive of them, we have only a handful of names. Nor would it be worth our while to invent as many names as natural kinds, even if we were in principle committed to developing an accurate taxonomy. As long as biologists have the language of molecular biology, they can characterize the many variations in genetic structure that underlie kinds of biological individual, and will not need names for all the kinds. But that seriously undermines Putnam's account of general names. Since, on my account, both professional biologists and ordinary folk will draw the boundaries of nature with a very broad brush, it is not true that our use of general names is consistently underpinned by certain underlying properties of the things in question, and, a fortiori, it is not true that the extension of the names is determined by those underlying properties. Nor, of course, is it true that the extension of a general word is determined by the real features of objects, rather than by human decision. For, in introducing and using general names, we must decide how closely we wish our names to reflect the full range of natural kinds, and how far we are prepared to extend our use of existing names to individuals that share some genetic features of our original stereotypical individuals, but not others. In other words, we must decide to what extent our natural kind classifications are to ride roughshod over the real underlying similarities and differences in nature.

Two objections

Before closing this chapter, I want to consider two objections to my account of biological natural kinds. The first objection concerns the status of formal taxonomy. I began by entertaining the thought that every species is a natural kind, determined by a real essence, that is, by a property or set of properties necessary and sufficient for membership of the kind. I went on to reject it, on the ground that species were not determined by real essences, and finished by arguing that on my conception of natural kinds there may be far more natural kinds than species. However, I consistently rejected any anti-realist or instrumentalist account of formal taxonomy. According to me, a formal taxonomy is supposed to tell us what kinds of thing really exist in nature. But I also resisted Dupré's 'promiscuous realism', and insisted that, although many systems of classification are available to us, a formal taxonomy has a special or privileged status. Two connected questions immediately arise. First, am I guilty of inconsistency? If I deny that species are typically natural kinds, am I not thereby committed either to anti-realism or to instrumentalism or to promiscuous realism? Second, what do I take taxonomists to be doing? If they are not marking out natural kinds, what are they doing?

The answers to those questions emerge as soon as we pick out one important thread in my account of natural kinds. At the centre of my account is the notion of an intrinsic property, a property that does not consist in a relational dependence on something else. For example, as I have argued throughout this book, biological kinds are determined by intrinsic properties, for they are determined by genetic properties. And the genetic features of an organism logically do not consist in a relational dependence on something else. In contrast, the biologist's conception of a species is rather more complex. As I argued earlier, the interest in intrinsic properties is certainly there, for the biologist is concerned to explain and predict the behaviour of plants and animals, and the fundamental engines of structure and change are genetic. But the conception of a species also has at its centre the notion of a certain historical development, that is, the evolution of populations of plants and animals from earlier populations. That complexity of interest has of course emerged comparatively recently. Until biologists became preoccupied with historical evolution, taxonomists took their lead from

Linnaeus, and were engaged in a neo-Aristotelian search for the intrinsic substantial forms that marked off one kind from another. But since the publication of *The Origin of Species*, biologists have become keenly interested in descent. Their account of species is an account of stable populations of interbreeding individuals, often geographically isolated from other populations, and that account is meant to fit into an overall historical picture of the descent of various populations from others by natural selection.

Indeed, if I may be permitted a slight digression, I suggest that there is something to be said for the pessimistic view that modern taxonomy is fundamentally inconsistent, for it is in effect a vain attempt to reconcile Linnaean and Darwinian ambitions. Since Darwin, the only sensible taxonomic project consists in discovering which groups of individuals are descended from which, and which sets of individuals are capable of interbreeding. Any attempt to graft on to that project the further project of distinguishing so-called species is a pointless relic of Linnaean taxonomy. It is pointless because, apart from considerations about descent and potential interbreeding, there are no further facts, no real joints of nature, that could be commemorated in a story about species.

However, since it would take us out of our way to pursue that pessimistic view, I shall return to the main track, and conclude that I am not guilty of inconsistency. I can deny that species are typically natural kinds, but resist anti-realist or instrumentalist accounts of formal taxonomy. My account of natural kinds, and the biologist's account of species, do rather different work. My account of natural kinds is concerned exclusively with the intrinsic features, and the causal powers, of individuals, and must therefore rest on considerations about genetic structure. In sharp contrast, the biologist's account of species rests both on considerations about intrinsic genetic properties and on considerations about the historical relations between different groups of individuals. If Richard Dawkins is right,[15] the two sets of considerations are of course intimately connected, since historical descent must be explained by natural selection, and the fundamental mechanism of natural selection is genetic. For it consists in the selection and replication of the 'successful' genes and the disappearance of the 'unsuccessful'. So it is right to interpret a formal taxonomy realistically and non-instrumentally, for it is, at least in intention, part of an account of real historical relations between populations. And it is also right to resist promiscuous realism, for the biologist's interest in the causal powers of things, in the fundamental genetic mechanisms of change, is enough to justify the special status of formal taxonomies.

The second objection springs from a passing remark in my discussion of the first objection. I suggested that perhaps modern taxonomy reveals an inconsistency of purpose. Given Darwin's theory of evolution, the only sensible taxonomic project is to establish which groups of individuals are descended from which, and which groups are capable of interbreeding with which. But taxonomic practice suggests that taxonomists are still influenced by the quite different, and by now redundant, Linnaean project of discovering the substantial forms that determine species. But, it will be said, my final account of biological essences reveals a rather similar inconsistency. On the one hand, I am impressed with the Darwinian arguments against determination of species by genetic real essences. But on the other, I still regard individual plants and animals as members of natural kinds, and attempt to avoid the apparent contradiction by allowing that species are not natural kinds, and that the number of natural biological kinds will be much greater than the number of species.

But why do I insist on treating *individuals* as members of natural kinds at all? Why do I not simply treat kinds of *gene* as natural kinds, and treat individuals merely as the vehicles within which the members of genetic natural kinds work out their various strategies for self-replication? After all, one central part of my account of natural kinds is the claim that the intrinsic properties that determine natural kinds either are, or are irretrievably connected with, the causal powers of individual members of the kinds. And, although of course individual plants and animals have causal powers, the causal powers that make them biological individuals are, or are irretrievably connected with, the causal powers of their genes. The objection is that my preoccupation with individuals is a relic of the Linnaean interest in the substantial forms of individuals. Given Darwin's theory of evolution and the molecular biology that has informed and expanded it, I should surely abandon that preoccupation, and thereby bring the natural kinds of biology much nearer to the natural kinds of physics and chemistry.

I rather suspect that this objection is not as serious as it seems, but, in replying to it, I am still strongly inclined to say that there are both kinds of gene and kinds of individual plant, or individual animal. There are two connected thoughts here. The first thought is that, throughout this book, I have deliberately left room for different levels of natural kinds, for example, have allowed that there are kinds of particle, kinds of atom, kinds of molecule, kinds of complex molecule, and so on. And as long as no object belongs to more than one kind at a given level, nothing of embarrassing consequence is likely to follow. Furthermore, when the features of a kind at one level clearly depend directly on the features of a kind at a lower level (as happens in the case of chemical and physical kinds), there is a lot to be said for the claim that there are natural kinds of different levels. Problems are only likely to arise when there is a possibility of multiple realization, or, in other words, where features at one level cannot be connected directly or tidily with features at some lower level.

Second, the case under discussion is precisely a case where the features of kinds at a higher level (the level of individual plants and animals) depend directly on features of kinds at a lower level (the features of the individual's genes). As I have already said, in the case of plants and animals, the main engines of structure and change are genetic. That being so, it is perfectly natural to carry on and claim that there are kinds of individual, whose real essences are genetic: membership of a kind of individual plant, or individual animal, is determined by genetic structure. Moreover, there is an interesting sense in which the dependence runs the other way as well, in which the features of genes depend on the features of individuals. A Darwinian theory of evolution is a theory about the appearance of new genetic structures by random mutation, and their survival or disappearance as a result of natural selection. Now the forces of natural selection cannot work directly through genes: they must work through individuals. That is, the ability of certain genes to survive depends entirely on the ability of their individual owner to survive long enough to reproduce itself. In short, the relation between genetic structure and the features of individual plants and animals is so close that there is a strong case for continuing to insist that there are both natural kinds of gene and natural kinds of individual, and that together they illustrate the claim that there may be natural kinds at different levels of size and structure.

Notes

1   See, for example, S.J. Gould (1991b), ch. I.
2   J. Dupré (1981), p. 88.
3   See S.J. Gould (1990), ch. 1.
4   One of the most interesting recent cases is the continuing analysis of fossils discovered in the Burgess Shale. See S.J. Gould (1991b).
5   J. Dupré, op. cit., p. 82.
6   S.J. Gould (1991a), pp. 160-1.
7   J. Dupré, op. cit., p.89.
8   See particularly the essay on family resemblances in G. Baker and P. Hacker (1980).
9   L. Wittgenstein (1953), Pt I, §§ 66-7.
10 L. Wittgenstein, op. cit., Pt. I, §§ 217, 219, 241.
11 Strictly, of course, 'the Putnam who wrote the papers collected in Putnam (1975)'.
12 J. Dupré, op. cit., p. 82.
13 J. Dupré, op. cit., pp. 80 and 81.
14 S.J. Gould (1991a), p. 161.
15 See R. Dawkins (1976 and 1989) and (1982).

6 Individual essences

Background

In this chapter I want to talk about individual essences. So far I have explored the view that certain *kinds*, namely natural kinds, have essences. That is, I have explored the view that some individuals, quantities of stuff, events, states and processes belong to certain kinds in virtue of their intrinsic properties, properties that are both necessary and sufficient for their being members of those kinds. Gold, carbon, water, elms, human beings, narcissi, etc., all have real essences that demarcate the relevant natural kinds. The essences are natural rather than nominal, de re rather than de dicto, and may well not be reflected in the necessities of our language. It is de re necessary, but not de dicto necessary, that gold has the atomic number 79, that water is H_2O, that chimpanzees have a certain genetic constitution, that AIDS is a breakdown of the immune system caused by HIV, and so on. The only important qualification of that general view was spelled out in chapter 5. I found that no biological kinds higher than species are determined by genetic real essences, and eventually I conceded that not even species are determined by real essences. It followed that there are far more biological natural kinds than species, and that we only have names for comparatively few biological natural kinds. So it is not strictly true that there is a natural kind *human being*, or a natural kind *mountain ash*, or a natural kind *chimpanzee*, determined by a genetic real essence. However, in the interests of brevity I shall continue to use species as examples of natural kinds, and will only acknowledge the important qualification when something significant threatens to turn upon it.

To repeat: that is a view about the essences of *kinds*. It is a view about the essential qualifications for membership of a kind, and the general thought is that any individual must have a certain property, a certain real essence, if and only if it is to be a member of a certain natural kind. In this chapter I want to consider a related but quite separate view, the view that certain individuals have *individual* essences, where an individual essence is some property whose possession is *either* both necessary and sufficient, *or* merely necessary, for an individual's being *that* individual. The two italicized expressions 'either' and 'or' reveal that there is immediately a problem, for there are two quite different views available. The view that there are essences of individuals might be the stronger view that there is at least one individual whose properties include a property necessary and sufficient for its being that individual; or it might be the weaker view that there is at least one individual whose properties include a property necessary for its being that individual.

Unfortunately, in the literature it is often quite unclear which view is under discussion. (I recently conducted an informal survey among some of my colleagues, and found that they could not agree on which prominent philosophers were defending which view.) One conspicuous exception is Wiggins, who makes it quite clear that he is only defending the weaker view:

> Individuals have essences without which they would not 'be what they are' — would not exist; but (apart from logically particularized essential properties like *necessarily identical with Caesar*) their essences are shareable. The requirement that essences should be unique to particulars ... is seriously contaminated with confusion.[1]

I plan to attack both elements of the stronger view, and, if my attack is successful, I shall thereby refute the weaker view. That is, if I show that there are no properties that are necessary, and no properties that are sufficient, for an individual's being that individual, then I will have shown that there are no properties that are necessary.

So let us return to where we were. So far I have been defending essentialism for kinds, the view that an individual must have a certain property, a certain real essence, if and only if it is to be a member of a certain natural kind. I now wish to consider the view that there are individuals with individual essences, where an individual essence is a property either necessary, or necessary and sufficient, for the individual's being that individual. The two views are connected because, if there are any individuals with individual essences, the best candidates, indeed the only serious candidates, would seem to be individual members of natural kinds — individual chimpanzees, elms, humans, daffodils. But the two views are different, as we can see if we set them out, with appropriate labels, side by side. To remind us that the necessities in question are de re, not de dicto, I shall borrow Wiggins' useful de re operator 'NEC'.[2]

Essentialism for kinds (EK): For any individual and for any natural kind, and as a matter of necessity, that individual has a certain real essence if and only if it is to be a member of that kind. Formally:

$$(x)(N) \text{ NEC } (Nx \leftrightarrow (\exists R)(Rx)). \tag{EK}$$

Strong essentialism for individuals (Strong EI): Loosely: there are individuals (namely, individual members of natural kinds) that have individual essences, features whose possession is both necessary and sufficient for their being the individuals they are. More tightly: there is at least one individual, and at least one property, such that, as a matter of necessity, the individual's having that property is necessary and sufficient for its being that individual. Formally:

$$(\exists x)(\exists P)(Px \text{ \& NEC } (y)((y = x) \leftrightarrow Py)). \tag{Strong EI}$$

Weak essentialism for individuals (Weak EI), the view that there is at least one individual that has a property necessary for its being that individual, emerges when we weaken one connective in strong essentialism for individuals:

$$(\exists x)(\exists P)(Px \text{ \& NEC } (y)((y = x) \rightarrow Py)). \tag{Weak EI}$$

Now, we can suppose, quite reasonably, that we may substitute names of natural kinds on 'N', names of real essences on 'R', and names of either on 'P'. In context, (strong) essentialism for individuals will then involve a commitment to this proposition:

$$(\exists x)(\exists R)(Rx \text{ \& NEC } (y)((y = x) \leftrightarrow Ry)). \tag{EI*}$$

In other words, possession of the real essence of a natural kind is necessary and sufficient for the identity of certain individuals. Membership of a natural kind determines their identity as *those* individuals. EI* is undoubtedly a very odd proposition, for reasons that I shall discuss later on. But the crucial point for the moment is that it is difficult to see how we could move from EK to strong EI, and in turn to EI*, without being guilty of a crude modal shift. Necessarily membership of a natural kind depends on having a certain feature (the real essence), but it does not seem to follow that individual members of a natural kind necessarily have that feature, if they are to exist at all.

Moreover, whether or not one accepts EK, there is a familiar objection to the whole idea of an individual essence. It rests on the premiss that there are no individuals as such, only individuals of certain kinds. I cannot point to an individual, but only to an individual daffodil, or an individual table decoration, or an individual item for sale, or whatever. Objects have properties, but are not separate from their properties. Failure to appreciate that fact will rapidly lead to a search for bare particulars or Lockean substrata. It follows that there are no individual essences as such; there are only individual essences relative to a kind, or essences under a certain description. Nothing is essential to the individual Julius Caesar, though something may be essential to him qua man, or qua Roman, or qua Emperor, or qua Wiggins' most memorable example. Qua man, Julius Caesar might not have been Emperor, and could not have been a goldfish. Qua Wiggins' most memorable example, Julius Caesar might well have been a goldfish, a Louis XV escritoire, or a prime number. As Locke remarked,

> take but away the abstract *ideas* by which we sort individuals and rank them under common names, and then the thought of anything *essential* to any of them instantly vanishes ... None of these [sc. features] are essential to the one or the other, or to any other individual whatsoever, till the mind refers it to some sort or *species* of things.[3]

Historians will note that the great and good give us no consistent advice on the matter. Kripke and Wiggins accept both EK (essentialism for kinds) and weak EI (weak essentialism for individuals), and Wiggins appears to think that EK entails weak EI.[4] Locke treats EK with considerable sympathy before eventually rejecting it but, as we have just seen, denies that individuals have individual essences. In one place in the *Metaphysics*, Aristotle seems to deny that there are individual essences, for in Z, IV, 1030a6 he tells us that 'there is an essence only of those things whose formula is a definition', and in Z, XV, 1039b27-8 that 'there is neither definition nor demonstration of sensible individual substances'. But in Z, IV, he also raises a question about what-it-is-to-be-you, and in Z, VI, 1032a6 ff., he uses Socrates as an example to illustrate his conclusion that there is a sense in which it is absurd to separate a thing and its essence. In other words he appears to take an interest in the essences of individuals.

I want to begin my own modest contribution to the discussion of individual essences by examining an argument that promises to carry us from EK to strong EI, from a commitment to essences of kinds to a strong commitment to essences of individuals. I repeat that I only propose to discuss strong essentialism for individuals. Furthermore, for the most part, I will ignore exegetical questions about the exact commitments of various other writers. First, I must clear a little more undergrowth, and defend my rather casual remark that, if there are any individuals with individual essences, the best candidates, indeed the only serious candidates, would seem to be members of natural kinds. That remark will surprise many readers, because the philosophical literature is full of discussions of the essences of such things as individual artefacts.

Kripke, for example, claims that his table could not have been made from a different block of wood, or made of ice. We could certainly have made an exactly similar table from another block, or from ice, but it would not be *that* table:

> though we can imagine making a table out of another block of wood or even
> from ice, identical in appearance with this one, and though we could have put
> it in this very position in the room, it seems to me that this is *not* to imagine
> *this* table as made of wood or ice, but rather it is to imagine another table,
> *resembling* this one in all external details, made of another block of wood, or
> even of ice.[5]

Kripke seems to have nothing more than intuition to support his attempt to
investigate the individual essences of artefacts and other members of non-
natural kinds, and there are important arguments against even attempting
such an investigation. I shall discuss one of them in the next section, and
will eventually reject it, but there are other, much more secure arguments
that we can consider very briefly straightaway. One argument concerns the
specific case of artefacts, and rests on the thought that it does not matter in
the slightest what artefacts are made of, as long as they perform, or are
capable of performing, the appropriate function. What makes a table a table
is its ability to support my books, crockery and other small portable
possessions, not its being made of any particular materials. Indeed, if I were
to engage in loving restoration, in the style of the ship of Theseus, carefully
replacing each piece of ageing wood with a new piece of ice, it would still
be numerically the same table when the systematically piecemeal restoration
were complete. If anything is essential to the table, it is its functional role,
not its composition. So it is absurd to suggest that a particular table could
not have been made of quite different materials.

But there is also a general reason for thinking that members of non-natural
kinds do not have individual essences. Remember that an individual essence,
strongly interpreted, would have to be an intrinsic property or set of
properties necessary and sufficient for the individual's being that individual.
In chapter 2, I picked out two main groups of non-natural kinds, dependent
kinds (e.g. *table, cliff, dinner, north wind*) and real but superficial kinds
(e.g. *tree, shrub, pebble*). (For present purposes we can ignore the final
group, hybrid kinds.) Generally something is a member of a dependent kind
in virtue of a relational dependence on something else, and is a member of
a real but superficial kind in virtue of a real (even intrinsic) but
comparatively superficial property, which in many cases will prove to be a
cluster property. Now I assume that an individual essence must be intimately
connected with the property or set of properties that determine membership
of the kind. If we were to reject that assumption, the search for individual
essences would have no rational constraints, and would quickly degenerate
into an unmotivated exchange of contrary intuitions. But if we accept the
assumption, members of non-natural kinds will not have individual essences,
for the properties determining dependent kinds are relational rather than

intrinsic, and the properties determining real but superficial kinds are superficial.

The reasons are these. Where the determining properties consist of cluster properties they cannot of course be characterized in terms of necessary and sufficient conditions. But even where the determining properties do not consist of cluster properties, they cannot constitute individual essences. One simple and obvious consideration, which unfortunately applies only to the case of dependent kinds, is that individual essences would have to be intrinsic properties, and dependent kinds are determined by relational rather than intrinsic properties. Another, much less obvious, consideration applies to both dependent and real but superficial kinds. Consider for example a table (*table* being a dependent kind) that has been moved to a quite different planet, inhabited by beings quite different from ourselves. Perhaps they use the quondam table as a footstool. The original individual has clearly survived, but what is its essence? The essence cannot be its being a table, because it is no longer a table: when its relational properties changed, it ceased to be a table, and became a footstool. Similarly, consider a shrub (*shrub* being a real but superficial kind) that has been pruned of all its side stems, leaving a single central stem, branching six feet above the ground. The original individual has clearly survived, but what is its essence? The essence cannot be its being a shrub, because it has ceased to be a shrub, and is now a tree. So in both these examples the search for an individual essence founders on the assumption that an individual essence must be intimately connected with the property or properties that determine membership of the kind. The individuals survive, but are no longer members of the relevant kind. So I shall continue to suppose that, if there are individuals with individual essences, the best candidates, indeed the only serious candidates, are individual members of natural kinds.

From kinds to individuals?

We can now move on. In the rest of this chapter I plan to do three things. First, I shall construct and examine a general argument that promises to carry us from EK to strong EI, from a commitment to essences of kinds to a commitment to essences of individuals, strongly interpreted. Second, I shall consider and reject all the candidates for the status of individual essences. Finally, I shall consider whether we should draw any conclusions about the criteria of identity of members of natural kinds. First, then, let us turn to the general argument, designed to show that a commitment to essences of kinds implies a commitment to essences of individuals. I strongly suspect that a weaker version of the argument is implicit in chapters four and five of Wiggins' *Sameness and Substance.* Compare for example the following:

> the whole justification of our criterion for essential properties is the claim that there can be no envisaging this or that particular thing as having a different principle of individuation ... from its actual principle.[6]

However, since I am not absolutely sure that I have understood him, and since he seems to be in favour of weak, rather than strong, essentialism, I must press on on my own.

The argument that I am trying to construct rests on the thought that, if we are to allow that there are individual essences, we must concentrate on individual members of natural kinds, such as elms, chimpanzees, tigers and daffodils; that there is not the slightest chance of discovering individual essences in the case of individuals that are not members of natural kinds, such as tables, nations, cricket matches and breakfasts. I have just given one general reason for supposing that it is vain to search for the individual essences of members of non-natural kinds, but the argument I want to consider begins by offering us a quite different reason. The argument begins with the thought that membership of a natural kind (*elm, chimpanzee, tiger, narcissus*), unlike membership of other kinds (*table, cricket match, glacier, pebble, shrub*), is intimately connected with the notions of identity and individuality. Being *that* individual has a great deal to do with being a member of a natural kind, and so with having a real essence, with having the property essential for membership of the kind. If any individuals have individual essences, such essences will prove to be precisely those essences that determine, or are closely connected with, membership of a natural kind.

Connections between the notions of a natural kind, of identity and individuality, emerge in various ways. The basic point, on which everything depends, is that an individual is a member of a natural kind in virtue of some intrinsic property which permits scientific generalization. An elm is an elm, a chimpanzee a chimpanzee, a narcissus a narcissus, in virtue of some intrinsic property or set of properties, irrespective of any relation the animal or plant may have to something else, and irrespective of any of its purely superficial properties. The intrinsic properties in question typically determine many of the other properties of the individual, including many that Locke would have included in the 'nominal essence', and there are laws of nature governing its origin, growth and development. An elm could not appear from a narcissus bulb, nor turn into a chimpanzee. That in turn means that the criteria of identity of individual plants and animals are, as it were, given by nature, or, to vary the idiom slightly, by the intrinsic 'natures' of individuals of that kind. What counts over a period of time as one and the same elm, or one and the same chimpanzee, or one and the same narcissus, is determined directly by the natures of such things, and by the laws of physics, chemistry and biology. A fortiori, it is in no way determined by human interest, convenience or convention.

In contrast, membership of a non-natural kind is not in virtue of any such profoundly significant intrinsic property of the individual. Broadly speaking, it is either in virtue of its relational dependence on something else, or in virtue of purely superficial properties that do not support scientific generalization. First consider dependent kinds. Something is a table if and only if it performs a certain function, and its performing that function will depend very much on where it is, on local conditions, such as local gravitational forces, and the peculiar features of the beings (e.g human beings) for whom it performs the function. Something is a cliff if and only if it is a quantity of solid material in a certain place, but if it were in a different place it would be something else (e.g. part of the sea bed). Something is breakfast if and only if it promises nourishment to humans at a certain time of the day, but the same food at another time would be lunch or tea or dinner, or pure self-indulgence. And so on. Tables, cliffs and breakfasts do not have natures which lend themselves to scientific generalization, and there are no laws of nature governing tables as such, or cliffs as such, or breakfasts as such. There are therefore no laws constraining the ways in which such objects may change without losing their identity. What counts as one and the same table, or one and the same cliff, or one and the same breakfast, depends very much on its relation to something else. In some of these cases, decisions about identity are no more than that: decisions. We get no help from nature, as it were, in deciding whether we have the same Louis XV escritoire we started with, much mended and restored, or the same meal we began eating some time ago, or the same cliff that has been affected by erosion and landslip. We must say whatever it seems most convenient to say. The decisions will not necessarily be arbitrary in any pejorative sense of 'arbitrary', and may be marked in part by a due respect for various features of the individuals in question. But there will be no sense in which nature offers us answers to questions about their identity, answers which we are expected to discover.

Substantially the same point applies to the members of real but superficial kinds, to clouds, trees, shrubs and pebbles. They do not have natures, and there are no laws of nature governing clouds as such, or trees as such, or pebbles as such. There are therefore no laws constraining the ways in which such objects may change without losing their identity. So we get no help from nature in deciding whether we have the same tree we started with, or the same cloud, or the same pebble. Although our decisions will not be arbitrary, and will be marked by a due respect for the objects' various properties, we must ultimately say whatever it seems most convenient to say.

This general point is so important in what follows that it would be helpful,

I think, to baptize it in some way. I shall therefore say that there are 'stable' criteria of identity only in the case of members of natural kinds. The criteria of identity of members of non-natural kinds are 'unstable', in the sense that they seem to depend, not on profoundly significant intrinsic features of the individual in question, but either on an indefinitely large number of facts about its relation to other things and to the general situation in which it finds itself, or on superficial properties that do not allow scientific generalization. In another, much more fashionable jargon, I might say that it is only in the case of members of natural kinds that we can in principle identify individuals across possible worlds.

There is, however, a complication. As I have already pointed out on several occasions, an individual may be a member of several kinds, natural and non-natural. It may be both a goat and the main butt of the Colonel's sense of humour and the regimental mascot. It may be both an elm and a landmark and a traffic hazard and the subject of a poem. In the first section of this chapter, I rehearsed a general objection to the claim that there are individual essences, an objection which hinged on the claim that there are no individuals as such, only individuals of a certain kind. But doesn't that immediately raise a problem? If individuals are individuals only relative to a kind, and if an individual can be a member of several kinds, natural and non-natural, then it will make no sense to say that there are stable criteria of identity in the case of members of natural kinds, but not in the case of members of other kinds. For in every case we are talking about precisely the same individual, now under a natural kind name, now under a non-natural kind name. So I should not claim that *members* of natural kinds have stable criteria of personal identity, and that *members* of other kinds do not, but rather that identity relative to a natural kind description is determined by the nature of the individual, so described, whereas its identity relative to some other description is determined either by its relation to other things, or by purely superficial properties. But in the absence of further argument, that would not show that there is a special connection between the notions of a natural kind, of identity and of individuality. At most it would show that criteria of identity relative to a natural kind description are 'stable', whereas criteria of identity relative to other descriptions are not.

Some readers will no doubt be reminded of Locke's general remarks about identity at the beginning of Bk. II, chapter XXVII of the *Essay*. He argues that identity is always relative to an 'idea', that we may only talk about identity under a description, and that an identity decision under one description does not commit us to a similar decision under another description. For example, as we discover later in chapter XXVII, we are under no obligation to give the same answer to the questions: Is A the same man as B?; Is A the same person as B?; Is A the same material substance as

B?; Is A the same immaterial substance as B? The overall impact of Locke's proposal is slightly diminished by his tendency to regard material substances not as individual objects but as quantities or 'parcels' of matter, which for our purposes do not count as proper individuals at all, but his general point is still extremely interesting.

However, despite that complication — that one individual may fall under several descriptions — we should not yet abandon our search for a close general connection between the notions of a natural kind, of identity and of individuality. As John Mackie has argued,[7] although we may need to talk of identity under a description, and although an identity decision under one description does not automatically commit us to a similar decision under another, there is no doubt that we give, and should give, special weight to a decision under a natural kind description. That decision seems to regiment, though not strictly to entail, all the others. Consider one familiar example. Some philosophers, over-impressed by Locke, have tried to argue that an individual might be the same *man* I met yesterday, but not the same *official* (because he has changed his job), and conversely that an individual might be the same *official* I met yesterday, but not the same *man* (because he has replaced the original holder of the office). Mackie is surely right to insist that that will not do, and that we must tie the two sets of identity decisions together. It would at best be very misleading to claim that successive holders of the same office count as one and the same official, and that promotion from one office to another yields the same man, but a different official. And what should we say when different men perform the same duties in rotation, for example when one is the stationmaster during the day, and the other is the stationmaster during the night? It would be absurd to suggest that there is one and the same official throughout. The sensible course is to say that we have the same official if and only if we have the same man. Furthermore, the reason is not far to seek. Clearly we do use many terms that are not natural kind terms in counting, identifying and re-identifying, terms such as 'official', 'table', 'cliff', etc. But although they might therefore appear to be genuine substance concepts, their use is parasitic on the use of natural kind terms. We cannot count officials unless we can first count human beings, and we cannot count tables unless we can first count well-defined quantities of wood; and so on. The criteria of identity associated with membership of a non-natural kind are dependent on the criteria of identity of members of appropriate natural kinds.

So, at least for the moment, we can pursue the suggestion that there is a special, or especially close, connection between the notions of a natural kind, of identity and of individuality. And, since membership of a natural kind is determined by a certain real essence, that is, by the possession of the property that makes the individual a member of that natural kind, we may have stumbled upon a direct route from EK to strong EI. In other words, we may have discovered a general argument to show that anyone who accepts essentialism for kinds is thereby committed to strong essentialism for individual members of those kinds. The individual essences of proper individuals will be the properties that determine their membership of the relevant natural kinds. Compare Wiggins again:

> Essences of natural things ... are not fancified vacuities parading in the shadow of familiar things as the ultimate explanation of everything that happens in the world. They are natures whose possession by their owners is the precondition of their owners being divided from the rest of reality as anything at all.[8]

Set out formally, the argument would be as follows:

(1) If an individual is to be a proper individual, it must have stable criteria of identity.
(2) If it is to have stable criteria of identity, it must be what it is in virtue of an intrinsic property which permits scientific generalization.
(3) If it is to be what it is in virtue of an intrinsic property which permits scientific generalization, it must be a member of a natural kind.
(4) So if an individual is to be a proper individual, it must be a member of a natural kind.
(5) But if it is to be a member of a natural kind, it must have a certain real essence. (This claim is EK, essentialism for kinds.)
(6) So if it is to be a proper individual, it must have a certain real essence. (This in effect is strong EI, strong essentialism for individuals.)
(7) Thus the individual essences of elms, chimpanzees, daffodils, etc., are precisely those properties that make them individual members of their respective natural kinds.

So we seem to have a direct route from essentialism for kinds to strong essentialism for individuals.

It should be noted, or perhaps strictly footnoted, that the argument may require a further assumption, if we are to avoid an embarrassingly rich choice of real essences. It may require the assumption that no individual can be a member of more than one natural kind *at each level*. The point of the assumption, and of the reference to 'levels', is this. Someone might argue that in an obvious sense a human being is a member of many natural kinds — of a certain sub-species (*Homo sapiens sapiens*), of a species (*Homo sapiens*), of a genus (*Homo*), of a family (the Hominids), of an order (the Primates), and so on. Now, we saw in chapter 5 that species strictly are not natural kinds, because they do not have real essences, properties necessary and sufficient for membership of the species. And the considerations leading to that conclusion showed equally that no other taxonomic categories (e.g.

genus, family, order) are strictly natural kinds. But even if that is true, there is another sense in which a human being is a member of more than one natural kind. For he or she, or parts of him or her, are quantities of water, hydrochloric acid, strings of protein, and so on. So again we might wish to talk of levels of kinds, from the level of particles, to the level of atoms, to the level of simple molecules, and so on, up to at least the level of the species — or at least to the level of the kind that finally replaced the species in the argument of chapter 5. For the purposes of this chapter, we should concentrate our attention at the level of the species (or its replacement kind), and the suggestion is that an individual human being has an individual essence, to wit, the property that makes it an individual member of the species *Homo sapiens* (or its replacement kind).

The talk of levels raises many problems, but mercifully we do not need to pursue them, because the argument does not work. There are three main difficulties. The first difficulty takes us back to my general project. At the beginning of the chapter, I explained that there is a weaker, and a stronger, version of essentialism for individuals, and that I proposed to discuss the stronger. So I am concerned to examine arguments for the view that there are individual essences in this sense: there is at least one individual whose properties include a property necessary and sufficient for the individual's being *that* individual. So there is little point in isolating a property that is merely necessary to the individual, for other individuals may share it, even possess it equally necessarily. The property in question must also be peculiar to that individual, and its possession sufficient for its being *that* individual. Consider the properties that are implicitly on offer in the argument under discussion. They are the properties that are the real essences of natural kinds, the properties that make something an elm or a chimpanzee or a tiger or a narcissus. But it is obvious that many chimpanzees, or many elms, or many tigers, or many narcissi, can, and indeed must, share the properties that make them all members of the relevant natural kind. Hence, even if it were true that there is an intimate connection between the notions of a natural kind, of identity and individuality, even if it were true that the only proper individuals were members of natural kinds, and even if it were true that members of natural kinds had certain properties essentially, we would still not have the bones of an general argument for individual essences in the strong sense, for properties whose possession was both necessary and sufficient for individuals' being precisely the individuals they are. We would at best have an argument for the weaker view that there is at least one individual whose properties include a property necessary for its being that individual.

Of course, the obvious reply is that my general project is too restricted, and that I should not confine my attention to strong essentialism for individuals. If the general argument above proves that certain properties are necessary for the identity of certain individuals, then it has yielded an interesting result, for it is a defence of weak essentialism for individuals. But this reply will not go through, since there are two further difficulties, which make it impossible to accept the argument as a defence of weak essentialism. The second difficulty is this. The argument turns on the claim that, if an individual is to be a proper individual, it must be a member of a natural kind (step (4)). And that claim is very odd. After all, for many years, analytical philosophers, and particularly those with Kantian interests, have regarded tables, chairs and other artefacts as paradigm examples of individuals that play a crucial rôle in our picture of the world. They have been equally ready to regard members of real but superficial kinds — trees, shrubs, rocks — as paradigm examples of individuals. Surely tables and chairs, trees and shrubs, are proper individuals if anything is!

It is certainly true that the criteria of identity of tables and chairs depend less on their intrinsic properties than on their relation to other things, and in particular on their functional relation to us and our needs. Roughly, something counts as one and the same table, or one and the same chair, over time, if it is a material object that consistently retains a certain continuity of function over that time. It is also true that the identity of trees and shrubs, as such, cannot turn on facts about underlying natures. No doubt we can imagine circumstances in which our decisions about the identity of tables and chairs, or trees and shrubs, would have to be rather different. For example, in a very unstable world, in which there were violent or variable gravitational forces, a table might cease to count as a table if no longer screwed to the floor; and if woody plants could never consistently be relied on to produce either a single stem or a number of stems, we might lose the distinction between trees and shrubs. Finally we should admit that identity decisions associated with membership of a non-natural kind may in practice be determined or regimented by some other identity decision associated with membership of a natural kind. The expression 'same ornament' or 'same official' may be tied to the expression 'same *Ficus benjamina*' or 'same man'.

But those concessions, important as they are, hardly undermine the claim that tables, chairs, and, mutatis mutandis, many other members of non-natural kinds, are proper individuals. The concessions might strengthen the case against the individuality of cricket matches, nations and the average taxpayer, but that case is already very strong. Such things are probably best understood as the properties or states of genuine individuals, as belonging to Aristotle's category of quality rather than to his category of substance. But tables, chairs, trees and shrubs have a strong claim to be treated as individuals. Whatever ingeniously contrived possibilities can be seen to hold in other possible worlds, in the actual world persistent and solid lumps of stuff move about and are classified as individual objects, which persist and change. Their criteria of identity are perhaps less 'stable' in the sense I attempted to explain, and the notion of individuality is perhaps less secure than in the case of members of natural kinds. But it still does not seem to follow that tables, chairs, coins, banknotes, trees, shrubs, clouds and pebbles are not proper individuals at all. Indeed, it is very difficult to see how furniture and antique dealers, bank clerks and burglars could go about their lawful and unlawful business, unless there were generally agreed and usable criteria of identity for such things. So we should reject step (4) of the argument. Since that step is a provisional conclusion which follows from three premises, we must reject at least one of the premises, and I suggest that the troublesome premiss is step (1). That is, it is just not true that, if an individual is to have stable criteria of identity, it must be what it is in virtue of an intrinsic property which permits scientific generalization.

The third difficulty is that the conclusion of the argument is ambiguous. On one interpretation it does not, after all, amount to essentialism for individuals, and on the other interpretation it amounts to essentialism for individuals but does not follow from what has gone before. Let us recall the final stages of the argument:

(4) So if an individual is to be a proper individual, it must be a member of a natural kind.
(5) But if it is to be a member of a natural kind, it must have a real essence.
(6) So if it is to be a proper individual, it must have a certain real essence.
(7) Thus the individual essences of elms, chimpanzees, daffodils, etc., are precisely those properties that make them individual members of their respective natural kinds.

Now let us take a careful look at the phrase 'real essence' in step (6). It can only mean one of two things: 'real essence of the relevant kind' or 'individual essence'. If it means 'real essence of the relevant kind', then (6) certainly follows from (4) and (5), but the conclusion is too weak. We have at most established that proper individuals must have a property that qualifies it for membership of a natural kind; in other words, it must have the real essence of a kind. But we have not shown that that individual has an *individual* essence. If, on the other hand, we take the expression 'real essence' in (6) to mean 'individual essence', then the argument is invalid, for 'real essence' in (5) unequivocally means 'real essence of the relevant kind'.

Individual essences: the candidates

In the previous section, I attempted to construct a general argument to show that anyone committed to a doctrine of natural kinds will be committed to a doctrine of individual essences. I did not enquire in detail into the possible candidates for the title of individual essences, save to suggest in passing that only members of natural kinds could seriously pretend to have individual essences, and that therefore the essences would probably be those properties that were essential to membership of the natural kinds. Insofar as I failed to produce a satisfactory general argument, some oblique doubt will have been cast on the search for individual essences. In this section I propose to go more directly to work. If there are individual essences, it must be possible to identify them. I shall examine all the plausible candidates that I can think of, and shall argue that none of them fit the bill. I shall conclude that there are no individual essences.

I have of course just dealt with one obvious candidate. If an individual essence (in the strong sense under discussion) is a property whose possession is both necessary and sufficient for an individual's being that individual, and if (as I argued earlier) we only have a chance of finding individual essences in the case of members of natural kinds, then perhaps the properties in question will be those properties essential to membership of natural kinds, the real essences that make elms elms, chimpanzees chimpanzees, tigers tigers and narcissi narcissi. But, since there are many elms, many chimpanzees, many tigers and many narcissi, the real essences of the kinds can at best be necessary for the individuals' being precisely those individuals, can at best be parts or elements of the individual essences. They are not sufficient.

Those who favour weak essentialism for individuals will not of course be dismayed, but I have to add that it is difficult to see how the properties in question could even count as necessary to the identity of individual members of natural kinds. Earlier I set out my main reason, which was briefly as follows. First, we cannot talk about individuals in total isolation from their sortal characteristics, and different sortal characteristics will almost certainly yield different considerations about identity and individual essence. If we are not to look in vain for bare particulars or Lockean substrata, we must recognize that there are no individual essences as such, even in the weak sense; there are only individual essences relative to a kind, or essences under a certain description. Nothing is essential to the individual Julius Caesar, though something may be essential to him qua man, or qua Roman, or qua Emperor, or qua Wiggins' most memorable example. The eventual success of that general argument waited upon my attempt to construct a general argument for individual essences, but unfortunately I failed to find one. I therefore conclude that our first candidate fails: the properties that determine membership of natural kinds are neither necessary nor sufficient for the identity of individuals.

Perhaps a second candidate could be used to fatten up the first. The individuals in which we are interested are in space and time, so perhaps we should regard the occupation of an ordered series of places and times as an individual essence, or as a crucial element of an individual essence. As we all know, in the philosophy industry we often appeal to spatio-temporal continuity in discussions of identity. The appeal is particularly strident where it is necessary to deal with puzzle cases involving princes and cobblers, Doppelgänger of Guy Fawkes and the like, or where we need to separate identical twins, or more generally to enforce a distinction between qualitative similarity and numerical identity. In the Oxford of the fifties and sixties, the phrase 'spatio-temporal continuity' rang out wherever two or three metaphysicians were gathered together. A visiting Martian might have reasonably supposed that we all knew what it meant.

But it is clear that the occupation of a particular spatio-temporal position, or more strictly, of a particular ordered series of spatio-temporal positions, is not an individual essence or even a crucial element of an individual essence. Anything we care to mention might not have been in exactly *those* places, at exactly *those* times. For example I was conceived, carried, delivered and have lived at a certain unique series of places and times. Now (to take the case of spatial position first) I can see no difficulty in the suggestion that I might have been conceived, carried, delivered and might have lived at a series of places quite different from the series I have occupied in the real world. Had my parents decided to emigrate to Australia shortly before my conception, they would have provided a perfect illustration of that possibility. And in those circumstances, it is clear by parallel reasoning that someone else might have occupied exactly the same series of places that I have actually occupied. Had my parents decided to emigrate shortly before my conception, and had their vacant house then been occupied by a couple with similar reproductive ambitions, another child might well have followed the spatial route that I have actually followed.

I admit that the case of temporal displacement is trickier, and plausible counterfactual tales about shifts of temporal position are more difficult to construct. However, I think that, with a certain imaginative effort, it can be done as follows. In a human female (and mutatis mutandis in all other female mammals) the fertilization of ovum by sperm is contingent upon an enormous number of background conditions. Indeed, that is merely to apply a general and commonplace remark about any causal transaction. So, in order for *this* ovum to be fertilized by *that* sperm at *that* time, an enormous number of background conditions must be fulfilled. As with any causal transaction, the background conditions might be fulfilled rather earlier or rather later, or a small alteration in a crucial condition might advance or retard the effect. In many processes, whether chemical or bio-chemical, a small variation in temperature is sufficient to advance or retard the effect. But it then follows that my conception might have happened slightly earlier or slightly later than the time at which it actually happened. But if such a small temporal shift is possible in one generation, it is possible in many other generations. Let us therefore consider the possible worlds in which, throughout my ancestral line, each conception happened slightly earlier than it otherwise would have done, and the possible worlds in which, throughout my ancestral line, each conception happened slightly later than it otherwise would have done. Presumably, corresponding adjustments in the reproductive histories of related families would also have to occur, but I think that we can safely assume that they could indeed occur. Since, over many generations, the effect of a series of very small temporal shifts will be magnified, there will be possible worlds in which I occupy a much earlier set of temporal positions than the set I actually occupy, and possible worlds in which I occupy a much later set of temporal positions than the set I actually occupy. Furthermore, of course, in some of those possible worlds, someone occupies exactly the same places and times that I occupy in this world. Put very simply: I might have lived much earlier, and I might have lived much later; and if I had, someone else might have occupied the vacant middle spatio-temporal ground.

If we combine these reflections about spatial and temporal position, it follows that my spatio-temporal route through the world is neither necessary nor sufficient for my being the individual I am. We do not find in spatio-temporal position the makings of an individual essence. Furthermore, nothing would be achieved by combining the second proposal with the first, by arguing that an individual essence consists in *both* membership of a natural kind *and* occupation of a particular series of spatio-temporal positions. Consider once again the example I just sketched. There will be a possible world in which I occupy a set of times earlier than the times I actually occupy, and a possible world in which I occupy a set of times later than the set I actually occupy. In both worlds there will be both logical and geographical room for another human male to occupy the vacant middle spatio-temporal ground, the ground that I occupy in the actual world. He and I would both be members of the same natural kind, and we would occupy the same spatio-temporal positions, but we would not be the same individual (or in another idiom, 'counterparts' of each other). In sum, whether we adopt the first proposal (that membership of a natural kind determines individual essences), or the second (that spatio-temporal position determines individual essences), or a combination of both, we are still no nearer finding individual essences for plants and animals.

A third proposal has been very popular, in one form or another, in the literature on individual essences. It is the claim that an individual essence consists in facts about the individual's origin. Kripke, for example, argues that Queen Elizabeth II could not have been the daughter of Mr. and Mrs. Truman, that a counterfactual tale, of dirty tricks involving bedpans or the discreet machinations of adoption agencies, would not be a story about Queen Elizabeth II, but a story about a numerically different, though very similar, individual.[9] And Graeme Forbes has offered a general account of the essences and origins of individuals, with the aid of the notion of a 'propagule':

> the oak tree's propagule is its acorn, while a human's propagule is his zygote, whose propagules are in turn the sperm and egg whose fusion that zygote is.[10]

Generally, X is a propagule of Y if and only if X immediately generates or immediately develops into Y. The individual essence of an individual will be its having developed from, or having been generated from, a particular propagule or set of propagules. If Forbes is right, he has given a general justification for Kripke's intuitions, since Elizabeth II's individual essence consists in her having developed from a particular zygote, which in turn developed from a particular sperm and a particular ovum, and so on. However we count or collect our propagules, on Forbes' account she could not have been the daughter of Mr. and Mrs. Truman.

I think that there are at least three objections to this fourth proposal, to the suggestion that individual essences consist in facts about origin, and in particular facts about 'propagules'. First, the choice of origin as the crucial determinant of an individual essence seems wholly arbitrary. As John Mackie argues, we could equally well claim that facts about the *future* history of the individual determine its essence, that it is destination rather than origin that is crucial.[11] For example, we could argue that Elizabeth II is the individual who eventually becomes Queen of the United Kingdom, and, with Philip's assistance, produces Charles, Anne, Andrew and Edward. An individual in another possible world who satisfies precisely those ambitions, despite being the daughter of Mr. and Mrs. Truman, is the same individual as our own dear Queen. Mackie explains in detail why it is natural for us to share Kripke's intuitions, but rightly concludes that such intuitions at best reflect de dicto rather than de re necessities.

Second, as another distinguished member of the Mackie family, Penelope, points out, Forbes' attempt to generalize considerations about origin, with the help of the notion of a propagule, does not work.[12] His suggestion is that the individual essences of plants and animals consist in their having had particular propagules, that is, certain entities from which they were immediately generated or from which they developed. He remarks airily that the relational property of being a propagule holds across either fission or fusion, but that remark seems to be fatal, at least as far as fission is concerned. A characteristic feature of many plants and animals is that they divide, or are the result of division. Indeed, as we shall see later in the chapter, thrifty gardeners make good use of that important fact. So it is common to stumble upon two plants — or, in the case of animals, identical twins — that have the same propagule. On Forbes' proposal, it would follow that the two individuals that result from the division have exactly the same individual essence. And that is absurd.

Perhaps some pressure could be applied to the horticultural examples, because so-called division in horticulture typically involves separating viable parts of a single tangled mass, smaller parts of a large and complex propagule. So it might reasonably be argued that the divisions do not come from the same propagule within the meaning of the act: one plant comes from the left-hand section of the original, another from the right-hand section. But it is not possible to deal with other examples in the same way. Cell division does not involve anything that could decently be regarded as the separation of the parts of a tangled clump. Since identical twins result from cell division, they are a genuine counter-example to Forbes' view. Identical twins have numerically the same propagule. But they are distinct individuals and therefore cannot have the same individual essence.

Third, any attempt to ground individual essences in considerations about origin is entirely contrary to the Aristotelian spirit of essentialism. 'For of the other categories none can exist independently, but only substance.'[13] If the notion of an individual essence is to make any sense, we must surely regard individuals with essences, neo-Aristotelian 'substances', as individuals that are what they are in virtue of some significant intrinsic property, quite independently of other things. The central governing thought has to be the thought that *that* individual is *that* individual, whatever else exists, and whatever is going on around it. It is that individual in all possible worlds in which it exists, however radically those possible worlds may differ from the actual world and from each other. But if its being that individual cannot depend on anything else, if it is indeed something that exists independently of other things, then, a fortiori, its being that individual cannot depend on any considerations about its origin. Whatever feature, if any, makes it the individual it is, that feature must be intrinsic or non-relational.

So the third proposal fails, and we must move to a fourth, which involves specifying a relevant property by using a proper name. So, for example, the individual essence of Aristotle will be the property of being-identical-with-Aristotle; the individual essence of Fido will be being-identical-with-Fido; and so on. Some philosophers have spent very little time and energy on this proposal. Penelope Mackie, for example, simply remarks that individuals have such properties 'trivially', and in a 'banal sense'.[14] Furthermore, the arguments used to defend the proposal are distinctly fishy. One striking example is the suggestion that it is merely an application of the logical truth that everything is identical with itself.[15] Aristotle is necessarily identical with Aristotle, and with nothing else; Fido is necessarily identical with Fido, and with nothing else; and so on. But that involves an extraordinary logical sleight of hand. Consider the general background logical principle, which we are invited to interpret as the claim that everything is identical with itself:

$$(x)(x = x).$$

The proposal is in effect an invitation to detach the expression ' $= x$' and to treat it as a predicate-schema which can be transformed into a genuine predicate by substituting a name for the individual variable. But what meaning can we attach to ' $= x$'? There seem to be two, and only two, possibilities: either it means 'is identical with x' or it means 'is identical with itself'. Even if the first alternative (that ' $= x$' means 'is identical with x') were intelligible (and I am not at all sure that it is), it would be too weak, for it fails to do justice to the thought that the general principle with which we began (the principle that $(x)(x = x)$) is a necessary truth. That is, the general principle is not to be interpreted as the weak claim that, for any x, x has the interesting property of being-identical-with-x. It is supposed to be some kind of necessary truth that everything has it! And the second alternative (that ' $= x$' means 'is identical with itself') is too strong, for there are many occurrences of ' $= x$' which clearly cannot be interpreted as 'is identical with itself'. For example, when I wish to point out that an individual y is identical with an individual x, by remarking ' $y = x$', I do not mean that y is identical with itself.

But even if the arguments in favour of this fourth proposal are fishy, and even if the properties in question are 'trivial', I think we need to discuss the proposal as patiently as we can. After all, better arguments may appear, and trivial properties are still properties. I think that the wise move is to argue that the properties of being-identical-with-Aristotle or being-identical-with-Fido are not genuine properties at all. I confess that I am seriously handicapped by not having a general theory of properties, but I want to argue that a property that is necessarily possessed by one and only one individual is not a property at all. Traditionally the problem of universals arose from thoughts about there being One over Many, about there being words that could apply in principle to any one of a potentially large number of things of the same kind. A property that is necessarily rather than contingently possessed by no more than one thing is not a property at all. (One could make a related point about attempts to treat existence as a property in standard formulations of the ontological argument: a property that is necessarily rather than contingently possessed by everything is not a property at all.)

One obvious reply is that there are many examples of genuine properties that are necessarily possessed by one and only one individual, especially in mathematics. For example there is necessarily one and only one number that is an even prime, and there is one and only one number that is the sum of eight and fifteen. So, it will be said, there can be nothing absurd in the suggestion that Aristotle or Fido could have a property necessarily possessed only by Aristotle, or only by Fido. (Presumably there are also examples of properties that are necessarily possessed by every individual in a given domain: in number theory every individual is a number.) But that reply will not do. There are at least two differences between properties such as that of being an even prime and properties such as that of being identical with Aristotle. First (though this remark may not be very significant), numbers are not spatio-temporal individuals, whereas Aristotle, Fido, etc. are. Second (and this is certainly significant), the property of being an even prime is logically connected with other properties of the individual in question. Given the position of the number two in the series of natural numbers, it is necessarily prime, necessarily even, and necessarily the only even prime. In contrast, it is difficult to see how the property of being identical with Aristotle is logically connected with Aristotle's other properties, or, to be strict, logically connected with them in an appropriate way. If being identical with Aristotle is to be the individual essence of Aristotle, then it must be connected with his other properties in such a way that it is a necessary, and not just a contingent, truth, that there is one and only one thing that is identical with Aristotle. That is, we have to rule out the possibility that, in another possible world, there is an individual that shares all the actual Aristotle's properties, but lacks the extra and elusive property of being identical with Aristotle.

What are his 'other properties'? They include his being human, being Greek, being interested in philosophy, etc., and no doubt in the actual world a sufficiently rich list of his properties will in some sense determine his being the one and only individual that is identical with Aristotle. After all, in the actual world there are workable criteria of personal identity! But all those properties are properties that could be shared by other individuals, even in the actual world — properties such as being human, Greek, interested in philosophy. And, as I argued in my discussion of the second proposal, even the property of occupying a particular series of places and times, which is certainly possessed by one and only one individual, does not yield an individual essence. Thus, by constructing an example similar to the examples I used in that discussion, we could show that in a possible world somewhat different from our own, there is an individual who shares the actual Aristotle's properties, including his spatio-temporal positions, but who is not Aristotle. In imagination, as it were, we shift the actual Aristotle forwards or backwards in time, leaving room for the other individual to occupy the middle spatio-temporal ground, ground occupied in the actual world by Aristotle. Thus Aristotle's 'other properties' do not entail that he is necessarily the one and only possessor of the property of being identical with Aristotle.

Alert readers will no doubt point out that none of those remarks rule out weak essentialism for individuals. For I have only shown that there is no set of properties sufficient for being-identical-with-Aristotle; I have not shown that there are no properties necessary for being Aristotle. They might include, for example, the properties that he can share with others, such as being human, being Greek, being a philosopher. But I would appeal once again to my general scepticism about referring to the essences of individuals, tout court. It may make sense to talk about the properties Aristotle necessarily has, qua Greek speaker, or qua husband, or qua famous writer, but it makes no sense to ask which properties he has, simply as Aristotle. So I think that I can reject the fourth proposal, even as an argument for weak essentialism. Once again, the general argument is as follows. A property that is necessarily possessed by one and only one individual is either not a genuine property at all or is entailed by the individual's other properties. Given my general scepticism about talking of individual essences tout court, the property of being identical with Aristotle or being identical with Fido neither entails, nor is entailed by, Aristotle's or Fido's other properties, so it is not a genuine property at all. The fourth attempt to discover some property that would count as an individual essence, whether in the strong or in the weak sense, therefore fails.

Before concluding that there are no individual essences, I must look briefly at a fifth and final candidate. Throughout this discussion, I have assumed that an individual essence would have to be a property or set of properties necessary and sufficient, or merely necessary, for the individual's being that individual. But some philosophers might reject that assumption and argue that an individual essence is not a property at all. It is rather a certain 'thisness', a *haecceitas*, as medieval philosophers would have called it. Aristotle has the haecceity of Aristotle and Fido has the haecceity of Fido. Whatever other changes an individual may undergo in its translation to other possible worlds, it retains its haecceity and is therefore unequivocally still *that* individual.

It soon becomes clear that this proposal is at best useless and at worst ridiculous, for reasons that are very similar to the reasons we had for rejecting the fourth proposal. We need only confront a simple question: Do haecceities entail, and are they entailed by, properties or not? Does Aristotle's haecceity entail, and is it entailed, by his being Greek, human, a philosopher, etc., or not? Our discussion of the previous proposals rules out the first alternative (that haecceity and properties are logically equivalent). Since there are no properties or sets of properties logically necessary and sufficient for Aristotle's being Aristotle, there are equally no properties or sets of properties that entail, and are entailed by, a certain Aristotelian haecceity, a thisness peculiar to Aristotle. And the second alternative (that haecceity and properties are logically independent) is simply ridiculous. If properties do not entail, and are not entailed by, haecceities, then properties and haecceities could run quite free of each other. Someone with all of Aristotle's properties could fail to be Aristotle, and an individual with none of Aristotle's properties — for example the number 28, or my favourite camellia plant, or Beethoven's last string quartet — could possess his haecceity and so be Aristotle. That, I suggest, is ridiculous. I conclude that there are no individual essences.

Natural kinds and identity

I began this chapter by wondering whether someone committed to a doctrine of natural kinds was thereby committed to individual essences (in a suitably strong sense). I constructed a general argument designed to illustrate the commitment but argued that it failed, and I then went on to argue that there are in any case no individual essences. However, it is possible that a related but less extreme position is available, which combines a commitment to natural kinds with a view about the criteria of identity of individual members of natural kinds. Even if we abandon the search for individual essences, we must still produce an account of the criteria of identity of human beings, chimpanzees and daffodils, and it is natural to argue that the criteria must be very intimately connected with their being members of natural kinds. Since an individual member of a natural kind has a real essence, which makes it the kind of thing it is, and since any changes it undergoes are governed by laws of nature, understood as de re necessary truths, any decisions about identity must be referred to, and settled by, nature. Whether I am confronted today by the tiger I saw yesterday, or by the elm tree I bought last year, depends ultimately on whether the object in front of me has developed from yesterday's tiger or last year's elm, in accordance with the de re laws of nature that govern tigers and elms.

Moreover, these de re criteria of identity will depend wholly on the important underlying intrinsic features of the things in question, namely those features (the 'real essences') that make them members of various natural kinds. They will not depend in any way on considerations about the existence of other things in the world, or on the individuals' relations to other things, or on purely superficial properties. In particular, they will not depend on human decision, nor thereby on peculiar human interests and concerns. It is nature that distinguishes one individual member of a natural kind from another, and determines what is identical with what over a period of time. Compare Wiggins:

> If there have to exist true lawlike principles in nature for the actual extension of a natural kind predicate to be collected together around the focus of an actual specimen, and if this is a requirement even for the sense of the predicate, then it is a condition of the very existence of fs, so defined, that certain lawlike sentences should hold true. Again, if these lawlike sentences are to have the character they are required to have for the sense of the predicate standing for the concept f, then they must determine directly or indirectly, in ways that we can uncover by empirical discovery, the characteristic development, the typical history, and the limits of any possible development or history of any compliant of f.[16]

In contrast, it will be said, criteria of identity for members of non-natural kinds work quite differently. If the ship of Theseus is rebuilt, plank by plank, and the old planks are re-assembled by some irresponsible shipwright, nature will be powerless to decide whether the spanking new ship, or the antiquated and leaky ship, is identical with the original. Our decision will not depend merely on the intrinsic features of the individuals in question, but on considerations about the existence of other things. For example, had we simply dismantled the old ship, without attempting to replace any of the components, and had then re-assembled the components at a much later date, we would have identified the later, elderly ship with the original. Had we replaced each plank as it was removed, and burned the old plank immediately afterwards, then we would have identified the spanking new ship with the original. When there are two ships at the dockside simultaneously, one very new and one very old, we may not be sure what to say, even when we know all the facts. Any final decision will inevitably be determined by our special interests and preoccupations. Again compare Wiggins:

> dispute might break out about this matter between priests who favoured the working ship and antiquarians who preferred the reconstruction ... Both are stuck with the identification *ship* but, having different interests, they seem not to mean quite the same thing by 'ship', and neither can base his view upon the 'law of development' of a ship, or suggest a programme of scientific research to force one particular resolution upon the question.[17]

I do not wish to explore the criteria of identity of members of non-natural kinds. (Wiggins does so, in a very interesting way.) I want rather to explore an apparent difficulty in the view that the criteria of identity of members of natural kinds are determined by nature, and by nothing else. In particular, I want to explore the claim that they are not determined by considerations about human interests and concerns. I am going to take Candide's advice ('il faut cultiver notre jardin') and consider examples of individuals which, even given the results of chapter 5, are surely members of natural kinds, namely plants. Philosophers interested in identity have exercised their minds over numerous puzzle cases, many of which are wholly unrealistic, well beyond the reach of present or even foreseeable technology. Some, indeed, are barely within the bounds of logical possibility. In contrast, the cases I am going to consider are entirely realistic, even mundane, and will be familiar to any devoted and prudent gardener. As every gardener knows, many plants can be divided: those growing from bulbs, corms and tubers (narcissi, begonias, gladioli, dahlias); herbaceous perennials (phlox, primulas, asters); many shrubs (hypericums, potentillas, berberis). More or less any plant that has a reasonably solid crown and an even spread of roots can be cut into pieces and replanted.

Now consider the following cases:

CASE A: I cut a plant down the middle. I carefully remove one half and burn it, leaving the remaining half in situ. What should we say? Surely, that the remaining half is identical with the original.

CASE B: I cut a plant down the middle. I carefully remove one half and plant it elsewhere. Unfortunately the remaining half dies from the shock of my intrusion, while the replanted half flourishes. What should we say? Surely, that the surviving half, the half that I moved, is identical with the original.

CASE C: I dig up a plant and cut it down the middle. I carefully plant each half elsewhere. Both the resulting plants do well. What should we say? We cannot talk of identity here. We cannot say that one of the plants is identical with the original, and the other is not, for neither plant has a greater claim than the other. Nor can we say that they are both identical with the original, for neither gardeners nor philosophers would do well to abandon the principle of the transitivity of identity. That principle would force us to say that, if each new plant is identical with the original, then they are identical with each other. The wise gardener simply says that the original plant has, or has been, divided. I suggest that the wise philosopher will follow suit.

CASE D: I cut a plant down the middle. I carefully remove half and plant it elsewhere. Unfortunately I plant it too near to a large and vigorous plant of the same kind, and the vigorous plant grows all over it, eventually fusing with it. What then? Surely, the remaining survivor of the original operation is identical with the original. The large and vigorous plant, fatter after the fusion, is neither identical with the original nor a division of the original.

CASE E: I cut a plant down the middle. I carefully remove half and plant it elsewhere. Unfortunately I plant it too near to a weak plant of the same kind, and the weak plant eventually fuses with its new and stronger neighbour. What then? The original plant has been divided, and the weak plant has fused with the new neighbour.

CASE F: A new shoot has appeared, some way from the main crown of the plant. I carefully remove it and plant it elsewhere. It is now not identical with the original, nor a division of the original. If the shoot was removed with a healthy section of root attached, it is an offset or a sucker. (Politically incorrect gardeners will call it an Irishman's cutting.) If it has no roots but grows roots after replanting, it is a cutting.

I could produce many more cases, for I have not yet mentioned the very common techniques of taking root cuttings, budding, grafting or layering. Nor have I mentioned the very exciting development of micro-propagation, where new plants are grown from microscopic fragments of a parent plant. But cases A-F will be sufficient for my purposes. The first general point to be made is that in all such cases decisions about identity and related matters are easily made, with the aid of the special vocabulary of divisions, cuttings, offsets, and so forth. Although we may finish up with rather more, or rather fewer, objects than we started with, we have no difficulty in arriving at an intelligible account of the relation between the original object(s) and the object(s) that survive.

But the second point is that these examples seem to be clear counter-examples to the view that the identity of members of natural kinds is determined by nature, by the intrinsic features of the individuals concerned and by the laws governing their changes and development. In these cases decisions about identity seem to depend, both causally and logically, on considerations about context, and particularly on human interests and concerns. Indeed, the decisions seem to be very much just that: a matter for decision. In these cases they *causally* depend on our being thrifty gardeners, on our interest in using divisions, offsets, cuttings and suckers, or in giving them to friends and neighbours. Nature takes us some way towards making a decision, but the rest is up to us. If our attitude to horticulture were rather different (for example, if we always scrupulously destroyed any material removed from a plant, for whatever reason), then our decisions about cases A-F might well be different. But it is not, so they are not. And the decisions *logically* depend on our interests, because any individual division or offset or sucker is not merely thought of as a quantity of natural stuff, or as an individual member of a natural kind. There is an implicit reference to human interest: the division or offset or sucker is thought of as an individual plant of possible interest to gardeners, rather than as a proper part of the original plant. Very generally then, it seems that the identity of such individuals does not depend on their underlying important intrinsic features, those that make them members of certain natural kinds, and on their growth and development in accordance with certain relevant laws of change. In cases A-F it depends crucially on what is happening elsewhere. For example, it may depend on what happens to the piece I remove, whether I destroy it, whether it survives in its new surroundings, whether it is swallowed up by a vigorous neighbour, and so on. And it will also depend on my actual or possible horticultural interests.

How much of the original claim is left? To what extent is it true that nature determines the identity of individual members of natural kinds? We must first recall that, although criteria of identity are rules for counting individuals of a certain kind, there are two separate, though clearly connected, counting tasks. One is to count individuals at a given time, and the other is to count them over a period of time. First, we want to know how many elm trees are in the garden at 3.00 p.m. today, and second, we want to know which one, if any, is identical with the tree planted by my grandfather forty years ago. My examples clearly undermine the claim that nature determines the proper way of completing the second task, for it is just not true that the identity of plants over time is determined by the intrinsic features which make them members of certain natural kinds, and by the laws of change appropriate to each kind. As we have seen, identity may be determined by various relational or non-intrinsic features, including a relation to human horticultural interests.

We might think, however, that nature can and does complete the first task, that of counting individuals of a certain kind at a given time. Assuming that an elm tree is an organic individual, with a number of interrelated parts, then it would seem to follow that nature swiftly determines how many organic individuals of that kind there are at 3.00 p.m. today. But sadly, it doesn't. Grandfather's elm may have produced a sucker from a root a little further down the hedgerow, and the sucker has grown tall. There is no definite 'natural' strategy for counting the number of elms here. Or perhaps he planted several elm saplings very close together and, over the years, each one begins to graft itself on to its immediate neighbours. Eventually there will be a single, if rather oddly-shaped, trunk, but for many years there will be no clear answer to questions about the number of elm trees. If it is possible to make a decision at all, the decision will depend on human interests and concerns. For example, if, as gardeners, we find that the tangled mass can be torn into as many sections as the original number of saplings, and that the sections can be replanted successfully in new places, then we might say that there are exactly that many elm trees in the hedge. If, as carpenters, we are interested in trunks rather than in roots, we will count an original tree and the tree that has grown from a sucker as two trees, and so on.

Hence very little of the original claim remains, at least, as a contribution to a discussion of identity. The laws of nature determine the development of individual members of natural kinds, and regulate division and fusion. They allow acorns to grow into oaks, and prevent oaks changing into chimpanzees, and so on. But they certainly do not yield unambiguous principles of counting, whether at a given time or over a period of time. Even in the case of members of natural kinds, identity does not depend on the purely intrinsic features of things. It depends on all kinds of considerations about context, and in particular on the interests of gardeners. So an interest in gardening should temper our philosophical ambitions. We should recall the words of Joseph Addison, writing in *The Spectator* in 1712:

> A garden ... is naturally apt to fill the Mind with Calmness and Tranquillity, and to lay all its turbulent Passions at Rest.

In particular, we should abandon any ambitions we might have had to use an account of natural kinds to clarify problems about identity.

Notes

1   D. Wiggins (1980), p. 120.
2   D. Wiggins, op. cit., ch. 4, passim.
3   Locke (1690), III, vi, 4.
4   See S. Kripke (1980), especially Lecture III, and D. Wiggins, op. cit., chs. 3-5.
5   S. Kripke, op.cit., p. 114.
6   D. Wiggins, op. cit., p. 122.
7   J.L. Mackie (1976), pp. 160-1.
8   D. Wiggins, op. cit., pp. 132-3.
9   S. Kripke, op. cit., p. 110f.
10 G. Forbes (1976), p. 133.
11 J.L. Mackie, op. cit., pp. 154-60.
12 P. Mackie (1987), pp. 188-90.
13 Aristotle, *Metaphysics*, Z, I, 1028a34-5.
14 P. Mackie, op. cit., p. 173.
15 Cf. the first few pages of S. Kripke (1971). Jonathan Harrison first alerted me to the oddities of this argument.
16 D. Wiggins, op. cit., p. 84.
17 D. Wiggins, op. cit., pp. 93-4.

References

ALTRAN, S. (1987), 'Ordinary Constraints on the Semantics of Living Kinds', *Mind and Language*, vol. 2.

ARISTOTLE, *The Complete Works: the Revised Oxford Translation*, edited by J. Barnes, Princeton University Press, 1984.

BAKER, G. and HACKER, P. (1980), *An Analytical Commentary on Wittgenstein's Philosophical Investigations, Volume I: Meaning and Understanding*, Basil Blackwell, Oxford.

DARWIN, C. (1859), *On the Origin of Species by Means of Natural Selection*, Murray, London.

DAWKINS, R. (1982), *The Extended Phenotype*, Oxford University Press.

DAWKINS, R. (1976 and 1989), *The Selfish Gene*, Oxford University Press.

DENNETT, D. (1978), *Brainstorms*, Harvester Press, Hassocks, Sussex.

DENNETT, D. (1987), *The Intentional Stance*, Massachusetts Institute of Technology Press.

DONNELLAN, K.S. (1966), 'Reference and Definite Descriptions', *Philosophical Review*, vol. LXXV.

DUPRÉ, J. (1981), 'Natural Kinds and Biological Taxa', *Philosophical Review*, vol. XC.

ELDER, C.L. (1989), 'Realism, Naturalism and Culturally Generated Kinds', *Philosophical Quarterly*, vol. 39.

FLEW, A.G.N. (1990), 'Hume and Physical Necessity', *Iyyun, The Jerusalem Philosophical Quarterly*, vol. 39.

FORBES, G. (1976), *The Metaphysics of Modality*, Oxford University Press.

GOULD, S.J. (1990), *The Panda's Thumb*, Penguin, London.

GOULD, S.J. (1991a), *The Flamingo's Smile*, Penguin, London.

GOULD, S.J. (1991b), *Wonderful Life, The Burgess Shale and the Nature of History*, Penguin, London.

GRAYLING, A.C. (1982), *An Introduction to Philosophical Logic*, Harvester Press, Hassocks, Sussex.

HARRÉ, R. and MADDEN, E.H. (1975), *Causal Powers*, Basil Blackwell, Oxford.

HART, H.L.A. and HONORÉ, A.M. (1959), *Causation in the Law*, Oxford University Press.

HOLLIS, M. (1987), *The Cunning of Reason*, Cambridge University Press.

HUME, D. (1739), *A Treatise of Human Nature*, edited by L.A. Selby-Bigge, Oxford University Press, 1888; second edition edited and revised by P. Nidditch, Oxford University Press, 1978.

KANT, I. (1781/87), *Critique of Pure Reason*, translated by N. Kemp Smith, Macmillan, London, 1929.

KIRK, R. (1994), *Raw Feeling*, Oxford University Press.

KRIPKE, S. (1971), 'Identity and Necessity', in M. Munitz, ed., *Identity and Individuation*, New York University Press.

KRIPKE, S. (1980), *Naming and Necessity*, Basil Blackwell, Oxford.

KRIPKE, S. (1982), *Wittgenstein on Rules and Private Language*, Basil Blackwell, Oxford.

LEIBNIZ, G.W. (1765), *New Essays on Human Understanding*, translated and edited by P. Remnant and J. Bennett, Cambridge University Press, 1981.

LOCKE, J. (1690), *An Essay Concerning Human Understanding*, edited by J. Yolton, Everyman's Library, Dent/Dutton, London, 1961.

MACKIE, J.L. (1974), *The Cement of the Universe*, Oxford University Press.

MACKIE, J.L. (1976), *Problems from Locke*, Oxford University Press.

MACKIE, P. (1987), 'Essence, Origin and Bare Identity', *Mind*, vol. XCVI.

McGINN, C. (1991), *The Problem of Consciousness*, Basil Blackwell, Oxford.

MILL, J.S. (1843), *A System of Logic*, Longman, London, 1970.

PARFIT, D. (1984), *Reasons and Persons*, Oxford University Press.

PUTNAM, H. (1975), *Philosophical Papers, Volume II*, Cambridge University Press.

RYLE, G. (1949), *The Concept of Mind*, Hutchinson, London.

SCHWARTZ, S.P. (1980), 'Natural and Nominal Kinds', *Mind*, vol. LXXXIX.

SMART, J.J.C. (1963), *Philosophy and Scientific Realism*, Routledge, London.

STRAWSON, P.F. (1959), *Individuals*, Methuen, London.

WIGGINS, D. (1980), *Sameness and Substance*, Basil Blackwell, Oxford.

WITTGENSTEIN, L. (1953), *Philosophical Investigations*, Basil Blackwell, Oxford.

WOOLHOUSE, R. (1971), *Locke's Philosophy of Science and Knowledge*, Basil Blackwell, Oxford.

Index